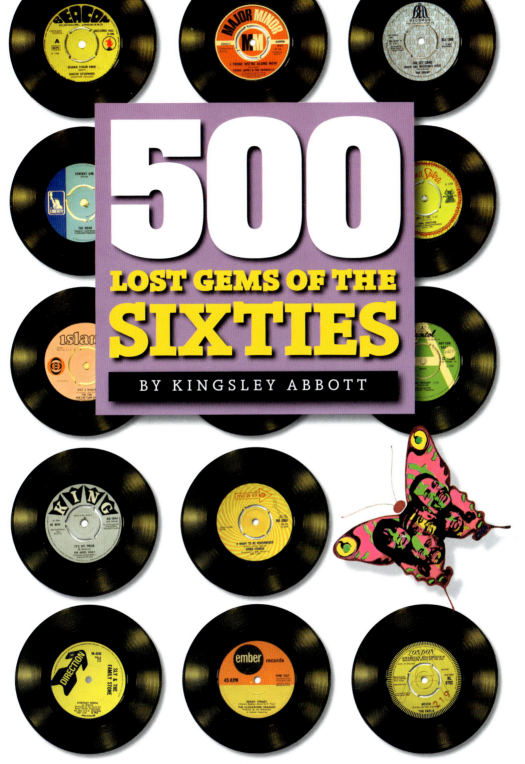

My! £3

500
LOST GEMS OF THE
SIXTIES
BY KINGSLEY ABBOTT

an
ovolo
book

Ovolo Publishing Ltd
1 The Granary, Brook Farm,
Ellington, Huntingdon,
Cambridgeshire
PE28 0AE

Text © 2008 Kingsley Abbott
This edition © Ovolo Publishing Ltd

Paperback ISBN: 978 1 905 959 075
Hardback ISBN: 978 1 905 959 068

Book Design: Gill Lockhart
Publisher: Mark Neeter

This edition first published in the UK by Ovolo Publishing Ltd,
May 2008 Printed in China by Asia Pacific Offset

For more information on Ovolo books please visit:
www.ovolobooks.co.uk or call: 01480 893833 (24 hours)

www.lostgems.co.uk

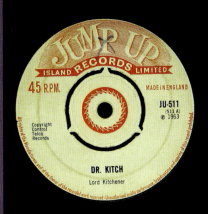

DR. KITCH
Lord Kitchener

SPANISH HARLEM
(Leiber—Spector)
SOUNDS INCORPORATED

HALF PAST MIDNIGHT (2.06)
(Emmerson)
THE STACCATOS
A Dasanda Production

AROUND AND AROUND (3.08)
(andaroundandaroundandaround)
(Crewe/Gaudio)
THE 4 SEASONS
Featuring the 'sound' of Frankie Valli
Arranged by Artie Schroeck
Produced and directed by
Bob Crewe

TINY GODDESS
(G. Spyropoulos—R. Singer—P. Campbell-Lyons)
NIRVANA
Produced by: Muff Winwood and
Jimmy Miller

THE THINGS WE DID LAST SUMMER
(Styne, Cahn)
SHELLEY FABARES
Arranged and produced by
Stu Phillips

INTRODUCTION

Prepare to be stunned, amazed and intrigued! The contents of this book could seriously alter your view of the Sixties – even if you were there. Collecting the true stories, gossip and details of 500 of the singles that failed to dent the top 10, yet are still worthy of inclusion in a volume such as this, goes to show how much of a melting pot of talent, creativity and energy the decade really was.

But, just how exciting can a book about 500 dollops of black plastic be? Read on through the decade and find out for yourself. But it's not just the groove, but in the grooves that you'll find the magic. Nuggets of information and connections between artists, producers and

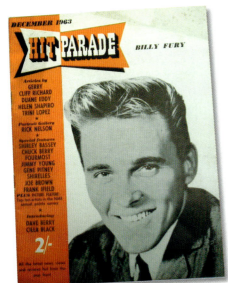

songwriters that you've either never known or forgotten about – depending on your age – offer a unique insight into the careers and artistic development of key (and not so key) performers over the ten years in question.

The genesis of this book is a combination of a love of vinyl records, spending too long logged-in to on-line discussion groups, and the excellent string of CD/vinyl re-issues by companies such as Ace, the Cherry Red group (Revola, RPM etc), Rhino, and Sundazed.

The idea behind this book is simple – to gather together a fantastic selection of Sixties pop releases that are not as well-known as they deserve to be.

The seven-inch single, which replaced the heavy, large, fragile, sonically-challenged and basically rubbish 78rpm disc, not only allowed a generation of Dansette record player-owning teenagers the freedom to play discs on small machines in their bedrooms, it also gave record companies the chance to issue multiple releases cheaply and easily.

The 45rpm single was the result of the so-called 'battle of the speeds' between Columbia and RCA Victor in America in the late Forties. The key elements of the seven-inch, 45rpm, vinyl record were that it was (comparatively)

unbreakable, big enough to handle easily, had a groove big enough to give a big sound, and yet was small enough to fit next to books on a shelf. (The other contender was the 33rpm album.)

With the seven-inch single came the development of smaller, more compact, portable record players. The effect of taking teen-listening out of the family living room, where parents tut-tutted at the hip-swivelling antics of Brylcreamed teen idols, and into the privacy of the teenage bedroom should not be under-estimated. The teen listening revolution had begun, and when the music industry as a whole started to understand the value of this new market, the ball was well and truly rolling.

The mid-Fifties saw the original rock'n'roll revolution, which the industry majors rapidly attempted to water down, often with white versions of the originals. This strategy broadly worked until the early years of the Sixties when the arrival of new young writers, producers and artists swept all before them, making the decade a memorable one…no, *the* memorable one. Between 1963 and 1967, sales of singles hit their all-time peak and bore witness to a huge surge of creativity within so many musical genres. The number of records appearing in each year in this book reflects this fact.

The book also echoes how the monopoly of the dominant record labels gradually gave way to a plethora of new, small, vibrant, entrepreneurial independents – eager to push on with their own musical preferences. Label and sleeve design also underwent a revolution – just flick through the 1960, 1961 and 1962 pages and compare them to the 1967, 1968 and 1969 pages. Colourful or what!

So, how were the singles in here chosen? Who acted as the St Peter at the gates of vinyl heaven and why did he choose as he did? The simple answer is that the choice is the

Do you agree with the tracks chosen for inclusion? Visit www.lostgems.com with your views

● Each must have been on a seven-inch single
● Selections were made on the basis of some specific interest, such as collectability, being a good example of a particular genre, being a good example of an artist's writing, production or ability, or simply that the record was not like any other.
● Finally, to narrow the list down, whether or not Kingsley thought that the record could or would be played on Radio 2's Sounds Of The Sixties (a real gem of a programme which thankfully isn't yet lost).

This last criterion proved most useful, inexact as it was, as it enabled him to make some harsh choices, and he is still rueful of some of the list that did not make the final cut. Ultimately, Kingsley was the final arbiter, and the book reflects his own assessments and tastes.

So there. We've done it. We've named the guilty party. But, to be fair, Kingsley has invested considerable time in consulting with many collectors and experts on the period to try to ensure that the selection is both balanced and entertaining.

Exact release dates are difficult, as labels sometimes lied or releases were simply delayed. Within each year, there has been no attempt to arrange chronologically – as this was simply impossible to confirm with any degree of accuracy – and, anyway, some records just cried out to be next to others.

There are certainly some occasions when a record was due to be released towards the end of a year and was held over until after Christmas. We have followed the year marked as the publication date on the record, unless we knew with absolute certainty that it was wrong. In terms of the book as a whole, following as it does the development of Sixties music through the decade, we don't believe that any harm will be done by following this arbitrary rule.

To keep your interest

completely subjective, unscientific view of Kingsley Abbott, and if you don't agree, then visit www.lostgems.com and let us know what you'd have chosen. But, for now, just enjoy the fact that this collection exists! What's key is that this book doesn't focus on the hits that everyone knows so well, but focuses on pop records that should have been hits, bigger hits, or at least regularly played.

Instrumentation, recording techniques, pop arrangements and the change in the role of the producer all combined to make the decade one of innovation and creativity.

We believe that this is the first book to celebrate the art (musical and otherwise) of the seven-inch single in its own right – rather than concentrating on specific artists or genres.

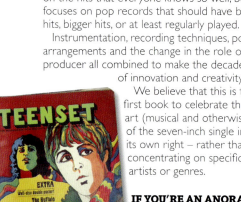

IF YOU'RE AN ANORAK THIS BIT IS FOR YOU:

The criteria for selection "is as follows", as Katie Boyle always used to say on the Eurovision Song Contest shows in the Sixties – yes, there were presenters before Terry Wogan.
● Each entry must have been a British release, A or B side, that appeared between January 1960 and December 1969.

We have scoured contemporary material for your visual delectation…

in 500 records, we've included a range of stories, plus quotes from the artists and from other interested parties. The great majority of the quotes have come directly from the artists especially for this book, but a few have been taken from other sources or from interviews Kingsley conducted in the past.

A book of 500 record labels might prove fascinating to some, but we felt that for the majority it would have created a book with astonishing visual tedium. So, for your titillation, we have scoured the contemporary material for adverts, artist pictures and other interesting ephemera. Deciding which labels to feature was also made partly on the basis of variety and colour, rather than, for example, always using dark EMI or London labels, love them as we all do.

While not all the choices are rare – and a few may be better-known to some of you – the contents are also intended for those of you born after 1955, for whom at least some of this book will be a novel voyage of exploration. It is our hope that every reader will find some things they didn't know about, some they can nod sagely about, some that they can mutter adversely about, and some that may just intrigue them. The great joy of all the records released in the Sixties is that it would be possible to produce another book with a totally different set of choices without too much, if any, diminution of quality (and who knows, we

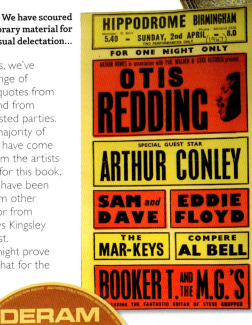

might even do it).

The values of the records included vary from about 10p to hundreds of pounds, and on occasion we have made reference to the worth. But this book is not about collecting records for their monetary value – it's about much, much more for a variety of other reasons, but most particularly for the enjoyment of the music contained within the grooves of these time capsules of pop history.

ABOUT THE AUTHOR

Kingsley Abbott has been involved with music since the early Sixties, when, as an active member of the Tamla Motown Appreciation Society, he would meet, greet and help promote Motown acts including Stevie Wonder, Martha & The Vandellas, Jimmy Ruffin and The Four Tops on visits to the UK. Soon after, he ran the Stevie Wonder UK Fan Club before and during Stevie's UK breakthrough. He met Fairport Convention at their first gig, and hung around helping out as roadie and general factotum, and now counts the band members as some of his oldest friends. Following a career in primary education, he has written books about Fairport, Motown, The Beach Boys and the *Pet Sounds* album. He has contributed to Mojo, Uncut and Shindig and is a regular writer and reviewer for Record Collector. He lives in Norfolk in a 300-year-old clay lump cottage.

THE SEVEN-INCH FORMAT

Most opinion about the seven-inch recorded format would date its arrival from the Fifties, but in fact the lineage goes back further.

Soon after the original cylindrical recorded formats of the earliest recorded sounds died out in the late eighteen hundreds, a German/Jewish American called Emile Berliner developed a flat seven-inch revolving format that played at approximately 70 revs per minute. In the early years of the 20th Century, the ten-inch format was introduced and rapidly became the dominant format for more than 40 years. The seven-inch was discontinued in 1907, and did not re-appear until the Forties, when RCA Victor led the way towards re-introducing the size.

RCA's rivals Columbia pulled off an industry coup when they introduced the lightweight vinyl ten- and 12-inch discs in 1948, though RCA themselves had attempted an introduction of light plastic longer-playing discs back in the early Thirties, but had given up owing to technical problems at the time.

In the Forties, RCA had a major advantage over Columbia, in that it was also involved in the manufacture of record players. This conjunction was one factor that led to the re-introduction of the seven-inch, one-song-per-side format that could offer three-minute songs drawn from Broadway hits, swing bands, and songs from the newly emerging concept of the teen-adored pop singers like Sinatra. It was a point where industrial hardware development exactly combined with changes in musical taste. Astute marketing executives also realised that there were new markets to sell to, as America and Europe emerged from the effects of war.

Columbia's introduction of long players was the single biggest nail in the coffin of shellac discs. Developments in the plastics industry led the record industry to see the value of exploiting different markets in a way that had not previously been possible, and the notion of the shorter, different-speed single took hold as a strong replacement for the ten-inch breakable disc.

Initially known as 'doughnut discs', owing to the large central hole in the US variety, the two single formats existed alongside each other for up to ten years as more and more people bought the newer and smaller players that allowed the stacked plastic discs to drop down one after the other.

The comparative unbreakable nature of the plastic discs, and their convenient bookshelf size, made them even more attractive to the emerging teen markets, and by the end of the Fifties the days of shellac discs were truly numbered, though it should be remembered that the format existed in certain parts of the world (for example, India) for several years more.

RCA Victor initially began to issue seven-inch records in different-coloured plastic according to the musical style represented. Proper classical music was found on ruby red, lighter popular classics appeared on dark blue, children's music on yellow, pop on black, International music on sky blue, folk and hillbilly on green, 'sepia' music (or blues and rhythm as it was termed then) on cerise. Albums were also issued in the late-Forties in the seven-inch format so that, for instance, four discs were stacked and played in side order 1-3-5-7- flip the stack over -2-4-6-8, enabling the format to cope with longer pieces of music or shows. However, for obvious continuity reasons, the single larger disc soon won out over this marketing idea.

Driven by the newly emerging youth markets with money to spend, the seven-inch single in the US helped fuel ever-larger sales of pop music, and the crossover arrival of rock and roll in the mid-Fifties ensured even more success. The situation was soon replicated in the UK, though the full force of seven-inch vinyl singles was not felt until the later Fifties, when the increasing number of smaller portable record players enabled teens and twenties to play their discs in bedrooms and other spaces rather that on the much larger radiograms that were usually in the established adult spaces within homes. The upsurge of jukebox culture associated with the arrival of skiffle, coffee bars and jazz clubs also had its part to play, and, once again, we witness the conjunction of musical taste and industrial development.

As the Sixties arrived, shellac was all but forgotten and the seven-inch 45s, as they were becoming known, helped to fuel a decade that saw previously unheard of sales figures on both sides of the Atlantic. While the US market was less dented by the effects of the war and led the way, the British teenager gradually had more spending power too. The Sixties were dominated initially by the manufactured, safe, teen idols, who were marketed to the same teen female markets that Sinatra had so successfully played to two decades previously. But they were also notable for the emergence of more male-orientated musical genres as the decade progressed. As record companies saw the chances of selling to these differing markets, the number of releases each week increased rapidly. This ensured that

The vinyl granules (above) are heated to produce the extrusion (below) that goes on the middle of the press (no, it's not what you think) before being squashed into shape by the stampers.

knowledge of, and purchasing of, the latest releases was one of the major aspects of shared youth culture – 45s were important to know about and to be able to talk about, fulfilling much of the ground taken today by computer games, DVDs and the so-called celebrity culture.

This book reflects the fact that so many records were issued. A block graph of the year-by-year inclusions would show a strong mid-Sixties peak reflecting the strong sales growth of the markets, especially post-Beatles, and the subsequent takeover in unit terms of album sales in the latter years of the decade.

During the Sixties also there was an explosion of creativity in terms of music available on singles, often begun and fuelled by American issues. Key genres such as the Beat influences, Folk Rock, Surf, Girl Groups, Soul and Psychedelia all had their roots in the US, and this book generally reflects that. The Sixties single was king – exciting, vibrant, often musically ground-breaking, and an essential part of youth culture. It was a wonderful decade to have lived through.

(With acknowledgments to 45 RPM, The History, Heroes & Villains of a Pop Music Revolution, by Jim Dawson and Steve Propes (Backbeat Books 2003), which is a fascinating book to read for the whole story.)

"Records might have looked very different had RCA issued singles in different-coloured plastic according to the musical style represented."

ACKNOWLEDGEMENTS

I am indebted to many people for a wide variety of reasons:

To Mark Neeter of Ovolo Publishing, who has been so enthusiastic about the book.

To Gill Lockhart, whose design ideas so enthused me that once seeing them I knew I was in good hands. Her job has been extreme in making it all fit.

To all the past and present staff of Record Collector, who have continually produced a great magazine and kept vinyl in our collective consciousness.

To all the record collector friends or contacts who have helped directly and indirectly on the project in terms of loans of singles, albums, memorabilia, scans, or allowed me to hear rare items from their collections: Roger Brown, Charlie Brennan, Andrew Doe, Stuart Talbot, Mick McMenamin, Charles Hedges, Jason Draper, Daryl Easlea, Andrew Vine, Stephen J McParland, Mick Patrick, Malcolm Baumgaut, Steve Byrne, Linda Stradling, Trevor Walker, John Purdue, Mick Grant, Toni Racklin, John Reed, Rob Harper, Martin Leversuch, Angie Dunlop, John Poole, Norman Tiplady, Brian Hinton, Graeme Milton, Peter Whitfield, Michael White, Alan Taylor, Pete Smith, Bob Stanley, and probably a few more whose names may have escaped me, for which I sincerely apologise. The book could not have happened without their loans, suggestions and help.

To all the artists who offered thoughts about their work. Without exception, response was almost instant, which both amazed and delighted me, and their stories made great additions.

Dedication
For William Oliver Drakard

SOURCES CONSULTED

As well as countless CD booklets and other ephemera including the Forbidden Fruit booklets, the following books have never been far from my side during the preparation of this book, and I would like to salute all the authors', contributors' and editors' hard and painstaking work that is within their covers:

Billboard Hot 100 Charts – The Sixties – Joel Whitburn – Record Research

40 Years of NME Charts – Dafydd Rees, Barry Lazell & Roger Osborne – Boxtree

Goldmine Standard Catalog of American Records – 1050-1975 – Tim Neely – Krause

Record Collector Rare Record Price Guide 2008 – Diamond Publishing

The Guinness Top Forty Charts – Paul Gambaccini, Tim Rice, Jonathan Rice – Guinness Publishing

Joel Whitburn's Bubbling Under The Billboard Hot 100 1959-2004 – Record Research

Fuzz, Acid & Flowers – Vernon Joynson – Borderline Productions

The London American Legend Vols 1 & 2 – David M. McKee – Athena Press

The Billboard Book of American Singing Groups – Jay Warner – Billboard

The Guinness Who's Who of Sixties Music – Ed. Colin Larkin – Guinness

Encyclopaedia Of British Beat Groups & Solo Artists Of The Sixties – Colin Cross, with Paul Kendall & Mick Farren - Omnibus

I would also acknowledge the work of countless others within the CD booklets, magazines and in other printed matter that I have consulted before and during this book's preparation.

reprise:

DINO, DESI
& BILLY

45 RPM

R.23047

RECORDING FIRST
PUBLISHED 1965
R.23047-A

NOT THE LOVIN' KIND
(Lee Hazlewood)
MECOLICO

fontana

TF 584
270147 TF

45

MONO
▽
A

Copyright
Control

270147 1F

NEIGHBOUR NEIGHBOUR
(A. Vollier)
THE ADLIBS
A Vee-Jay Recording

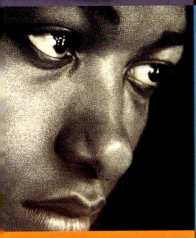

WONDERFUL, WONDERFUL
THE TYMES

LIBERTY

THIS RECORD MUST
BE PLAYED AT 45 RPM

PICCADILLY

THE
ROCKIN'
BERRIES

45RPM

7N.35270

R-1965
7N.35270-A

THE WATER IS OVER MY HEAD
(Kooper, Levine)
A. SCHROEDER MUSIC

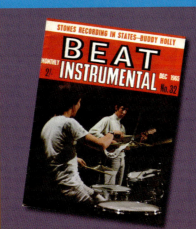

STONES RECORDING IN STATES—BUDDY HOLLY

MONTHLY

BEAT
INSTRUMENTAL

2/-

DEC 1965
No. 32

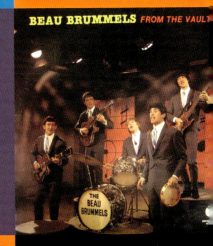

BEAU BRUMMELS FROM THE VAULT

THE
BEAU
BRUMMELS

HARLEM SHUFFLE
(Relf–Nelson)

Marc Records
U.S.A.

Time: 2.30

Sue
RECORDS

WI-374
(A)

BOB AND EARL

DECCA

REGD.
MADE IN ENGLAND
THE DECCA RECORD CO. LTD.

45 RPM

TRUE HIGH
FIDELITY

K/T
℗ 1965
Gauntlet
M. Ltd.

F.12271
s

DR.36798

SHUT 'EM DOWN IN LONDON TOWN
(Ford, Thomson)
THE MAJORITY
Music Director : David Whitaker
Production : Jim Economides

immediate
immediate
immediate
immediate
immediate
immediate
immediate

THE COLLECTION

Glancing through this list, we're sure you'll know some of the tracks, but others, while excellent in their own way, did not receive the credit they deserved. Time to make amends...

1960

Hit & Miss **JOHN BARRY SEVEN PLUS FOUR,** *20*
Piltdown Rides Again **THE PILTDOWN MEN,** *20*
Schoolboy Blues **BUZZY KING,** *20*
I Shot Mr Lee **THE BOBETTES,** *21*
Stay **MAURICE WILLIAMS & THE ZODIACS,** *21*
There's A Moon Out Tonight **THE CAPRIS,** *21*
Mr Lonely **THE VIDELS,** *22*
Tell Tommy I Miss Him **MARILYN MICHAELS,** *22*
He'll Have To Stay **JEANNE BLACK,** *22*

1961

September In The Rain **DINAH WASHINGTON,** *25*
I've Told Every Little Star **LINDA SCOTT,** *26*
Peppermint Twist (Part 1) **JOEY DEE & THE STARLITERS,** *26*
Those Oldies But Goodies **NINO & THE EBBTIDES,** *26*
"Nag" **THE HALOS,** *26*
Rama Lama Ding Dong **THE EDSELS,** *26*
Imagination **THE QUOTATIONS,** *26*
Cruisin' **THE HOLLYWOOD VINES,** *27*
More Money For You And Me - Medley **THE FOUR PREPS,** *27*
I'm Gonna Knock On Your Door **EDDIE HODGES,** *28*
Swingin' Low **THE OUTLAWS,** *28*
You'll Answer To Me **CLEO LAINE,** *28*
Two Timing Baby **CARTER - LEWIS & THE SOUTHERNERS,** *29*
Carolina **FOLKS BROTHERS,** *30*
Hurt **TIMI YURO,** *30*
I Like It Like That **CHRIS KENNER,** *30*
A Certain Girl **ERNIE K-DOE,** *30*
You Can't Sit Down **THE PHIL UPCHURCH COMBO,** *30*

1962

It Will Stand **THE SHOWMEN,** *33*
You Know What I Mean **THE VERNONS GIRLS,** *34*
Please Pass The Biscuits **JIMMY DEAN,** *34*
She's Gone **BUDDY KNOX,** *34*
Shout Shout **ERNIE MARESCA,** *35*

Mary Jane **ERNIE MARESCA,** *35*
The Things We Did Last Summer **SHELLY FABARES,** *35*
I'm Gonna Be Warm This Winter **CONNIE FRANCIS ,** *35*
42 In Chicago **MERLE KILGORE ,** *35*
You Won't Forget Me **JACKIE DE SHANNON,** *36*
Let Me In **THE SENSATIONS,** *36*
Pop Pop Popeye **THE SHERRYS,** *36*
The Cinnamon Cinder (It's A Very Nice Dance)
THE CINDERS, *36*
Let's Go (Pony) **THE ROUTERS,** *38*
Bye Bye Love **RAY CHARLES & THE RAELETS,** *38*
Desafinado **ELLA FITZGERALD,** *38*
This Song Is Just For You **HOUSTON WELLS AND THE MARKSMEN,** *39*
James (Hold The Ladder Steady) **CAROL DEENE,** *39*
Rinky Tinky Rhythm **ANITA & TH' SO AND SO'S,** *39*
That's All I Want **TERRY DAY,** *40*
Life's Too Short **THE LAFAYETTES,** *40*
I'll Do My Crying Tomorrow **THE TOKENS,** *40*
Twist And Shout **THE ISLEY BROTHERS,** *40*
Reap What You Sew **BILLY STEWART,** *41*
She's A Troublemaker **THE MAJORS,** *41*
Remember Then **THE EARLS,** *42*
What's So Good About Goodbye **THE MIRACLES,** *42*
Two Lovers **MARY WELLS,** *42*

1963

The Bird's The Word **THE RIVINGTONS,** *46*
Sandra **THE VOLUMES,** *46*
Never **THE EARLS,** *46*
Martian Hop **THE RAN-DELLS,** *47*
Candy Girl **THE FOUR SEASONS,** *48*
Killer Joe **THE ROCKY FELLERS,** *48*
I Wanna Be The Leader **THE MARCELS,** *48*
Maybe You'll Be There **BILLY & THE ESSENTIALS,** *49*
I Wonder What She's Doing Tonight **BARRY & THE TAMBERLANES,** *49*
A Little Like Lovin' **THE CASCADES,** *49*

Get Your Hat **DON & DEWEY**, 80
Let It Be Me (Je T'Appartiens) **BETTY EVERETT & JERRY BUTLER**, 80
Dancing Silhouettes **JACKIE DE SHANNON**, 80
Joy Ride **THE ROADSTERS**, 81
Drag **RONNIE & THE DEL-AIRES**, 81
California Sun **THE RIVIERAS**, 81
Hot Rod USA **THE RIP CHORDS**, 81
Please Don't Leave Me **THE CINDERELLAS**, 82
They're Jealous Of Me **EARL-JEAN**, 82
Goin' Places **THE ORLONS**, 82
Spanish Harlem **SOUNDS INCORPORATED**, 82
She Was My Baby **THE SHOUTS**, 82
Blowing In The Wind **STAN GETZ**, 82
Now We're Thru **THE POETS**, 83
All I Want Is My Baby **BOBBY JAMESON**, 83
Young Love **BO AND PEEP**, 83
So Much In Love **THE MIGHTY AVENGERS**, 83
Goodbye Dolly (Gray) **THE MASSED ALBERTS**, 83
Little Latin Lupe Lu **THE KINGSMEN**, 84
I Wonder **THE CRYSTALS**, 84
The Jerk **THE LARKS**, 85
The Crusher **THE NOVAS**, 85
Cross My Heart **THE EXOTICS**, 86
Here She Comes **THE TYMES**, 86
Shang A Doo Lang **ADRIENNE POSTER**, 86

1965

Home Of The Brave **BONNIE & THE TREASURES**, 89
I Want That Boy **THE CHANTELLES**, 90
He Knows I Love Him Too Much **GLO MACARI**, 90
Out In The Sun (Hey-O) **THE BEACH-NUTS**, 90
Hey Baby **THE HI-LITES**, 90
Thou Shalt Not Steal **GLENDA COLLINS**, 91
I Do **THE MARVELOS**, 91
I'm A Happy Man **THE JIVE FIVE**, 91
At The Discothèque **CHUBBY CHECKER**, 91
Hole In The Wall **THE PACKERS**, 92
Baby I'm Yours **BARBARA LEWIS**, 92
May The Bird Of Paradise Fly Up Your Nose **"LITTLE" JIMMY DICKENS**, 92
Genzene (What Have I Done) **THE SHANGAANS**, 92
The Lurch **TED CASSIDY**, 93
Incense **THE ANGLOS**, 93
Liar Liar **THE CASTAWAYS**, 94
I Ain't Gonna Eat Out My Heart Anymore **THE YOUNG RASCALS**, 94
Feel A Whole Lot Better **THE BYRDS**, 94

Sins Of The Family **PF SLOAN**, 94
Is This What I Was Made For **THE IGUANAS**, 94
Child Of Our Times **BARRY MCGUIRE**, 94
For You Babe **THE SPOKESMEN**, 96
It's All Over Now Baby Blue **LEROY VAN DYKE**, 96
Daddy You Been On My Mind **JOAN BAEZ**, 96
Can You Please Crawl Out Your Window? **THE VACELS**, 96
It Ain't Me Babe **JOE & EDDIE**, 96
We Didn't Ask To Be Brought Here **BOBBY DARIN**, 97
You Were On My Mind **WE FIVE**, 97
Let's Get Together **WE FIVE**, 97
Pied Piper **THE CHANGIN' TIMES**, 98
Come Away Melinda **WENDY HUBER**, 98
A Beginning From An End **JAN AND DEAN**, 98
Can't You Hear My Heartbeat **GOLDIE & THE GINGERBREADS**, 98
But You're Mine **SONNY AND CHER**, 99
Don't Talk To Strangers **THE BEAU BRUMMELS**, 99
I Still Love You **THE VEJTABLES**, 99
The Water Is Over My Head **THE ROCKIN' BERRIES**, 99
Dark Shadows and Empty Hallways **TAMMY ST JOHN**, 99
Around The Corner **THE DUPREES**, 100
New York's A Lonely Town **THE TRADE WINDS**, 100
Shut 'Em Down In London Town **THE MAJORITY**, 100
Little Surfer Girl **KENNY & DENY**, 101
Be My Guest **THE NITESHADES**, 101
Theme From "A Summer Place" **THE LETTERMEN**, 102
Beach Boy **RONNY & THE DAYTONAS**, 102
Tiger-A-Go-Go **BUZZ & BUCKY**, 102
She's Just My Style **GARY LEWIS & THE PLAYBOYS**, 103
The Little Girl I Once Knew **THE BEACH BOYS**, 103
The Monkey's Uncle **ANNETTE**, 103
(Here They Come) From All Over The World **JAN AND DEAN**, 104
You Really Know How To Hurt A Guy **JAN & DEAN**, 104
Give Us Your Blessings **THE SHANGRI-LAS**, 104
Right Now And Not Later **THE SHANGRI-LAS**, 104
Sailor Boy **THE CHIFFONS**, 104
My Place **THE CRYSTALS**, 104
I Don't Want To Be Your Baby Anymore **THE POPSICLES**, 105
The Sh-Down-Down Song **THE GINGER SNAPS**, 105
Cold Cold Winter **JEAN AND THE STATESIDES**, 105
Candy **THE ASTORS**, 105
It's Growing **THE TEMPTATIONS**, 106
I'll Always Love You **THE DETROIT SPINNERS**, 106
My Girl Has Gone **THE MIRACLES**, 106
Neighbour Neighbour **THE ADLIBS**, 106
I'm So Thankful **THE IKETTES**, 107
Johnny My Boy **THE ADLIBS**, 107

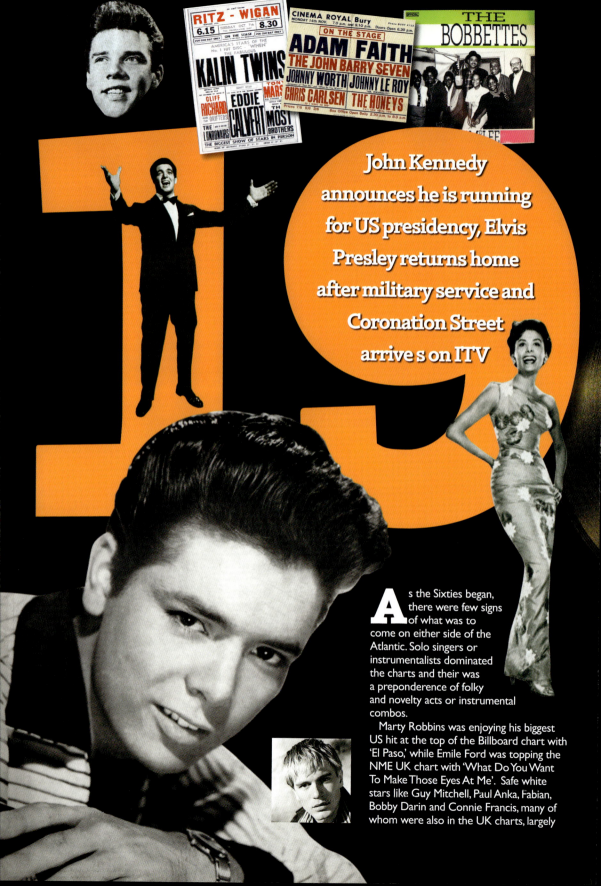

John Kennedy announces he is running for US presidency, Elvis Presley returns home after military service and Coronation Street arrives on ITV

As the Sixties began, there were few signs of what was to come on either side of the Atlantic. Solo singers or instrumentalists dominated the charts and their was a preponderence of folky and novelty acts or instrumental combos.

Marty Robbins was enjoying his biggest US hit at the top of the Billboard chart with 'El Paso,' while Emile Ford was topping the NME UK chart with 'What Do You Want To Make Those Eyes At Me'. Safe white stars like Guy Mitchell, Paul Anka, Fabian, Bobby Darin and Connie Francis, many of whom were also in the UK charts, largely

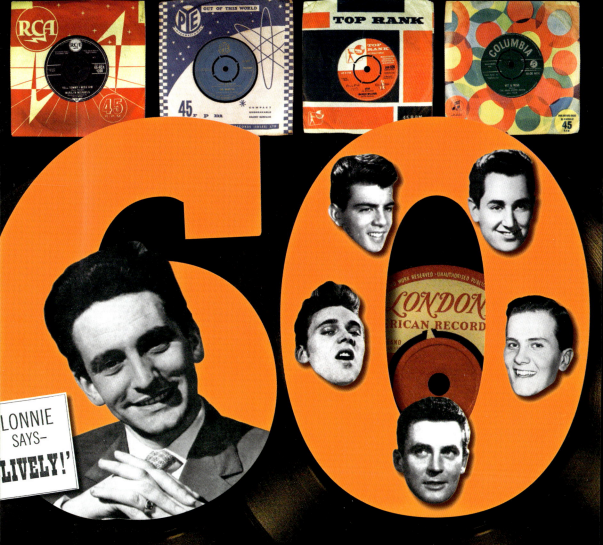

dominated the US charts.

Homegrown talent included Adam Faith, Marty Wilde, Cliff Richard, Alma Cogan and The Beverly Sisters. Guitar or piano instrumentals, or orchestral releases, could still expect to be heavy sellers, contributing to the still strong sales of sheet music.

Rock and Roll had been successfully watered down by many American companies, but there were a few glimmers of hope with medium-sized hits from Joe Turner, The Drifters, The Clovers and The Five Satins in the January 1960 US chart, while Freddie Cannon, Fats Domino, Sandy Nelson and Johnny & The Hurricanes all figured in the NME chart.

Melody Maker

November 19, 1960 FOR THE BEST IN JAZZ Every Friday 6d.

CHRIS BARBER pages 2 & 3

Publishers, songwriters, singers gripped by—

STRANGLEHOLD OF THE TOP 20 CHARTS

THE Top Twenty is placing a "stranglehold" around Britain's music business. And, as a result:

● GIRL SINGERS cannot get the right breaks;
● QUALITY SONGS are edged out—because writers cannot get them recorded;
● TEEN-BEAT FANS— who represent only a minority of Britain's music enthusiasts—are dictating the policies of the A & R men.

This was alleged on Wednesday by Bill Phillips, general manager (exploitation) of KPM Music. He declares: "The A&R men have not ring through with...

SUSAN MADE IT!

THE GOOD HUMOUR MAN

Piltdown Rides Again
THE PILTDOWN MEN
CAPITOL CL 15175

Another Saturday TV programme was The Lone Ranger, whose daring do-gooder deeds proved popular for many years. The rousing theme tune, adapted from Rossini's William Tell Overture, still evokes a call of 'Hi Ho Silver Away' from men of a certain age.

'Piltdown Rides Again' is another adaptation of the same melody, though without Rossini's name anywhere in evidence, and is a solid sax-led instrumental rocker much in the style of Lord Rockingham's 'Hoots Mon'.

Other Piltdown Men titles were McDonald's Cave, Fossil Rock, Goodnight Mrs Flintstone and Brontosaurus Stomp – no theme there then.

Hit & Miss
JOHN BARRY SEVEN PLUS FOUR
COLUMBIA DB 4414

What better way to start this book than with the record chosen by BBC TV as the theme for its long-running Saturday evening TV show, Juke Box Jury hosted by David Jacobs. This short show was one of the few places on TV or radio where we could hear new records as they were released, even if it was only a section of each, and where judgement as to their worth was given by a seemingly haphazard selection of personalities of the day. While we did get the occasional music star who had some knowledge, the panel more often consisted of conventional-looking DJs, actors, TV stars, whose knowledge of pop was usually limited. However, in its time the show included DJ Pete Murray, The Beatles and The Rolling Stones as panelists.

John Barry's striking guitar-led theme is forever linked with the show. The record was a hit in its own right, bouncing around the lower reaches of the top 30 for several weeks. Barry had appeared on shows like Oh Boy, and was active as a writer/arranger for Adam Faith, among others, but found his lasting fame in films, starting with his striking work on the James Bond Theme for Dr No.

Schoolboy Blues
BUZZY KING
TOP RANK JAR 278

In this song, poor Buzzy gets the schoolboy blues in a classic tale of 'Woe is me – we've split up.' For him, it's: 'No more record hops, No more soda shops,' so life is obviously hardly worth living (other than to make this rocking little record, which is helped along with a decent sax break).

It appears to have been Buzzy's sole UK release, and it fits solidly in the sub-genre of teen rockers that began with Frankie Lymon and included groups such as The Rocky Fellers (featured in 1963, see page 48).

I Shot Mr Lee
THE BOBBETTES
PYE INTERNATIONAL 7N 25060

The Bobbettes consisted of Jannie Pought (soprano), Emma Pought (alto), Helen Gathers (alto), Laura Webb (tenor) and Reather Dixon (baritone), who, back in 1955, had been part of a larger group called the Harlem Queens. They were between 11 and 15 years old in 1957 when they had their big hit 'Mr Lee' on Atlantic Records in the States.

The song was about their schoolteacher, who they were, let's say, not over keen on. The saga continued with 'I Shot Mr Lee', which was recorded in February 1959, though contractual problems and wrangles delayed its release until 1960. It is every bit as cute and infectious as its predecessor, and although simple in structure, it is instantly memorable, recalling a cheeky style of playground singing.

The two records were a big step away from the cleaner, Fifties girl group world of massed petticoats and hair bows – no mean feat for teenagers who wrote a good deal of their own material.

They broke up not long afterwards, but three of the original members did re-form the group for a while in the Eighties.

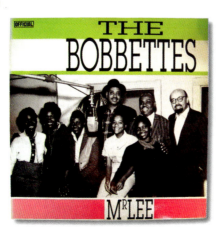

The Bobbettes with Ahmet Ertegun (right) and Big Joe Turner (back).

Stay
MAURICE WILLIAMS & THE ZODIACS
TOP RANK JAR 526

Stay made the top spot on the US Billboard charts on November 27, 1960 on the Herald label – one of several labels based at 1697 Broadway in Manhattan. Close to the New York music business epicentre (the famed Brill Building was 1619 Broadway and The Aldon Building 1650), 1697 housed many second-division companies.

Maurice Williams was already a veteran of the New York recording scene and had previously had the original version hit of 'Little Darlin'' with The Gladiolas. He teamed up with The Zodiacs (Charles Thomas, Henry Gaston and Wiley Bennett) to enjoy his biggest hit with 'Stay'.

The song is taken more slowly than the subsequent hit for The Hollies in the UK beat boom, and alternates between a mid vocal lead and a falsetto. It still stands as a great one-off single that was unlike any other of the time.

There's A Moon Out Tonight
THE CAPRIS
COLUMBIA DB 4605

Although released at the end of 1960, it took until February 1961 for the Capris' wonderful doo-wopper 'There's A Moon Out Tonight' to climb to its No3 peak on the US charts. It was originally released on the small

Planet label back in 1958, and re-appeared on the larger Old Town label run by the late Hy Weiss.

The Capris were five NYC Italian Americans from the Queens borough, and originally included tenor Mike Mincelli, lead singer Nick Santamaria (aka Santo), second tenor Vinny Narcardo, baritone Frank Riena, and bass man John Apostol. Later line-ups of the group replaced Narcardo and Apostol with Tony Danno and Tommy Ferrara.

'There's A Moon Out Tonight' stands as one of the strongest NYC doo-wop records, and it is hardly any wonder that it continued to be reissued – on the Lost Nite, Rommers and Ambient Sound labels, the latter being a very fine Eighties re-make.

London American Records Label

The history of the London American label is tied in with UK Decca's involvement in the American record industry. Decca originally set up US Decca as an outlet for UK product way back in 1934, but the war led to a withdrawal of US interests for the British record major that was not revived until a new outlet for our product was set up in 1947, called London Records. These records had the advantage of Decca's famed ffrr technology (Full Frequency Range Recording), used as an adaptation of submarine hunting technology during the war. London had its first US hit with, of all things, Gracie Fields' 'Now Is The Hour' in 1948.

After introducing two separately numbered Country and Western and Rhythm and Blues series, the label became an outlet for both UK and US releases. Gradually the American releases reduced in favour of the label being purely an outlet for British records.

However, in a key move, the New York-based label remained as a distributor for local American smaller companies and an agent for their overseas releases. In terms of British collectability, the start of the UK London HL series in 1954 is the recognised date when the label began to serve as an outlet for Rock and Roll items, and releases from labels such as Speciality, Atlantic, Dot and by the end of the decade even early Motown.

The importance of the London American label, as it was now called, reached its peak in the late Fifties and early Sixties when the number of releases and chart entries were the highest.

They did not have it all their own way, of course, with some rivals in the form of Pye's Top Rank, and EMI's Columbia, Parlophone and HMV labels all providing UK outlets for whichever US hits and labels they could make business contact with.

London American was probably the first UK label to be collectable in its own right, even though its catalogue was varied, including as it did, some decidedly middle-of-the-road items.

However, the sight of a yellow London demo still gets vinyl hunters' hearts racing, and the label retains a respected image with all collectors – and that is acknowledged by the inclusion of many records in this book.

Mr Lonely
THE VIDELS
LONDON HLI 9153

The Videls reached No73 on the US Billboard chart with the gentle 'Mr Lonely'.

It is sung by the Rhode Island group in the easy Dion & The Belmonts style that was so popular with all the white East Coast groups at that time.

The group was notable because it brought together the talents of Pete Andreoli (aka Anders) and Vincent Poncia, who would later go on to become excellent writers and producers working with Phil Spector, The Critters and others.

Tell Tommy I Miss Him
MARILYN MICHAELS
RCA 1208

He'll Have To Stay
JEANNE BLACK
CAPITOL 15131

1960 was possibly the peak of the 'answer-disc' phenomenon, because disc sales were rising steeply.

Record companies everywhere saw this route as a short cut to reasonable sales on the back of someone else's big hit. These two are two female responses to the American male hits of Ray Peterson's 'Tell Laura I Love Her' and Jim Reeves' 'I'll Have To Go' (though in the UK, it was Ricky Valance who scored the hit with Laura).

Both records here are respectable 'other side of the coin' variations of scenarios and both are handled well by their singers: Marilyn Michaels has just enough vibrato and reverb to suit, while Jeanne Black is more relaxed and laid back.

TOP
RANK
INTERNATIONAL

MADE BY ELECTRIC
AND MUSICAL
INDUSTRIES LTD.
IN GT. BRITAIN

45 R.P.M

JAR-526

Lorna
Music

ALLAN
(37)

STAY
(M. Williams)
MAURICE WILLIAMS
& The Zodiacs

The Capris
THERE'S A
MOON OUT
AGAIN!

COLUMBIA

MILLS MUSIC
NCB

MADE IN GT. BRITAIN

7XCA 25066   45

45-DB 4414

HIT & MISS
(Barry)
THE JOHN BARRY SEVEN
plus FOUR

PYE

45 RPM

7N.25060

I SHOT MISTER LEE
THE BOBBETTES

PYE RECORDS LTD.

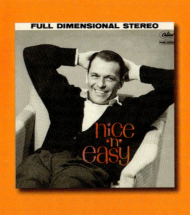

FULL DIMENSIONAL STEREO

nice 'n' easy

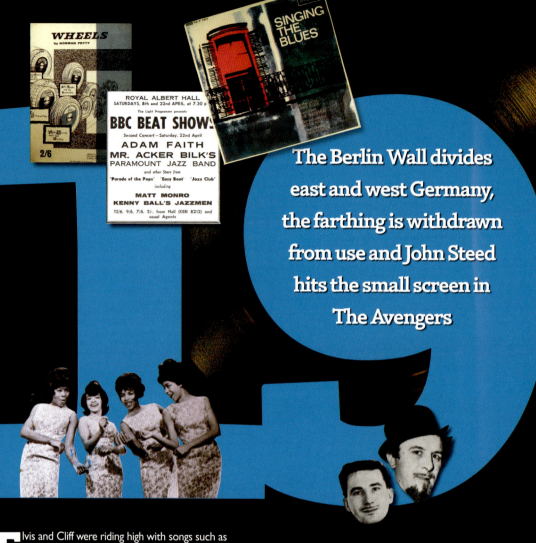

WHEELS
by NORMAN PETTY

2/6

SINGING THE BLUES

ROYAL ALBERT HALL
SATURDAYS, 8th and 22nd APRIL, at 7.30 p

The Light Programme presents

BBC BEAT SHOWS
Second Concert — Saturday, 22nd April

**ADAM FAITH
MR. ACKER BILK'S**
PARAMOUNT JAZZ BAND

and other Stars from
'Parade of the Pops'   'Easy Beat'   'Jazz Club'

including

**MATT MONRO
KENNY BALL'S JAZZMEN**

12/6. 9/6. 7/6. 5/-. from Hall (KEN 8212) and
usual Agents

The Berlin Wall divides east and west Germany, the farthing is withdrawn from use and John Steed hits the small screen in The Avengers

Elvis and Cliff were riding high with songs such as 'Wooden Heart' and 'Theme For A Dream' respectively, and the doo-wop revival, spearheaded by The Marcels' 'Blue Moon', served as an effective antidote to carefully packaged soloists.

The King Brothers were Britain's biggest male group, serving up their version of 'Seventy Six Trombones', but on February 9, The Beatles had debuted at The Cavern.

Bob Dylan had arrived in New York to begin to play early gigs at the Café Wha?, but he was not one of the other Bobbys — Messrs Vee, Rydell, Darin were the teen stars of the day, being industry-packaged as safe boys-next-door in the rapidly emerging teen market.

In the UK, the hippest thing for a night out was a Trad Jazz dance to watch Chris Barber, Kenny Ball or Acker Bilk and their bands. On both sides of the Atlantic, you could attend package shows such as the first Dick Clark Caravan of Stars featuring a troop of teen record stars performing three or four songs each.

Motown had its first US No1 with The Marvelettes' 'Please Mr Postman', and on September 15, a group of kids soon to be known as The Beach Boys ventured into a friend's West Coast studio to have a stab at recording a song called 'Surfin'...

Mercury RECORDS

Music For Every Mood

SEPTEMBER IN THE RAIN
(Dubin—Warren)
DINAH WASHINGTON
Orchestra conducted by
Nat Goodman

45-AMT
1162

THIS RECORD MUST
BE PLAYED AT **45** REVS PER
MINUTE

61

September In The Rain

DINAH WASHINGTON
MERCURY AMT 1162

Dinah Washington was a class act in every way. She reigned supreme in the Fifties covering every style from R&B, jazz and blues to pop, and won a Grammy for her recording of 'What a Difference A Day Makes' in 1959, which was to prove her biggest hit.

This sublime reading of 'September In The Rain', a mere two years before her accidental death at the age of 39, went by comparatively un-noticed despite its obvious quality.

Much loved for her sparkling and humorously confident personality, she once declared in London: "There is only one heaven, one earth, and one queen...Queen Elizabeth is an impostor."

I've Told Every Little Star

LINDA SCOTT

COLUMBIA DB 4638

Ms Scott is certainly at the pop, or popette, end of the spectrum, with no pretensions to be otherwise.

The early Sixties was an era of boy- and girl-next-door marketing, with many eager young singers ready to try their luck under the watchful eyes of guiding managers.

This Canadian American recording presents the Hammerstein/Kern song as typical cute pop, and was the first of half-a-dozen UK issues by Linda – 'Starlight Starbright', 'Count Every Star', 'Land Of Stars' (you get the picture).

Her UK album release is now highly prized by collectors.

Peppermint Twist (Part 1)

JOEY DEE & THE STARLITERS

COLUMBIA DB 4758

While this fast dancer number was a top 30 UK hit, these days it doesn't seem to get the airplay that it deserves – it is, without doubt, one of the top three Twist records there were.

The Peppermint Twist was named after New York's Peppermint Lounge on 45th Street, where all the glitterati of the day, from Jackie Kennedy down, could be found being hip with the new dance craze. The lounge itself was of no great size, being a long, thin bar with a dance space and small stage at the end. Joey Dee and his two pals were the house band and sometime-employers of the three girls who would become The Ronettes two years later.

Veronica, Estelle and Nedra honed all their moves at the Peppermint Lounge and look back on that time with pleasure, considering their time with The Starliters as a fun and friendly learning experience.

The record continues on side two, and is most memorable for its 'bop-shu-ah' backing vocals behind Joey Dee's exuberant lead..

Those Oldies But Goodies

NINO AND THE EBBTIDES **TOP RANK JAR 572**

"Nag" THE HALOS **LONDON HLU 9424**

Rama Lama Ding Dong THE EDSELS

PYE INTERNATIONAL 7N 25086

Imagination

THE QUOTATIONS

HMV/VERVE POP 975

1961 had seen the worldwide success of the Marcels' madcap version of the popular standard 'Blue Moon', and had helped to fuel what is now referred to as the neo-doo-wop era of 1961-1964.

In the classic doo-wop era of the mid-Fifties, many groups had stuck closely to a standard blended harmony formula, but The Marcels' arrangements brought both the bass and high tenor voices to the fore with distinct vocal lines that were often quite separate to the mid-range singers. Bass voice novelty intros became the new standard, as was the case with both the Edsels' and The Quotations' records. In The Halos' "Nag", the bass singer becomes the principal lead voice with the other answering him.

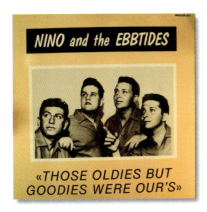

"THOSE OLDIES BUT GOODIES WERE OUR'S"

Cruisin'
THE HOLLYWOOD VINES
CAPITOL CL 15191

Issued as the B side to the group's 'When Johnny Comes Slidin' Home', 'Cruising' is, like the top side, a sax and guitar-led instrumental reminiscent in feel to Link Wray's 'Rumble' (which was deemed so insidious that is was banned at the time as likely to deprave kids). The Hollywood Vines were probably a studio-based group whose names may, or may not, be the same as the 13 that appear on the writing credits on both sides of the record!

Nino And The Ebbtides, by comparison, delivered their fine cover of Little Caesar and The Romans' original West Coast hit with 'Those Oldies But Goodies' in a more traditional classic doo-wop framework, but nevertheless became part of the revival in vocal groups.

Brooklyn-based The Quotations, a white four-piece made up of Richie Schwartz, Lew Arno, Harvey Hershkowitz and Larry Kassman, probably owed most to The Marcels, whose idea it had been to rip apart and update an old standard, and thus Imagination was given a similar treatment.

Nino and his gang were from the nearby Bronx and after several personnel changes they comprised Antonio (Nino) Aiello, Vinnie Drago, Tony Imbimbo and the youngest and newest member Tony Dibari, who actually sung lead on Those Oldies But Goodies.

By contrast, the black quintet The Edsels hailed from Ohio, and comprised brothers Harry and Larry Greene, George Jones Jr, James Reynolds and bass singer Marshall Sewell. The latter's deep tones lead off the famed intro of 'Rama Lama Ding Dong', which was to be immortalised as part of Barry Mann's tongue-in-cheek 'Who Put The Bomp' hit record.

Their hit enjoyed an 11-week run on the Billboard chart, reaching No21 in summer 1961, the East Coast sales being the best.

The Quotations

The Halos bass singer, Arthur Crier, wrote the comic '"Nag"' and the group presented it in a style that drew from the Coasters. Crier, along with Harold Johnson, Al Cleveland and Phil Johnson, were well-known on the NY scene as backing singers and were the male equivalents of The Cookies. They were used by producer Phil Spector as the vocalists behind Curtis Lee on his hit 'Pretty Little Angel Eyes'.

Along with Fifties doo-wop, the Sixties neo-doo-wop period is particularly collectable and all these four UK pressings would certainly be expensive – even if you could find them.

More Money For You And Me - Medley
THE FOUR PREPS
CAPITOL CL 15217

During the Seventies and Eighties, it became the norm for companies to issue session singers with record medleys of well-known hits – such as Gidea Park's 'Beach Boy Gold' and the 'Stars on 45' releases. Prior to this, The Barron Knights had set up a good comedy-based career using records that re-worked a succession of hits with a comic twist; this US hit for the usually straight-laced Four Preps was an early forerunner.

Collecting together 'Mr Blue', 'Alley Oop', 'Smoke Gets In Your Eyes', 'In This Whole Wide World', 'A Worried Man', 'Tom Dooley' and 'A Teenager In Love' and linking them with a loose 'funny' narrative, they gained a No17 US hit in October 1961.

On the 'live' recording from their On Campus album, the biggest audience reaction seems to come with the suggestion that while Dion was singing, The Belmonts might be found in the parking lot stealing hup-caps off the cars. Consequently, the Four Preps may not have wanted to share any concert bills with The Belmonts thereafter…

I'm Gonna Knock On Your Door

EDDIE HODGES LONDON HLA 9369

American Eddie Hodges managed to get to No37 in the UK chart in October 1961 with this rousing and enthusiastic rocker. Its B side was 'Ain't Gonna Wash For a Week', which The Brook Brothers rushed to cover for the British market, gaining a top 20 hit. Hodges stuck around for a few years, and had other releases in the UK on London, MGM and Stateside, the last of which saw him move from straight rock to folk rock with a cover of Dylan's 'Love Minus Zero – No Limit'

"...Topside bows in a new American beat singer, could be a sleeper'. It's the familiar 'jukebox' formula- but the foot-teasing ingredients are pretty potent." MELODY MAKER 1961

"That record was my first real try at recording a rock 'n' roll song. I fell in love with the music listening to Murray the K and all the other jocks on the New York stations.

My parents weren't sure about it due to all the bad press, but Archie Bleyer at Cadence Records helped me talk them into it. It was a dream come true recording it, with Archie doing the sound effects and all.

After it was released, there was no activity for a while and I thought the record was dead. Then, one day Archie called us and said the record had "broken" in Fargo, N.D. I had no idea where that was, but I was ecstatic. Before long, I was flying around the country on a record promotion tour. In the northeast, the R&B stations were playing it – they thought I was a young black girl." *Eddie Hodges, 2007*

Swingin' Low

THE OUTLAWS HMV POP 844

Though credited to 'Raymond' this relies heavily on the melody of 'Swing Low Sweet Chariot'. However, the quality and overall tone of the guitar lead takes it into very different territory.

This instrumental, The Outlaws first solo single, is from the Joe Meek studio, and features the original line-up with Billy Kuy on lead guitar. It made No46 in the UK for two weeks.

Joe Meek dreamed up a publicity stunt for the release. After dressing in Wild West gear, they hired a stagecoach and drove it down London's Oxford Street to the huge HMV store where they staged a hold up, demanding a copy of their new single (which they duly got after sheepishly having to part with the-then requisite amount of 6s 4d). The stunt continued with Joe waving posters and blasting out the recording from the stagecoach until they were politely asked to stop. The hoped-for press coverage never materialised.

The record itself is a prime piece of Meekabilia, with the bold guitar lines being interspersed with all manner of percussive noise, which sounds as if they were recording directly from his kitchen and someone is hitting every implement in sight – which may well have been exactly what was happening.

You'll Answer To Me

CLEO LAINE

FONTANA TF 267166

It is both the quality of the song and Cleo's vocal that make this release so attractive. The Sherman Edwards/Hal David song tells the age-old story of 'You'd better not treat him bad' with a simple but effective melody.

Cleo Laine wraps her husky and seductive tones around the lyric, managing to ignore the somewhat intrusive high string lines and the cooing chorus that adds little to the proceedings. Had this been recorded later, the producer and arranger may have had the courage to present it in a more stripped-down fashion, more like Ketty Lester's wonderful 'Love Letters'. No matter really, as this is still a five-star record that sits alongside Cleo's other great song of that time, 'Looks Like They're In Love.'

Two Timing Baby
CARTER-LEWIS & THE SOUTHERNERS
EMBER EMB S 145

John Carter and Ken Lewis arrived in London from Birmingham with the aim of making it in the music business. They managed it in fine fashion, although after this early release. They were to excel as writers, singers and producers with a string of hits to their credit from The Ivy league, The Flowerpot Men, White Plains and the lesser-known Friends, and Dawn Chorus (the latter two are featured in 1968 and 1969 respectively). These hits were the tip of the iceberg, especially in John Carter's case, as he has been active in the music business since 1961, including being the lead voice on The New Vaudeville Band's 'Winchester Cathedral' hit.

Carter-Lewis as a recording unit usually consisted of John and Ken with guitarist Lorne Green, bass player Ron Prentiss and drummer Bob Graham from The Outlaws. There was a shifting line-up in the road band that included drummers Viv Prince or Mitch Mitchell, bass Ron Clark, and the young guitarist Jimmy Page, who would sit in the Denmark Street Giaconda Café awaiting the chance of gigs. Page would soon join the recording unit, where his first recorded guitar solo can be found with Carter-Lewis.

'Two-Timing Baby' is an advanced group record for 1961, engineered as it was by Joe Meek's at his Holloway Road studio. Though very much a Carter-Lewis initiated recording, the familiar gallopy Meek drum sound is present.

In this instance, the recorded group was Chas Hodges and Bob Graham (both Outlaws), guitarist Albert Lee, and Meek collaborator Geoff Goddard on piano.

Carter-Lewis certainly provided a breeding ground for UK musical talent.

Carolina
FOLKS BROTHERS
BLUE BEAT BB 30

Way before there was any quantity of West Indian music on our airwaves, one or two records somehow crept in under the radar, and this one is reckoned by many to rank as this country's first ska record.

The recorded quality and even the performance of 'Carolina' was not perfect, being somewhat lo-fi even to ears then, but it had an immediate attraction and magic as a result of its seemingly lazy vocal delivery as the group clustered around a sole microphone.

Produced by Prince Buster, it featured three real brothers, John, Mico and Junior Folkes, together with the drumming of Oswald Williams (aka Count Ossie).

The Blue Beat label was gaining much credence with its releases of Prince Buster records, and this infectious record was also one of the trailblazers. The song was covered much later by Apache Indian.

Hurt TIMI YURO
LONDON HLG 9403

I Like It Like That
CHRIS KENNER
LONDON HLU 9410

A Certain Girl
ERNIE K-DOE **LONDON HLU 9487**

You Can't Sit Down
THE PHIL UPCHURCH COMBO
HMV POP 899

Back in 1961 people just enjoyed records without the need to pigeon-hole or categorise them.

However, 'I Like It Like That' and 'A Certain Girl' are now categorised as the New Orleans sound. The record industry sometimes used EPs to introduce genre music to audiences and 'Singing The Blues' is an example, including as it did the Chris Kenner track, alongside three other American hits. Common to all of them was a slightly lazy, beat driven by piano as much as guitar. Kenner's rendition of a song about a local music club was beguiling, and his loose style of singing cropped up later with his original recording of 'Land Of 1000 Dances,' his only other UK single issue.

Ernie K-Doe, by contrast, had several UK singles, including his third 'I Cried My Last Tear'.

Tucked away on the B side was 'A Certain Girl', which still appears in the Yardbirds' live sets.

The Phil Upchurch recording of 'You Can't Sit Down' was in its first Sixties incarnation on the HMV label, appearing as it did later in 1966 on a Sue label reissue, which paid heed to its growing popularity as an instrumental club sound that was ever-popular at places such as the Flamingo.

Leaving the Timi Yuro record until last is purposeful, as in many ways it was the one that began to explain why so many liked the other ones.

The Yuro record was unlike any other, as her emotional delivery seared through you. Here was a singer who was prepared to let go vocally, and didn't conform to the mannered delivery that was so prevalent on the radio at the time.

Yuro, born in Chicago to Italian/American parents, took the song all the way to No4 on the Billboard charts.

'Hurt' is the link with the other three records in this section: none of the vocalists conformed to usual stereotypes, even though the records were quite different. Perhaps strangely, the Upchurch instrumental was doing something similar in its own terms. There was an earthy, emotional quality. Real soul was coming.

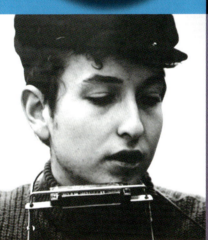

Music For Every Mood

LIBERTY

Produced by JOE MEEK of R.G.M. Sound for DECCA
TELSTAR ★ THE TORNADOES | DECCA F11 494

Frock & Roll Classics — MONO
THE GREAT **Carol Deene**
Johnny Get Angry

19

VOTED A UNANIMOUS HIT ON 'JUKE BOX JURY'
POP POP POP-PIE ORCHS IN THE PRESS
Recorded by THE SHERRYS on LONDON • SIMONE JACKSON on PICCADILLY

The musical world was well served by the music of New York's Brill Building writers, and more specifically the younger teams across the other side of Broadway at No1650, The Aldon Building. There, you would have found Carole King and Gerry Goffin, Barry Mann and Cynthia Weil and others whose output was catching teens' ears.

Cliff and The Shadows were riding high with 'The Young Ones' and 'Wonderful Land', and Telstar put Joe Meek's small bedroom studio fully on the musical map. The West Side Story soundtrack had taken musicals into new territory. The gang stand-offs presented in that film were replicated in real life. The world held its breath as America and Russia squared up to each other during the Cuban Missile Crisis.

There were race riots in the American South after James Meredith tried to enter the University Of Mississippi, and the first Motown Revue set off to spread the word far beyond Detroit. The Beatles entered the NME charts in October with 'Love Me Do', and William Perks (aka Bill Wyman) met and joined The Rolling Stones in December…

The Shanari...

The Crystals

Marylin Monroe dies, Nelson Mandela is arrested, the Cuban Missile Crisis is averted and The Beatles 'Love Me Do' is recorded

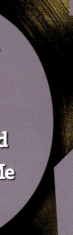

It Will Stand THE SHOWMEN
LONDON HLP 9481

At a time when the first great age of Rock & Roll had passed and had been replaced by the more manufactured paler imitation stars the companies could control, this magnificent issue from The Showmen stood as a beacon for the earthy power of the true spirit of the genre. The lyrics said it all: Rock and Roll will stand forever, and the way the group delivered it proved R&R/R&B grit was still alive.

The five-piece group revolved around the rough-cut voice of General Norman Johnson, and yes, General really was his first name. Beside him were tenor Gene 'Cheater' Knight, tenor Dorsey 'Chops' Knight, baritone Leslie 'Fat Boy' Felton and bass Milton 'Smokes' Wells.

Originally called The Humdingers, they began in Norfolk, Virginia and found their way to New Orleans, where they were developed by the combined talents of Joe Banashak and Allen Toussaint. 'It Will Stand' was their biggest hit, reaching No61 on Billboard, but the record has maintained a legendary status ever since. It was one of the tracks on the wonderful Singing The Blues EP in the last section.

General Johnson has maintained a long-running career that has included 'The Chairmen Of The Board,' and a great take on 'Rockaway Beach' cut as a one-off single with the late Joey Ramone.

Please Pass The Biscuits
JIMMY DEAN **CBS AAG 122**

Record buyers in the Fifties and Sixties liked a laugh, and sales of comedy and novelty discs remained strong, especially in America. Country singer Jimmy Dean cut this oddity as the B side to his self-penned 'Little Black Book', and it is a strange tale of youthful frustration, but not the sort you might expect.

It was Initially confusing to British ears because the biscuits referred to in the title are not our usual sweet temptations, but a side helping of bread for Sunday lunch. The poor boy has his chicken, chowder and tatties, but no one has thought to pass the bread down to the hungry lad who is too polite to reach across the table. The story is told with the help of a gentle chorus that comments on his plight, and eventually all the bread goes to the adults, and he is left unfulfilled.

You Know What I Mean
THE VERNONS GIRLS
DECCA F 11450

By 1962, the original much larger group of Vernons Girls (formed at the famed football pools company for staff recreation) had slimmed down to a sassy trio. They were given a Decca contract under the eyes of producer Jack Good and MD Charles Blackwell and achieved a top 20 hit with the A side of this record, 'Lover Please,' a fine cover of the Clyde McPhatter US hit.

'You Know What I Mean' was a tongue-in-cheek slice of Liverpool life, with the girls commenting on their current lads – a bit like The Shangri-Las transported from Queens to the Albert Dock. After its initial release the record was re-promoted as a double A side and had another smaller chart run.

The initial line-up was Maureen Kennedy, Frances Lee and Jean Owen, but personnel changed over time, with members often crossing over to British session singers who featured in groups such as The Breakaways and The Ladybirds.

The girls also cut another comedy side called 'Funny All Over', which is well worth finding, as well as some good girl group dance-based sides.

She's Gone
BUDDY KNOX
LIBERTY 55473

The well-respected Buddy Knox had enjoyed a good run of releases since his best-known hit 'Party Doll' back in 1957.

'She's Gone' found him working with renowned producer Snuff Garrett, who was then enjoying huge hits with Bobby Vee.

The bright and infectious rocker finds Buddy in a speeded-up Dion vein, while the B side has an obscure Mann/Weil song, 'Now There's Only Me', where Snuff Garrett returns him to 'Oh dear, poor me' Vee territory.

Shout Shout
ERNIE MARESCA
LONDON HLU 9531

Mary Jane
ERNIE MARESCA
LONDON HLU 9579

These two performances have a distinct Dion flavour, but it's hardly surprising in this case as Ernie Maresca had written 'The Wanderer' for Dion DiMucci and co-written 'Runaround Sue' with him.

Ernie was deeply involved with the Italian American New York group scene, and was a regular at Lou Cicchetti's record store (Cousins) on Fordham Road in the Bronx, between a wig shop and a menswear store. This small shop was the epicentre of many Bronx recordings and releases, as Cicchetti ran his own label that gave an outlet for local groups.

The Cousins label's biggest hit was The Regents' original recording of 'Barbara Ann', and Ernie wrote the follow-up, 'Runaround', for the Regents. 'Mary Jane' was the second of six singles he released in the UK, and was his follow-up to the much-played, but now seemingly forgotten, 'Shout Shout, Knock Yourself Out'. 'Mary Jane' was released a little too early for the title to be mistaken for a veiled drug reference, and is, indeed, about a girl he knows – though with lyrics like "Mary Jane, you give me a pain on the brain" we suspect that the relationship wasn't going anywhere.

Sadly, the record didn't either; even with a wandering higher falsetto line amid the insistent early Sixties-styled verses and chorus, though according to Ernie it was written back in 1957 as an attempt to impress friends.

"Writers at that time were getting lots of hits. Goffin & King and Greenwich and Barry wrote for established stars. Had I been with a bigger company, I could have had as many hits. I had 'Shout', which was a great happy song for that early Sixties time"

ERNIE MARESCA

The Things We Did Last Summer
SHELLEY FABARES
PYE INTERNATIONAL 7N 25166

I'm Gonna Be Warm This Winter
CONNIE FRANCIS
MGM 1185

42 In Chicago
MERLE KILGORE
MERCURY AMT 1193

1962 saw the charts dominate by the NY team of writers based at 1650 Broadway in the building run by Don Kirshner. Goffin & King, Mann & Weil, Kooper & Levine and many others plied their trade there with great effect. Kirshner's linked record label Dimension had a string of hits with well-crafted pop hits for Little Eva, The Cookies, Big Dee Irwin and Carole King herself. Carole's writing went a long way to kick-starting and defining teen pop of the Sixties, and her success had an immediate effect through the industry. These three records chimed with the seasonal weather theme of Carole's hit 'It Might As Well Rain Until September' to a greater or lesser degree.

Shelley Fabares was a well-known starlet on the West Coast who had hit earlier in the year with the slightly sickly 'Johnny Angel', but had now re-worked the Styne/Cahn standard into a cute poppy NY styled teen item, with a similar version of Neil Sedaka's 'Breaking Up Is Hard To Do' on the flip.

Connie Francis, a particularly well-established major star, also jumped onto the teen train with 'I'm Gonna Be Warm This Winter', giving herself an immediate contemporary feel with a release that had the New York sound written all over it.

Merle Kilgore, by contrast, was a country singer who had been around with highly collectable UK releases since 1954, and his '42 In Chicago' was a country/pop crossover song in a similar vein to Leroy Van Dyke's classic 'Walk On By'.

His deep voice observes that while it's 42 in Chicago and 81 in LA it's 10 below and freezing since his girl went away. It's a good example of the occasional sub-genre of heartbreak/ weather forecast recordings!

You Won't Forget Me
JACKIE DE SHANNON
LIBERTY LIB 55497

Let Me In
THE SENSATIONS
PYE INTERNATIONAL 7N 25128

Pop Pop Pop-Pie
THE SHERRYS **LONDON HLW 9625**

The Cinnamon Cinder (It's A Very Nice Dance)
THE CINDERS
WARNER BROS WB 86

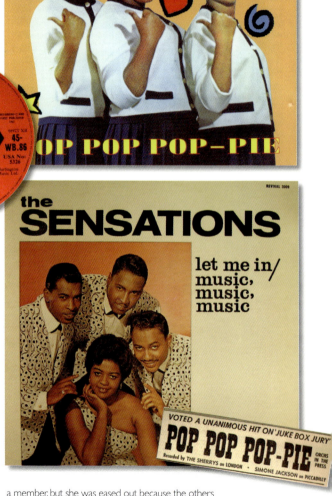

These four 1962 releases show the diversity of girl group records – and yes, the genre often has honorary releases by soloists (and even groups with chaps in) if the sound fits the overall accepted format.

Jackie De Shannon released several prime examples of the sound in her long career, such as the pounding 'Should I Cry'. Jackie's songs, which are always immediately catchy, stay with you – 'You Won't Forget Me' even underscores the point lyrically. With a cascading piano behind her, the song is one of the strongest from her time with Liberty Records.

The Sensations''Let Me In' was released on the old murky-blue Pye International label. The label changed from this often-unreadable colour to the much-loved yellow and red in 1962.

The Sensations, featuring Yvonne Baker who wrote the song and was the sole female member, were from Philadelphia and included bass Alfonso Howell, baritone Tommy Cooke and tenor Richard Curtain alongside the featured Yvonne. They had released one other song, 'Music Music Music', in the UK the previous year, and their attractive group song provided the basis for Ellie Greenwich and Jeff Barry's soon-to-be-hits as The Raindrops, especially 'What A Guy', which was written with The Sensations in mind.

The Sherrys were another Philadelphia-based group guided by John Madara and Dave White, who figure later here with work on records by Len Barry and The Spokesmen. 'Pop Pop Pop-Pie' originated as a dance in New Orleans specifically for Chris Kenner's 'Something You Got' local hit, and the dance quickly spread to local prominence.

The Sherrys comprised Delthine and Dinell Cook, their cousin Charlotte Butler and Delores 'Honey' Wylie. The Cook sisters were the daughters of Little Joe Cook, who had hit earlier with his version of 'Peanuts', and the girls were often used as back-up singers on local records such as Bobby Rydell issues.

At one stage, the later Motown star Tammi Terrell was

a member, but she was eased out because the others apparently didn't like her.

The group mostly stuck to girlie dance songs, although their song 'That Boy Of Mine' in 1963 is a genre corker.

The Cinders was really a one-off Marty Cooper production, arranged by the famed Jack Nitzsche in the style of the Gary US Bonds, Curtis Lee and Jimmy Soul hits – that is, with a lot of extra sounds of partying interspersed with easy sing-along lyrics and a rasping sax break.

Despite featuring both male and female voices, this qualifies as an honorary girl group record through the cutesy end of chorus interjections of: "It's A Very Nice Dance."

Girl groups

One of the definitive genres of the early Sixties was the girl group. It was a sound that roughly straddled the years 1960-1965, and the standard of releases were remarkably consistant.

This is because, almost without exception, the genre was writer/producer led and coincided with a time when music industry people realised the financial power of the teen market and the growing sales of singles to young girls especially.

The well-crafted hook-laden pop single was an ideal vehicle for the various lyrical permutations of teen romance and emotion. Although there are plenty of examples of Fifties girl groups, the true pop market releases can realistically be dated from The Shirelles wonderful 'Will You Love Me Tomorrow' from 1960, Carole King and Gerry Goffin's first major hit. By 1962, with the help of dance record hits from acts such as Little Eva, The Marvelettes, The Orlons and The Sherrys, the genre was well-established in the US, with increasing attention in the UK.

Dimension Records in New York and the newly established Phil Spector-led Philles Records in LA took girl groups to even greater heights, as the power of the productions and the sheer quality of the immediately accessible songs gave hit after hit – and caused every label and every producer to issue girl group records.

They are now established as a solid area of record collecting, with the later, more soul-tinged, releases often crossing over into Northern Soul territory.

Further fine examples appear later in this book, but for further reading we recommend John

The Marvelettes

Clemente's Girl Groups – Fabulous Females That Rocked The World (Krause 2000) or Charlotte Greig's Will You Still Love Me Tomorrow (Virago 1989).

The Shangri-las

The Crystals

Let's Go (Pony)
THE ROUTERS **WARNER BROS WB 77**

The Routers were one of many studio-based group names used by producer Joe Saraceno on the West Coast. The 'members' were usually the local key session players, although pictures of the road band for the Routers reveal a young Scott Engel (Walker) as the sometime bass player.

Saraceno was notable for building his instrumentals around instantly recognisable riffs, such as this ten-strike handclapping pattern with 'Let's Go' tacked on the end, which has dominated sports stadiums ever since. It's probably the best-known instrumental of the Sixties that few could actually put a name to.

The bracketed addition of Pony was to tie into yet another dance craze, but proved unnecessary.

Desafinado
ELLA FITZGERALD
VERVE VS 502

They say class will out, and it is indeed true here. The much-loved first lady of jazz eased herself easily into the early Sixties cool Bossa Nova popularity.

Both in the US and the UK, the work of Stan Getz, Charlie Byrd, Jobim and Astrud Gilberto's unforgettable 'Girl From Ipanema' seduced everyone.

Ella's take on the vocal version of the better-known Stan Getz and Charlie Byrd's 'Desafinado' was sheer magic, and every bit as important a part of the early Sixties as anything else.

Bye Bye Love
RAY CHARLES & THE RAELETS
HMV POP 1589

Although both tracks on this record are 1962 recordings, they didn't actually emerge as a single in this form in the UK until 1967. However, it seemed more appropriate to include 'Bye Bye Love' in its correct year, when Ray Charles was releasing so much wonderful material in a number of different veins. His 1962 hits with 'I Can't Stop Loving You' and 'Unchain My Heart' had followed close behind classics such as 'Hit The Road Jack' and 'One Mint Julep' the year before, and his lesser-known interpretation of the old Everly Brothers hit deserves to be bracketed with these.

The power-swing of the orchestra and The Raelets carry an elongated intro before Ray comes in to take total control on a super-charged version that leaves you breathless.

This Song Is Just For You
HOUSTON WELLS AND THE MARKSMEN
PARLOPHONE R 4955

While plenty of acts in the US, including Ray Charles, were really developing country music, there were far fewer in the UK. Independent producer Joe Meek had a penchant for country songs and the associated cowboy imagery, which he had already begun to develop in a rock vein with The Outlaws.

Here, however, he plays it more traditionally with the first release from the Americanised, but British, act, Houston Wells And The Marksmen. The well-formed country-styled song achieves everything it sets out to do.

The group managed to get a small hit with their third issue 'Only The Heartaches', eventually clocking up some eight singles, two EPs and one rare Meek-produced album called, perhaps unsurprisingly, *Western Style*. There was also a Houston Wells and The Outlaws release, and other solo work from The Marksmen. Overall, the group's work with Joe Meek was probably among his most restrained productions.

James (Hold The Ladder Steady)
CAROL DEENE
HMV POP 1086

The attractive young British starlet Carol Deene was always on the verge of becoming a major star, yet never found the song that would give her a major breakthrough.

She had to settle for the lower fringes on the Top 30 with covers of US hits, more often than not with her versions of US star Sue Thompson's output – to the extent that it almost became a standing joke in the industry.

The John D Loudermilk song 'James (Hold The Ladder Steady)' was typically cute and cuddly fare, with Carol managing to extract every bit of emphasis from the song to make listeners think that it had been written especially for her.

She lost career momentum when a bad car crash in 1966 almost killed her, but thankfully she recovered to make more good records, though without the early, albeit limited, success.

A fine Nineties CD collection from Diamond Records of her work was sub-titled as 'Frock & Roll Classics', which just about says it all.

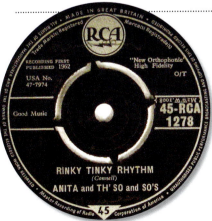

Rinky Tinky Rhythm
ANITA & TH' SO AND SO'S **RCA 1278**

Another song and performance from the land of cute was this B side (of 'Joey Baby', since you ask) from Anita and Th' So and So's, which exactly as it's written on the label. A male bass voice leads into female shoo-be-doos before the whole thing kicks into what is pretty much a nonsense song.

Led by a tack piano repeating a close approximation of the organ riff from Chris Montez's 'Lets Dance', lyrically it may be a dance craze item. It's certainly an infectious little side that should have been the A side.

There could possibly have been some link to Dave Cortez's 'Rinky Dink', which hit around the same time.

That's All I Want
TERRY DAY
CBS AAG 104

Although this is not the best song in the world, it is certainly a rocking and spirited performance and production from all concerned – and those concerned were some pretty key people in LA.

Terry Day is actually the late Terry Melcher, son of Doris Day, who was soon to get hits with future Beach Boy Bruce Johnston as Bruce and Terry and as The Rip Chords, before going on to become the first Byrds producer.

Working with him on this early disc, as he worked as a hotshot CBS A&R man, was Jack Nitzsche (whose name was spelt wrong on the label – not for the last time) and some of the key LA session players, most likely drummer Earl Palmer and the crew that had formed part of the Ernie Fields Orchestra a couple of years earlier. Their rocked-up version of 'In The Mood' had been a worldwide hit. They were also the same players who masqueraded as B Bumble & The Stingers on 'Nut Rocker'.

Terry Melcher's career is worth a book in its own right; it took in so much of what became really important LA rock and pop over the years.

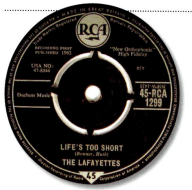

Life's Too Short
THE LAFAYETTES
RCA 1299

'Life's Too Short' is a decidedly different record, especially for 1962. Sparsely orchestrated, it consists of piano, bass and drumsticks on what sounds like a tabletop, apart from a unexpected few bars of sax added about a third of the way in.

The slightly offhand vocalist is trying to convince his girl to marry – or at least take things further – because he reckons there is so little time.

The whole strange effect is of a garage record a bit before its time. Quite unlike anything else.

I'll Do My Crying Tomorrow
THE TOKENS **RCA 1313**

To attempt to collect all The Tokens' records ever issued, either under their own name or as one of the many pseudonyms they used, would be a thankless task. It would, however, be a most rewarding one, as they maintained a steady quality control over their work, even though they took a few bizarre offshoot directions at times.

Back in 1962, still fresh from their huge hit 'The Lion Sleeps Tonight', they were still only operating as themselves and concentrating on being a great harmony group.

'I'll Do My Crying Tomorrow' is a full-blooded NY production number with big thumpy drums, plenty of percussion, and a string arrangement that goes over the top of everything else as the song builds.

The group comprised Phil and Mitch Margo, Hank Medress and Jay Seigal and it is the latter's soaring and effortless falsetto that drives this record. The song rarely appears on their compilations, and when it did, it was marked as 'previously unreleased'. We know better.

Twist And Shout
THE ISLEY BROTHERS
STATESIDE SS112

Had The Beatles not wrenched the song apart to make it totally their own, this may have stayed one of the great unknowns, though the small print credits would probably have rescued it from total oblivion.

Produced by co-writer Bert Russell (aka Bert Burns) and arranged by Teacho Wiltshire (well-known and respected names, you understand), the group settle into vocals every bit as frenetic as The Beatles, albeit without the climatic build that Mr Lennon led so effectively.

The backing is a glorious cacophony with horns gradually entering and building their role, while the drummer seemingly works to his own script entirely using an ever-widening array of fills.

It was one of the earliest releases on the highly collectable Stateside label (formed by EMI as a counter to Decca's London American outlet).

Reap What You Sew

BILLY STEWART
PYE INTERNATIONAL 7N 25164

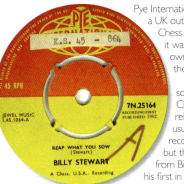

Pye International provided a UK outlet for Chicago's Chess label until it was given its own label later in the decade.

The earliest sought-after Chess releases were usually blues recordings, but this one from Billy Stewart, his first in Britain, was quite different and would have proved difficult to categorise at that time.

The simple backing with girl chorus allowed Stewart to deliver the sort of tenor vocals he became known for: breathy, emotional and liberally expansive with word repetitions, all of which made him both instantly recognisable and arresting to listen to.

This churchy tale was not too many steps away from a sermon, and was, in retrospect, one of the stepping stones to what we now call soul.

She's A Troublemaker

THE MAJORS **LONDON HLP 9627**

The Majors were a one-girl, four-boy vocal group who worked in and around New York, made up of Idella Morris, Ronald Gathers, Frank Trout, Eugene Glass and Ricky Cordo. They had already enjoyed a hit with 'Wonderful Dream', which had entered the Billboard Hot 100 one place below The Beach Boys' 'Surfin' Safari'. The Majors' record leapfrogged the Beach Boys and led the way up to is peak at No22 before being overtaken again.

The Majors' sound rested on a R&B-tinged, male falsetto-lead voice. Ricky Cordo's vocals once again led their follow-up 'She's A Troublemaker' although this one only lasted one week in the US chart, at No93.

Both songs, a couple of subsequent issues, and a very rare album were issued in the UK, where, despite some radio play, they never got the attention that they deserved.

Sam Cooke

If ever anyone deserved a spotlight it was Sam Cooke, whose early crossover from gospel to pop led the way for hundreds of other black artists.

As the lead voice of The Highway QCs at only 15, Sam developed a fan base that increased when he joined The Soul Stirrers at age 19.

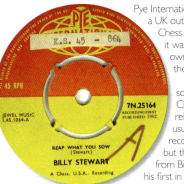

By 1957, when he was in his mid-twenties, he signed with Keen Records, where he had a string of pop hits with 'You Send Me', 'Only Sixteen' and '(What A) Wonderful World'.

A move to RCA in 1960 brought more hits with 'Chain Gang', 'Twisting The Night Away', 'Cupid' and 'Another Saturday Night'. At that time, Sam was astutely setting up deals that would give him control and ownership of his work, an unprecedented move for an artist at the time. He had also set up SAR Records as an outlet for himself and artists such as Billy Preston, The Valentinos and Johnnie Taylor.

Sam possessed a beautifully mellifluous voice that had a special purity of tone, and it effectively helped to usher in the pop soul era by bridging the gap between Ray Charles and the more pop-orientated mid-Sixties artists.

He was shot and killed in December 1964 after a seedy motel incident, but despite this his influence remains strong.

A posthumous hit, 'Shake', had a real gem on its B side: 'A Change Is Gonna Come' was a soaring and emotional ballad that anticipated the power of the civil rights movement, and remains a glorious testament to his talent.

> "Music is simple, man. Don't make it so they need to figure it out. Keep going back to the same thing, and repeat it. You get a melody, you stick to the melody. That's why my songs hit. Cause people like to sing along."

SAM COOKE TALKING TO BOBBY WOMACK

What's So Good About Goodbye

THE MIRACLES
FONTANA H 384

Two Lovers

MARY WELLS
ORIOLE CBA 1796

These two are early Motown issues that came well before the formation of the Tamla Motown stand-alone EMI label, and even before the run of wonderful records that emerged on EMI's Stateside label.

Berry Gordy had been working on finding a regular UK home for his Detroit output since his company's inception in 1959, and Fontana (with four issues) and Oriole (with 19) were the labels he tried after the initial 11 issues on Decca's London American.

Needless to say, all these early releases are extremely collectible with The Miracles weighing in at £200-plus and Mary Wells at £75. Taken as a pair, they represent the two-pronged attack of early Motown – R&B-based group sounds and soloists – while their common link is that William Smokey Robinson wrote both sides of each record.

The key to understanding Motown's success is to remember that it was founded by a songwriter, Berry Gordy, who recognised the raw talent in Smokey. The two topside songs are also good examples of Robinson's craft; the first, 'What's So Good About Goodbye', represents his ability to weave a song around a title idea, while 'Two Lovers' is a prime case of his story songs with a twist.

The Miracles at this stage included Smokey and his wife Claudette Robinson, Bobby Rogers, Warren 'Pete' Moore and Ronnie White.

Initially, The Miracles' records were almost under-orchestrated, being built around guitarist Marv Tarplin's skilful lines, and this one is glorious in its simplicity. Smokey's voice, still a little untutored, has enough personality to carry the song and hold your attention, while Mary Wells' voice is considerably smoother than the raunchy delivery on her Motown debut with 'Bye Bye Baby'.

'Two Lovers' talks of two different men she loves, but the song cleverly reveals at the end that it is actually one man with a split personality. It has a gorgeous melody, and every aspect of the record is just about perfect, including a great flip with Operator. Practically every Motown issue on Fontana or Oriole is deserving of a place in this book, but these are especially fine contenders to represent the early days of a growing force in pop music.

Remember Then

THE EARLS
STATESIDE SS 153

The Earls were normally pictured as a four-piece from the Bronx made up of Larry Figueiredo (aka Chance), Bob Del Din, Jack Wray and Eddie Harder, though personnel changed. At least one album cover shows a seven-piece, including a black member. Lead voice Larry Chance was always a set member, and he still keeps the name alive on the oldies circuit.

'Remember Then' was a big US hit for them, and was one of the last old-styled doo-wop records with its Re-Mem–Mem-Remember-Member bass intro, which was copied note-for-note by Showaddywaddy in the Seventies.

The follow-up issue, 'Never', is also highly collectable, as both are fine vocal group records.

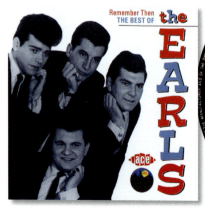

PYE INTERNATIONAL
45 RPM
1.45.1166-A
EDWIN H.
MORRIS
7N.25166
RECORDING FIRST
PUBLISHED 1962
THE THINGS WE DID LAST SUMMER
(Styne, Cahn)
SHELLEY FABARES
Arranged and produced by
Stu Phillips

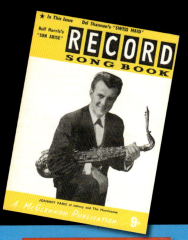

★ In This Issue   Del Shannon's 'SWISS MAID'
Rolf Harris's
'SUN ARISE'
RECORD
SONG BOOK
JOHNNY PARIS of Johnny and The Hurricanes
A McLennon Publication   9d

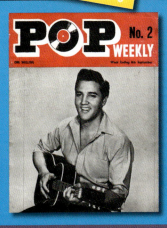

POP WEEKLY   No. 2
ONE SHILLING   Week Ending 8th September

MADE IN GT. BRITAIN
Stateside
45 RPM
SS 112
Sherwin
Music Ltd.
BIEM/NCB
45KR-3023
"Wand"
Recording
RECORDING FIRST
PUBLISHED 1963
TWIST AND SHOUT
(Medley—Russell)
THE ISLEY BROTHERS
Arranged by Teacho Wiltshire
Produced by
Bert Russell
E.M.I. RECORDS LIMITED

ORIOLE
ORIOLE AMERICAN
Sound
45 r.p.m.
CBA 1776
TWO LOVERS
MARY WELLS
YOUNG—
NEW—
EXCITING
ORIOLE RECORDS LIMITED, LONDON, W.1.

LET'S GO (PONY)
(L. & R. Duncan)
45 R.P.M.
WARNER BROS
WB RECORDS
RECORDING ℗ AND
FIRST PUBLISHED 1962
45-WB.77
USA No:
5283
West-Giant
Music
THE ROUTERS
Produced by Joe Saraceno

45
AAG 104
(4-42427)
California Music
AAG-104.18
Recording First
Published 1962
THAT'S ALL I WANT
TERRY DAY
with Jack Nitzsche and
his Orchestra
MADE IN ENGLAND

Verve Records
MADE UNDER LICENCE FROM
METRO-GOLDWYN-MAYER INC., OWNER OF THE TRADE MARK "VERVE"
45 r.p.m.   U.S.A. Recording
45VK 10274A   45-VS 502
RECORDING FIRST
PUBLISHED 1962
DESAFINADO
(Slightly out of tune)
(Jobim—Mendonca—
Cavanaugh—
Hendricks)
ELLA FITZGERALD
Orchestra Conducted
By Marty Paich
Essex Music Ltd.
Mecolico
MADE IN GT. BRITAIN

RCA
45-RCA 1319
I'LL DO MY CRYING TOMORROW
THE TOKENS
45 R.P.M.
MADE IN ENGLAND

Glenda Collins

HMV RECORDS POP 1233

PERSONAL MANAGERS: DAVE MORRIS AND ERIC COLLINS
142 CHARING CROSS ROAD, LONDON W.C.2. TEM 3917/COV 0140

IF YOU'VE GOT TO PICK A BABY

Position	Artiste	Last Week
	eat Britain's only Pop Star Chart	
	OP STAR TOP 20	
1	ELVIS PRESLEY	1
2	CLIFF RICHARD	2
3	BEATLES	7
4	BILLY FURY	3
5	ADAM FAITH	4
6	SHADOWS	6
7	BOBBY VEE	14
8	BRENDA LEE	5
9	JOE BROWN	8
10	JOHN LEYTON	11
11	HELEN SHAPIRO	11
12	MARTY WILDE	9
13	FRANK IFIELD	16
14	R'D CHAMBERLAIN	12
15	JAYWALKERS	19
16	MIKE SARNE	15
17	SHANE FENTON	
18	EDEN KANE	13
19	TORNADOS	17
20	DEL SHANNON	

US President John F Kennedy assassinated, Great Train Robbery nets £2.6m, first episode of Dr Who on BBC and Profumo affair rocks the Conservatives

Bo Diddley

The Rolling Stones

Phil Spector

The Beatles 'From Me To You'

's Issue

RECORD SONG BOOK

THE BEATLES

A McGLENNON PUBLICATION

Twist and Shout • Boys

Twist and Shout THE BEATLES

After a couple of years marking time, the Sixties cranked up several gears as The Beatles swept all before, and the term 'Beatlemania' was coined. Almost overnight, record company A&R men rushed around like headless chickens, signing up any reasonable regional groups they could find, having realised that the market no longer desired the packaged pretty boys, at least not individually.

The US/UK chart entry balance swung dramatically in favour of the home side, though plenty of good American music still got through. On the West Coast, producer Phil Spector was building his Wall Of Sound with previously unheard of numbers of musicians and singers, and with fine choices of songs that he astutely called 'little symphonies for the kids'. The Cold War continued and support for CND grew; Martin Luther King made his 'I Have A Dream' speech, and President Kennedy was shot in Dallas, sending the whole of the States into shock.

The year ends with 'I Want To Hold Your Hand,' and 'She Loves You', plus The Beatles' Sunday Night At The London Palladium performance ringing in everyone's ears.

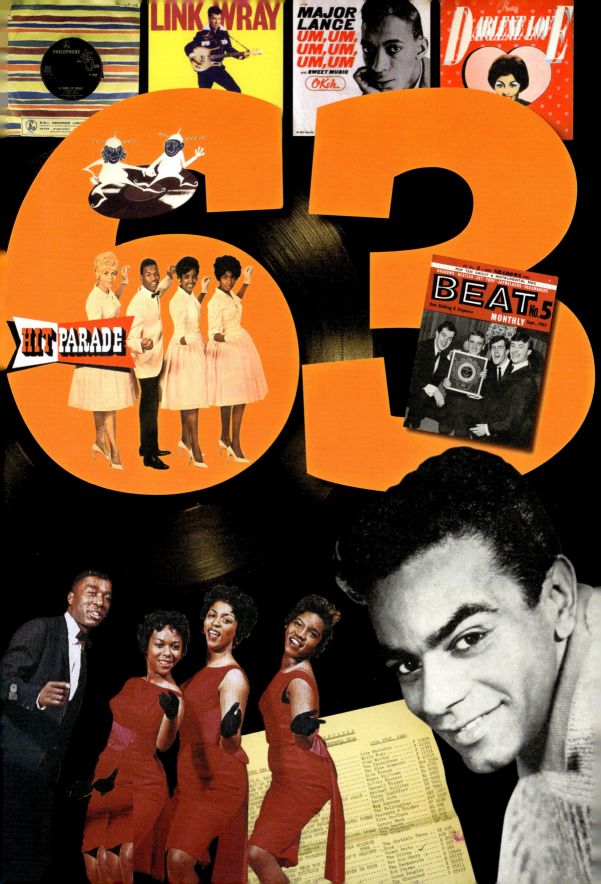

PAPA-OOM-MOW-MOW
MY REWARD
LOVE PILL
I'M LOSING MY GRIP
MAMA-OOM-MOW-MOW

THE BIRDS THE WORD
CHERRY
HAPPY JACK
LITTLE SALLY WALKER
STANDING IN THE LOVE LIN

THE RIVINGTONS

"PAPA-OOM-MOW-MOW"

Sandra
THE VOLUMES
LONDON HLI 9153

The Volumes hailed from Detroit and comprised lead singer Edward Union, tenor Lawrence Davis, tenor Larry Wright, baritone Joe Travillion and bass Ernie Newsome. They formed in 1960, and managed a string of releases on various labels until 1968 when they called it a day.

'Sandra' is an unashamed copy of the Four Seasons' sound that had taken the world charts by storm in 1962, and is now a prized item for group collectors.

It is representative of the move from the sparser doo-wop sounds of the very early Sixties into a fuller-sounding pop production led by the Four Seasons.

> **VOLUMES: Sandra; Teenage Paradice (London HL 9733).** From a group who had a big U.S. hit with "I Love You" comes this Four Season styled effort with plenty of gimmicks thrown in. Medium paced with a bass voice and falsetto mouthing the praises of the girl.

The Rivingtons from left:
Sonny, Carl, Rocky and Al

The Bird's The Word
THE RIVINGTONS
LIBERTY 55553

This slice of vocal group mania was the fourth of seven releases that the Los Angeles-based group put out on the US Liberty label, but only two of these made as far as UK release – their signature song 'Papa-Oom-Mow-Mow', which was cut in one take, and this throat-destroying ode to the joys of The Bird dance.

Their four-piece line-up of lead Carl White, Al Frazier, John 'Sonny' Harris and bass man Turner 'Rocky' Wilson Jr had decided on a novelty approach akin to The Coasters with more vocal distortions. The group had had a variety of personnel since the late Forties, and a family tree would throw up the names of The Lamplighters, The Tenderfoots, Four After Fives, The Sharps and The Crenshaws, before their brief hit period as the Rivingtons. 'Papa-Oom-Mow-Mow' and 'The Bird's The Word' were amalgamated and recycled as 'Surfin' Bird' by The Trashmen in 1964.

Never
THE EARLS
LONDON HL 9702

This was a good, but rarely heard, follow-up to the group's 'Remember Then' of the previous year. Still relying on the bass voice intro, the group take a fuller-than-usual part in the song's structure, with plenty of harmonised ascends, stops, starts and shoo-bops behind lead Larry Chance's proclamation that he's had it with girls since his special one walked away.

Back to the stairwell chaps…

Martian Hop
THE RAN-DELLS **LONDON HLU 9760**

The Ran-Dells took gimmickry to new heights in 'Martian Hop', a song which Radio Luxembourg played quite frequently at the time. Its electronic sound effects from Fifties sci-fi B movies were mixed in with childlike doo-woppish vocals that aimed at being reflective of a Martian vocal group.

Though structured in time-honoured fashion with a nifty key change at the appropriate point, the recording was like no other, which is probably why it is so collectible on both sides of the Atlantic, especially ones with of the wacky US picture sleeves used for early copies.

The Ran-Dells were three New York teenagers, Steven Rappaport and his two cousins Robert Rappaport and John Spirt. Via an introduction from Gerry Goffin, they managed to catch the ear of Don Kirshner at 1650 Broadway who released them on his subsidiary label Chairman. They made two other US-only discs, 'Sound Of The Sun' and 'Wintertime', both of which are similar-sounding and enjoyable.

> 66 **"I created that electronic sound in college, at Brandeis University** (which had one of the first electronic music labs in the country), using many relatively small boxes. Each was about 8" x 8" x 12", IIRC. We had four-track tape machines. I sped the song up from the 15 inches per second that it was recorded to 16 ips, so about 7%. I cut a demo in Atlantic City for $25, but I never considered the demo a master. Not enough sound, no modulation (raised 1/2 tone after second verse), not nearly as professional a sound as the released version. I am proud of 'Martian Hop' – you can hear the original demo on my website. "
> *Steven Rappaport*

Stateside Records

"Stateside was set up by EMI with the very specific aim of trying to destroy London American as the market leader of exciting US product," said Derek Everett, who, as a young up-and-coming EMI employee, was charged with the task of overseeing the new label in 1962.

EMI quickly realised that there were plenty of US labels who did not have a real grasp of the European markets, and that by making quick contact with any smaller labels not already in deals with London, there were avenues to follow.

Whereas London's output was varied and wide-ranging, Stateside tended to concentrate on the pop and emerging soul areas of the markets. They quickly formed a good relationship with Berry Gordy and his staff at Motown, which led to some 45 releases on Stateside between October 1963 and March 1965 (against London's earlier 11), which paved the way for the formation of the stand-alone Tamla Motown UK label in March 1965. The Four Seasons, The Chiffons, various neo-doo-wop groups and other pop goodies that are now considered highly desirable to collectors could be found on Stateside, as could the often rare album compilations that appeared in small numbers.

Derek Everett also tried Vee Jay Blues material by the likes of John Lee Hooker and Jimmy Reed, but missed out when he turned down a deal with Donny Kirshner's Dimension label when he was offered Little Eva's 'Locomotion' hit, thinking it was just another American dance song.

The deals that Stateside did set up, though, go some way to explaining why Beatles' material appeared at first in the States on so many labels. After their main link Capitol turned the group down, EMI went to several of the Stateside-linked companies, like Vee Jay, Swan and Tollie, just to get The Beatles' hits onto the US market. When the group did finally break through on Capitol in early 1964, these smaller outlets cleaned up with the songs that they had the rights to.

These days, Stateside collectability has increased sharply, mainly on the back of interest in its soul releases.

The label has also been revived in recent years with a series of re-releases of Sixties material aimed at soul collectors.

Candy Girl
THE FOUR SEASONS
STATESIDE SS 216

Just as they did with the few Beatles tracks they held the rights to, the Vee Jay label milked the success of the Four Seasons for all they were worth, with single and album issues at almost two-monthly intervals.

The Seasons had hit the US No1 spot with 'Sherry' at the start of 1962, and followed it immediately with two other No1s, 'Big Girls Don't Cry' and 'Walk Like A Man'.

At this stage, the group worked solely under their shared name, rather than the later Frankie Valli-led title, and they were rare among vocal groups in that they actually did play the instruments on their records, usually just adding a drummer.

They were self-contained in other ways too. Writing was usually by producer Bob Crewe and group member Bob Gaudio, the vocal arrangements came from bassman Nick Massi, and the group business side was taken care of by Nick DeVito. Apparently, promoters and others always paid up to Mr DeVito!

'Candy Girl', notable for the fact that it wasn't written by the immediate group, was a summer 1963 hit in the US, reaching No3, but it was one that didn't do so well here. Consequently, it has not always made it onto the many Seasons compilations.

It is a Latin-ish sound with lighter instrumentation rather than the heavier sounds everybody was used to, though this was balanced by the good-value flipside 'Marlena', which stayed firmly in their hit zone.

Killer Joe
THE ROCKY FELLERS
STATESIDE SS 175

Oh, they were so cute! Four Filipino boys, Junior, Tony, Albert and Eddie, along with their dad 'Pop' Maligmat, were all proficient on a variety of instruments. Yet it was the kiddie lead (long before the Jackson or Osmond families had the same idea) that really swung it for this infectious song.

Killer Joe, obviously older and more streetwise, is dancing with our young hero's girl, and he is quite naturally incensed, but also pretty unsure who she might go home with. This was put to a great Latinish rhythm track, with the cowbell on overtime. Killer Joe was a real chap called Frank Piro, who had made a name for himself as a Jitterbug champion in the Forties and was well known in the Sixties as a society dance instructor to the likes of Jackie Kennedy and the Duke and Duchess of Windsor. Indeed, he taught the Frug to guests including Andy Warhol at Jackie's first big dance party after her husband's assassination, and also taught the Watusi to the likes of Margot Fonteyn and Lucy Baines Johnson. Well, somebody had to….

I Wanna Be The Leader
THE MARCELS PYE INTERNATIONAL 7N 25201

By the time the 'Blue Moon' Marcels released 'I Wanna Be The Leader', their last in Britain, they had an all-black line-up consisting of their distinctive lead singer Cornelius Harp, bass man Fred Johnson, tenor Ron Mundy, tenor Allen Johnson (Fred's brother) and baritone Walt Maddox. Fred and Walt kept a version of the group on the road for 25 years.

This song is an answer to Johnny Cymbal's 'Mr Bass Man' hit. Here, there is a struggle by the tenor to regain the key role, having been usurped by the prominence of the bass man on records, ironically dating back to the Marcels' own 'Blue Moon' hit. He claims we'll never hear him singing do-do-do-doop-doop, but wants to sing the words written on his heart. This was the first – and only – Marcels' UK issue with a label that you could comfortably read the small print on, owing to the severe dark blue of the previous design. Despite this, all their UK issues are collectable and all are great fun.

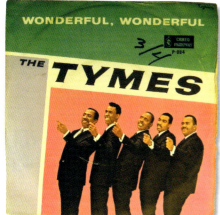

Maybe You'll Be There
BILLY & THE ESSENTIALS **LONDON HL 9657**

I Wonder What She's Doing Tonight
BARRY & THE TAMBERLANES **WARNER BROS. WB 116**

A Little Like Lovin'
THE CASCADES **RCA 1358**

Wonderful, Wonderful
THE TYMES – **CAMEO PARKWAY P 884**

My Heart Said (The Bossa Nova)
TIPPIE & THE CLOVERS **STATESIDE SS160**

This clutch of vocal group records proves they didn't need vocal gimmicks to make good sounds.

Billy & The Essentials (five lads from Philadelphia, pictured right) and Barry & The Tamerlanes (a studio-based Californian three-piece of Barry DeVorzon, Bodie Chandler and Terry Smith) both re-cycled the white group sound with two good songs.

The Cascades were well-known for their 'Rhythm Of The Rain' hit, but had failed to follow it up. 'A Little Like Loving' was the B side to 'Cinderella', and a much stronger song in a New York Latin production style, while The Tymes were sticking with their 'So Much In Love' mode with a cover of Johnny Mathis' "Wonderful, Wonderful", which – if anything – was even stronger.

The Tymes, who later slimmed down in numbers, were made up of lead vocal George Williams, tenor Al Berry, tenor George Hilliard, baritone Norm Burnett and bass Donald Banks.

Lastly in this batch, Tippie & The Clovers provided evidence of the songwriting prowess of Jerry Leiber and Mike Stoller. The famed writer/producer duo teamed up for this outing with Barry Mann and Cynthia Weil on a song that combined the best of

Broadway pop writing with the new Bossa Nova craze that received much attention at the time.

By 1963, The Clovers were down to a trio that included long-term members Buddy Bailey, Harold Winley and Harold Lucas, following a time in the Fifties when the group had actually splintered into two units.

All good records deserving better, yet strangely none of them were picked up on by any British groups.

I May Not Live To See Tomorrow
BRIAN HYLAND
HMV POP 1113

A Touch Of Venus
JOHNNY ANGEL
PARLOPHONE R 5026

I Saw Linda Yesterday
DOUG SHELDON
DECCA F 11564

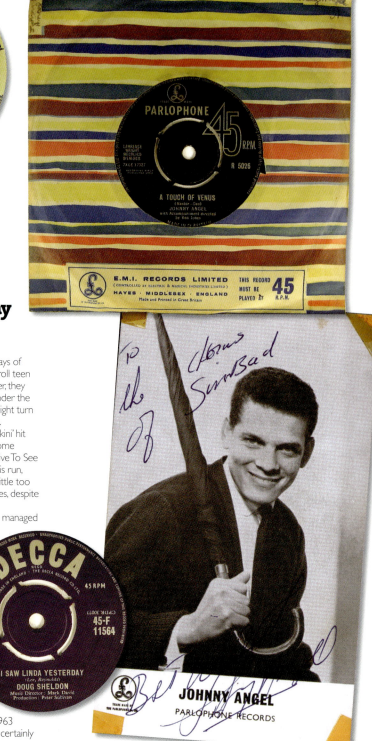

By 1963 and the arrival of The Beatles, the days of the non-threatening, boy-next-door rock 'n' roll teen idols were well and truly numbered. However, they continued to put out records, presumably under the assumption that the crazy new hairy ones might turn out to be just an unpleasant dream…but no.

Mr Hyland, responsible for the 'Itsy Bitsy Bikini' hit of summer 1960, had peaked with 'Ginny Come Lately' and 'Sealed With A Kiss'. 'I May Not Live To See Tomorrow' was another stab at continuing his run, but, as you can judge from the title, it was a little too depressive and down-beat to sell many copies, despite its overall good sound.

Johnny Angel — yes, there really was one — managed seven releases on Parlophone, of which this is the last. He was a pleasant London boy, with the archetypical camel-coated cigar-chewing manager.

'A Touch Of Venus' was an excellent example of the well-crafted pop song being shouldered aside by the newcomers.

Doug Sheldon got a deserved No37 UK hit with 'I Saw Linda Yesterday', a cover of Dickey Lee's US hit that was very much in Dion mould. Doug had a dozen UK single releases usually covering American material, plus a collectable EP that included a far-sighted 1963 cover of The Miracles' 'Mickey's Monkey'. He certainly should have had a few big hits.

Detroit City

BOBBY BARE
RCA 1352

Shutters And Screams

BEN COLDER
MGM 1191

Funny How Time Slips Away

JOHNNY TILLOTSON
LONDON HLA 9811

This trio come from a time before country music had become slick, when country songs were, arguably, more memorable.

Bobby Bare's 'Detroit City' is a classic of its type, being a gentle jog-along clip-clop song in which he bemoans being in the big city rather than back at home with his girl and familiar surroundings. He wants to go home…oh, how he wants to go home…

Ben Colder (aka Shep Wooley) is a different vein of country. It is a re-write of Jerry Wallace's 'Shutters and Boards' in Addams Family/Munsters mode, complete with bubbling and rattling and the campest owl effect you'll ever hear. Ben has great fun with the lyrical references to Frankenstein et al.

Johnny Tillotson's disc was the last he released in the UK on London before his move to MGM, and it was a part of a long run of classy pop songs with a distinct country edge. This must have been one of the earliest covers of a Willie Nelson song, and Johnny's youthful version lets the song carry it.

Come Dance With Me

JAY & THE AMERICANS **UNITED ARTISTS UP 1039**

I'll Take You Home

THE DRIFTERS **LONDON HLK 9785**

These are two out-and-out New York records with all the wonderful trappings associated with that period. The Atlantic Records/Leiber & Stoller Latinised big-city feel is all over these two lesser-known examples of each group's work – the two songs are so close in melody, tempo and feel as to be practically interchangeable!

Jay & The Americans were onto their second Jay by this stage: Jay Traynor having given way to Jay Black as lead vocalist. Jay 2 joined Kenny Vance, Sandy Deane, Marty Saunders and Howie Kane, and together they made a string of great, beaty ballads and power pop dancers including 'Living Above Your Head' for United Artists.

Coming from New York doo-wop backgrounds, several members were able to turn their hands to various vocal group styles, including a nifty car song called 'Top Down Time' in 1964 as The Rockaways. They also once cut 'Things Are Changing', an equal-opportunities promotional track for The US Advertising Council's campaign in 1966, which was notable because it used the same Phil Spector-produced backing track that reputedly features the only known Spector/Brian Wilson collaboration. The Blossoms also used the same track for a fine version with a Darlene Love lead.

In 1963, The Drifters still benefited from the fine lilting voice of Rudy Lewis, who died a year later.

Their run of fabulous hit records began in 1953 and lasted well into the Seventies – during that time there has been an incredible 58 official group members, not counting the many so-called Drifters groups that have been, and still are, out there on the live circuit trying to trade off the name.

Most collectors would probably agree that the early Sixties was the time of their very best recordings, but the quality runs so deep that even this is questionable.

This Little Girl
DION CBS AAG 145

Walking Proud
STEVE LAURENCE CBS AAG 166

Everybody Go Home
EYDIE GORME CBS AAG 170

I Can't Stop Talking About You
STEVE & EYDIE CBS AAG 178

When the press first began to quiz John Lennon and Paul McCartney about their songwriting collaborations, they often cited Carole King and Gerry Goffin as their role models. On the evidence of these four songs, all Goffin/King numbers, it's not hard to understand why. They show how adept the pair were at turning out a run of high-quality songs that were right on the button market-wise, something Lennon and McCartney aspired to do in their early days.

Dion slips effortlessly into 'This Little Girl' which would almost certainly have been written with him in mind. It's an absolute natural for him – he is able to sing an out-and-out pop song yet retain a bit of street edge to it.

Both Steve and Eydie were more mainstream, but the songs work equally well with their incredibly structured simplicity of lyrical idea and execution. Steve Laurence had also recorded the pair's 'Go Away Little Girl', while Eydie Gorme had hit with 'Blame It On the Bossa Nova', while together they had enjoyed a big UK summer hit with 'I Want To Stay Here'. 'I Can't Stop Talking About You' was a faster song compared to the hit, but no less attractive.

Taken together, these four represent Goffin and King at their peak – all deserved to be bigger sellers.

Little Band Of Gold
JAMES GILREATH
PYE INTERNATIONAL 7N 25190

Although little is written or known about Mr. Gilreath, 'Little Band Of Gold' was actually a UK top 30 hit. Its unusual time shifts and jerky high brass insertions made it unlike anything else and hence caught the public ear enough to gather sales. Gilreath only had one other UK release, a song called 'Lollipops, Lace and Lipstick'.

Pretty Thing
BO DIDDLEY
PYE INTERNATIONAL 7N 25217 (R&B SERIES)

Pye International's R&B series was differentiated from their usual label by its black overprinting with the release details. 'Pretty Thing', as raw a bluesy rocker as you would want, appears here with a writing credit for E McDaniel, Bo's real name – though the same song has a Willie Dixon credit on the most recent Chess label collection of Bo's best work. It all goes to show just how murky and difficult song credits can be, especially during the old blues and R&B days when players often learnt songs from each other, or freely borrowed or adapted others' work to the extent that they genuinely wouldn't know whose tune it originally was.

Bo Diddley almost certainly holds the record for the number of times he managed to get his own name into the titles of his songs, possibly for self-aggrandisement, or possibly as a form of de facto copyright protection! Either way, he made some cracking music with his immediately recognisable rhythmic guitar playing, and this is one that got away in the UK.

Poet & Peasant
PETER JAY & THE
JAYWALKERS **DECCA F 11659**

If You Gotta Pick A Baby
GLENDA COLLINS **HMV POP 1233**

Back at 304 Holloway Road, Joe Meek was keeping busy with both instrumentalists and soloists. Norfolk's Peter Jay and his gang had managed a hit with 'Can Can '62', and had decided to keep in the well-trodden track of rock groups re-working accessible classical tunes with this sax-led arrangement of the overture to Franz Von Suppe's nineteenth century light opera. Poor Franz does not get any mention on the label, but may well not have wished to recognise the jerky version of his memorable melody, which can immediately be likened to the feel of the intro to Cliff Bennett's 'One Way Love'.

Joe Meek's production is reasonably straightforward in this case. Alongside drummer Peter Jay, you would have found Lloyd Baker, Mac McIntyre, Peter Miller, Tony Webster, Johnny Larke and Jeff Moss, and collectively they could sometimes be found providing the main back-up work on package tours.

> GLENDA COLLINS: If You've Got To Pick A Baby; In The First Place (HMV POP 1233). Brash, attacking effort from Miss Collins as she chants. Joe Meek wrote the top side, and it has the echoey RGM sound, of course

The Glenda Collins record is more of a case of 'all bells and whistles' as it is a full-on Meek sound. In fact, it is one of his strongest and best of the period. Joe wrote the song, which is way above many of his efforts, and worked really hard on overdubs to the basic track to make it as commercial as possible.

Glenda Collins had been around for a few years and had a genuinely strong pop voice, but she never quite made a breakthrough despite many very fine recordings for Meek and others. The 'Instrumental Accompaniment' alluded to on the label was The Outlaws, who were then virtually working as Meek's house band. Their line-up at this point was Richie Blackmore on lead, Chas Hodges on bass, Ken Lundgren on rhythm, and Mick Underwood on drums. Blackmore was still very young, but evidently coping very well with everything asked of him.

Both sides of the single were cut live with The Outlaws and Glenda had to sing each song approximately 15-20 times before Joe was satisfied. Sometimes they would do whole run-throughs, but on other occasions Joe would rush out of his control room yelling instructions after only a few bars. The pounding commercial sound should have given Glenda a hit, so why didn't it make it?

Joe Meek's Studio

London's Holloway Road is, and was then, a really busy thoroughfare, so it puzzling why Joe Meek considered it a good site to live and have his studio.

The dark entrance stairway led from street level to the first floor landing with rooms off that: smaller room to the rear, medium-sized middle room, and a wider front room that crossed the width of the property over the shop front of the leather goods shop beneath. This was echoed on the second floor.

Joe's office was the first floor front room and he sat with his back to the street window. The middle room was his living room and kitchenette, set out with a couple of small settees where he held business meetings during the day when he wasn't recording. The second floor housed the studio at the front, the control room in what would have normally been the middle bedroom, and a bathroom/loo to the rear.

The main control room gizmos were set up on the wall facing the studio, and the floor was almost invisible for the mass of wires running everywhere. It was only a matter of a few steps from this room into the studio as the two open doors were adjacent to each other. The doors to both the studio and control room were always open to allow the mass of cabling to connect, so anyone on the landing had to remain very quiet.

The studio set-up had the drum set to the far left next to an upright piano, there was a space for the singer's mic behind the door, and the guitarists had low sitting spaces in a line between the door and the front window, making them visible to anyone on the landing. The bass drum was packed with heavy material, and more material was available to lay over the snare and toms.

Joe operated like a coiled spring moving in and out of each room (there was no connecting intercom), and the effect of the whole thing in operation was that of somewhat haphazard mania, but with a professional spirit of a team working together. Joe, acting as both engineer and producer, knew what he wanted to achieve, and, although he was direct and brusque at times, the whole proceedings were conducted in quite a gentlemanly manner.

Surf and drag music

The surf and drag music craze had become as popular as the actual sports in the US by 1963, with instrumental hits leading the way. It was a comparatively easy bandwagon to jump on for most people, and bands and record companies began to alter titles of existing music to fit the theme for new releases to try to grab some of the action.

Dick Dale, by contrast, was a full-blooded surfing beach guy. His music reflected the power of the sport, 'Let's Go Tripping' and 'Miserlou' even being heard in England. However, most of the lifestyle and terminology was alien to our ears, and EMI's cheap in-house advertising paper, Record Mail, attempted to introduce us to the aspects of the sport and music, even before the Beach Boys really took hold. They were hoping that Dale could break through worldwide.

Aside from a handful of hits the music, the genre remained firmly rooted in California until the harmony vocal sounds led by The Beach Boys and Jan & Dean began to be heard.

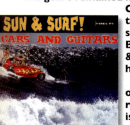

The number of surf/drag race related record issues in 1963/4 was huge in the US, and because of the relatively short-lived popularity are now ever more collectible, especially for some of the rarer album releases that were ignored in what was essentially a singles-based genre. Many groups and musicians got their feet wet when they started with surf music, including Frank Zappa, Jim McGuinn, The Turtles and Lou Reed, and there were many related oddities including a surf vocal by the dancer Sir Robert Helpman!

Baja/Kuk
THE ASTRONAUTS
RCA 1349

The Lonely Surfer
JACK NITZSCHE
REPRISE R 20202

The Original Surfer Stomp
BRUCE JOHNSTON COMBO
LONDON HL 9780

Boss
THE RUMBLERS
LONDON HLD 9684

Four On The Floor
THE SHUT DOWNS
COLPIX PX 11016

The Scavenger
DICK DALE & HIS DEL-TONES
CAPITOL CL 15320

The Astronauts from landlocked Colorado lead off our surf and drag selection with a great slippery-sounding instrumental called 'Baja', named after one of the best surf spots. On its flip was 'Kuk', a fun vocal track that bemoaned the difficulty non-participants had in understanding surf terminology – "How I wish I knew what they were talking about" was the tagline for each chorus. The few that heard it in the UK understood completely. The Astronauts proved to be a fine vocal/instrumental unit that went on to make several good, collectable albums.

Jack Nitzsche's record, 'The Lonely Surfer', was a moody and melodious deep guitar-led tune, somewhat like Duane Eddy, with a rich palate of instrumentation behind it. Jack was better known as an arranger at the time, working mainly with Phil Spector crafting the Wall Of Sound, but went on to make many fine instrumental film soundtracks.

Future Beach Boy Bruce Johnston had been active on the West Coast since 1958, working mainly with small independent labels like Del-Fi, which released this strong cut. He backed it with a Pyjama Party (the B side title) album that appeared at least twice under different group names. The Surfer Stomp was the dance that could be seen at beach parties and in some of the famed Beach Movies put out by American International Productions.

The Rumblers' 'Boss' was the group's first UK issue (there was one more single on King in 1965), but they also somehow got an EP and even an album released on London, both titled *Bossounds*. Needless to say, these are both rare. 'Boss' is an atmospheric guitar, sax and drums workout, which is every bit as good as the better-known hits, and was almost certainly cut by experienced session guys.

The Shut Downs' 'Four In The Floor' (an allusion to the gears we are reliably informed) was also likely to have been cut by session guys, and in this case produced a fast guitar-led rocker with overdubbed car noises. It subsequently proved so popular in fan circles that it became one of the earliest drag tunes to be bootlegged purportedly for a Norwegian Rockin' Cats car club. The two EPs of The Rockin' Cats that we know of show immaculate taste in rocking instrumentals. Strangely enough, 'Four In The Floor' appeared on the Colpix label as an output from Donny Kirshner's NY-based Dimension label. It may have been licensed in from a producer as it sounds like a West Coast recording.

Finally, the master himself, Dick Dale. Dick had moved from surf to cars on singles and albums, and though famed as a guitarist, this car song is one of his vocal tracks, and he packs plenty of power into it. Essentially, he reckons the Scavenger (a fast car) can beat all the others, identified by a myriad of numbers like 426. Aside from the obvious macho posturing, surf and drag songs were lyrically quite straightforward. 'The Scavenger' has an intro of squealing tyres that gives way to a squealing sax break to keep the many aficionados of that instrument very happy.

"Those Del-Fi recordings are basic and fun, and it gave me a chance to bring great looking girls to the recording sessions!"
BRUCE JOHNSTON

Highland Fling
DOUG SALMA AND THE HIGHLANDERS
PHILIPS BF 1279

Arresting (or, arguably, in need of being arrested) is the best word to describe this one-off single. Anticipating the heavy stomp sound of the Strangeloves a couple of years later, we get bagpipes against drums, bass and handclaps with a simple song extolling the joys of doing the Highland Fling. Along the way, there is an early lyrical reference to 'hippies' and even Annie Laurie gets a look in.

It is believed that the whole strange mixture was the brainchild of West Coast producer Gary Paxton and some of his mates.

Jack The Ripper
LINK WRAY AND HIS RAY MEN STATESIDE SS 217

Guitarist Link Wray had emerged with the menacing sound of his 'Rumble' hit, and here he stays broadly in the same zone with 'Jack The Ripper'.

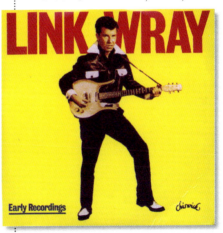

The record is notable for the tonal variety of his guitar work, which varies from deep, fuzzy sounds to rich and rounded higher lines set against up-front electric bass (a new toy at that point) and drums.

He is to be applauded for resisting the temptation to open the tune with ghoulish sound effects, an option that would have proved irresistible to most of his contemporaries.

Bird Stompin'
JOHNNY AND THE VIBRATONES
WARNER BROS. WB 107

This glorious happily manic instrumental is another disc from the Paxton stable. Johnny extols the qualities and excitement of Bird Stompin', which is more likely to be a dance than an early cure for avian flu. It has a cacophonous mix of sax, guitar and organ, with vocal interjections from Johnny.

The B side, 'Moving The Bird', is presumably what you did after the stomping! It would be interesting to know just how many collections include this one…

I Know (You Don't Love Me No More)
BERYL MARSDEN
DECCA F 11707

British covers of American R&B material often fell short of the mark, but this one is totally convincing. Barbara George's original probably became better known as a result of its inclusion on the first issue of Sue Records compilation album *The Sue Records' Story*, rather than from its single release in 1962.

This was the first of several great singles that Liverpudlian Beryl cut before she joined Shotgun Express alongside Rod Stewart in 1966. She began her career early in her teens and was quite different from the eyelashed and petticoated princesses that made up the majority of the Brit girls of the day.

She still plays to fans at Liverpool's Cavern Club wearing a mini dress!

"The majority of female singers that made the charts were Susan Maughan types: pretty songs and party clothes. But in Liverpool you had to be one of the boys."
BERYL MARSDEN

"We'd do concerts with The Beatles and come on half way through the show. Our debut single 'I Don't Care' got a lot of airplay and was almost a hit, but we struggled after that."
EDDIE AMOO

I Don't Care
THE CHANTS
PYE 7N 15557

Another bunch of original Cavern Club regulars were The Chants, a five-piece group much enamoured with US doo-wop sounds.

Formed in 1962, and briefly managed by Brian Epstein, the group consisted originally of Eddie Amoo, who wrote 'I Don't Care', Joe Ankrah, Eddie Ankrah, Alan Fielding and Nat Shalma, although several other names passed through their ranks before they broke up. Some interesting rare footage of them performing appeared in the BBC's Soul Britannia series.

Their first issue 'I Don't Care' is an American-styled vocal group stomper with plenty of handclaps and harmonies. Its flipside is a good version of The Del-Vikings' 'Come Go With Me'.

Eddie Amoo went on to co-form the Seventies hit group The Real Thing following a series of excellent Chants records throughout the Sixties.

It's You
THE VISCOUNTS
PYE 7N 15536

The Viscounts formed in London in 1959 and signed to Pye Records. Pye stuck solidly with the trio until 1963, seeing them as a group to match the-then popular King Brothers, producing the easily-digested pop that was so often of US origin.

The line-up consisted of the soon-to-be producer/manager/songwriter Gordon Mills, who was involved with writing both sides of this Beatles-influenced issue. By summer 1963, when this emerged, the full effect of the Moptops was being felt and the UK music industry was in the early stages of hyperdrive in their rush to either cover Beatles' album tracks or have existing groups adapt to the template. This is a clear case of the latter, with distinct feels being injected from the Beatles catalogue: the intro apes 'From Me To You', there is a harmonica from 'Love Me Do', and the build-up vocals are from 'Twist And Shout'. To its credit, the record still manages to be itself, and stands as a solid example of Beatles-led Brit pop of the time.

Talking About You

THE REDCAPS

DECCA F 11789

Another fine example of The Beatles' effect is this second of three issues by The Redcaps on the Decca label – who were desperately trying to make up for letting the Liverpool group slip so spectacularly through their fingers.

The Redcaps, a rock/R&B outfit from Walsall near Birmingham, were scooped up when every London-based A&R man began to frantically comb the country to find bands who spoke with regional accents.

This cover of the Chuck Berry number is convincing in every way, as was their earlier version of the Isley Brothers' 'Shout'. Lead singer Dave Walker shows a driving vocal delivery uncannily like John Lennon's on this track. He later briefly joined Black Sabbath in place of Ozzy Osbourne.

Ooh! 'E Didn't

JAN AND KELLY

PHILIPS 326567 BF

Quite, quite bizarre! Taking their cues from the street sass of The Vernon's Girls and Wendy Richard's character in Mike Sarne's 'Come Outside', the London duo catch up on last night's dating news. One of them had been out with a chap who, rather than attempting a bit of the other as was expected, and even hoped for, decided to spend the night yodelling – never the best chat-up career move.

Our lass is obviously disappointed but, distressingly, decides by the last verse and chorus to take the 'if you can't beat 'em, join 'em' approach. The duo also released titles including 'Oo I Can't', 'I Could Have Died', 'Make Me A Doormat', followed by 'And Then He Kicked Me'. What took him so long?

Birthday Party
THE PIXIES THREE
MERCURY AMT 1214

What A Guy
THE RAINDROPS **LONDON HL 9718**

When The Boy's Happy (The Girl's Happy Too)
THE FOUR PENNIES
STATESIDE SS244

I Want A Boy For My Birthday
THE COOKIES **COLPIX PX 11012**

Let's Start The Party Again
LITTLE EVA **COLPIX PX 11019**

Walk Me Home (From the party)
CLAUDINE CLARK
PYE INTERNATIONAL 7N 25186

"I'm so happy and elated that people remember these songs. We never knew what was going to be put out, until we heard them on the radio. We often thought they were demos for other people!"

MARGARET ROSS OF THE COOKIES

Stand well back – It's party time in girl group land, that venue for lyrical triumphs and disasters for the uber-excited or sobbing teen girl, with imagery straight out of the pages of Jackie or the Happy Days adventures of Richie Cunningham's little sister.

Producers of girlie sounds, more often than not also the writers of the scenarios, knew how to encapsulate the true feelings of a key slab of the record-buying market. These examples of the craft show just how high the standard had been set.

The Pixies Three were a white trio in The Angels mould. Producers Madara and White, who we have already met, wrote 'Birthday Party' for them, sadly their sole UK issue.

The Raindrops were a vehicle for writer/producers Ellie Greenwich and Jeff Barry, intended for studio demo output. 'What A Guy' was in fact written with The Sensations in mind, but as it came out so well the pair got a deal with it and it was a US hit. Ellie then had to recruit her sister Laura to make up the numbers for personal appearances. As The Raindrops, Ellie and Jeff made some splendid singles and an album, although one of the best, 'Let's Go Together', was only released as a US single.

The Four Pennies were the Chiffons in disguise, and as such put out two singles, 'My Block' being the second.

'When The Boy's Happy' is a joyous up-tempo romp with a rolling Spectorised backing track, and was so good that it qualified for a late Seventies UK re-issue, which is a little easier to find than the

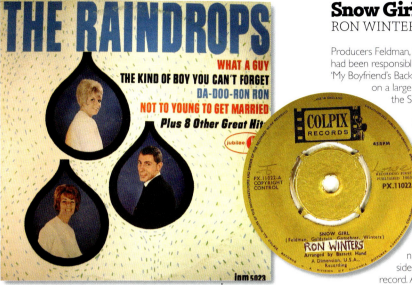

Snow Girl
RON WINTERS COLPIX PX 11022

Producers Feldman, Goldstein and Gottehrer had been responsible for the sassy Angels' hit 'My Boyfriend's Back', and their names pop up on a large number of hits throughout the Sixties.

The trio, who were to become The Strangeloves in the mid-Sixties, were experimenting with a mixture of the Bo Diddley beat and their later Strangeloves thumpy sound in this rare one-off UK release from Ron Winters. Ron puts a teen male vocal on top of everything, and although he is named as a co-writer on each side, it is decidedly the producers' record. As with many Colpix issues, this originated on Don Kirshner's Dimension label, but is unlike other issues there.

rare original Stateside release.

The Cookies sing the first verse of 'I Want A Boy For My Birthday' together, and then Earl Jean coos seductively on her own, while Margaret Ross and Dorothy Jones take the Greek chorus positions supporting her. Together they made some quite varied records, including 'Will Power', 'Chains' and 'Don't Say Nothing Bad About My Baby', but the single that eclipsed them all was their last for the Dimension label in the States called 'I Never Dreamed' – which for some reason was not issued in the UK.

The group were the absolute first call Manhattan studio backing singers, who included Little Eva in their ranks at various times. Margaret Ross was delighted to attend and sing at the 2005 New York launch of Rhino Records' superb box set of girlie sounds.

The late Little Eva, who was still in great voice when she toured the UK just a few years ago, will always be known for 'The Locomotion', though she made some other great recordings, of which 'Let's Start The Party Again' is a good example. In no uncertain terms, Eva stops everyone leaving and revives a flagging party with this mid-tempo dancer, which has obvious vocal back-ups from The Cookies and quite probably also Carole King, who co-wrote the song.

Philadelphia-raised soloist Claudine Clark is considered a part of the girl group genre by virtue of the sound and feel of her records. She sold a million in the US with her better-known 'Party Lights' single and followed it with a thematic *Party Lights* album, which did not include this track...

Claudine has chosen a lad at the party and is eager to get to the best bit – when she gets walked home and when some real action may happen. Let's draw a discrete veil because, of course, like the majority of the genre, she was a good girl.

Sue's Gonna Be Mine
DEL SHANNON
LONDON HLU 9800

Two Faces Have I
LOU CHRISTIE
COLUMBIA DB 7031

LOU CHRISTIE: Two Faces Have I; All That Glitters Isn't Gold (Columbia DB 7031). Two faces and two voices has Lou Christie. Proceeds to demontrate tha latter fact on top deck by varying from falsetto to middle register. The falsetto sounds not unlike a duck in pain. At first I thought that this was meant to be funny. Even if it was, it isn't, if you know what I mean.

With the continued and growing popularity of The Four Seasons, it was inevitable there would be plenty of copycat records, but it was not just groups that made them.

Del Shannon and Lou Christie were successful by 1963, with Del enjoying the higher profile. He had worked the rich 'Runaway' and 'Swiss Maid' seam pretty well, and had turned to a more contemporary feel with a song that married his own songwriting with some Seasons flavouring.

In the States, the record had come out on the new Berlee label, which Del formed after the start of a long-running legal battle with his early management. On the US, release the song is called 'Sue's Gotta Be Mine', (reflecting the actual lyrics sung) but somehow it was changed between the States and here. Bizarrely, the B side also changed from The US variant 'Now She's Gone' to the UK one 'Since She's Gone'. It did sell some copies but was not one of his bigger hits.

Lou Christie enjoyed a long writing partnership with Twyla Herbert and their songs maintained an extremely high standard throughout his Sixties hits. Lou was able to sing at length in both the tenor and falsetto ranges, and this song uses Lou's Frankie Valli-influenced high voice on the choruses, while his normal range takes the verses, with a bouncy and attractive track behind him. It was maybe too much of a contrast in the UK for him to break through at that point.

My Last Cigarette

SHEILA HANCOCK

DECCA F 11618

This is a wonderful, very British, oddity. The lovely and talented Sheila Hancock had made quite a name for herself as the character Carol in the popular BBC TV comedy drama The Rag Trade – popular enough for Decca to put her comedic talents on record.

'My Last Cigarette' describes the plight of the hardened smoker trying, without success, to give up the weed, which was quite radical when smoking still held a very accepted place in society.

The song that Sheila wheezes her way through was written by Sydney Carter – yes, the same man who was responsible for the school assembly staple 'Lord Of The Dance'. It also appeared at the time on an album called *Putting Out The Dustbin*.

Royal Flush

DON DRUMMOND

R&B JB 103

Dr Kitch

LORD KITCHENER

JUMP UP JU 511

Little was known in 1963 in most of Britain about the wealth of Jamaican music, but in London's more specialist shops it was possible to find some issues.

These two contrasting issues represent the diversity of what was on offer. The Don Drummond record is a quietly infectious, laid-back trombone-led instrumental that originates from N.D. Recordings in Jamaica. Notably, it has Mathew Mark from the Maytals on the flip as it was quite usual for Jamaican recordings to feature two separate, but probably studio or writer-related, songs on a single.

The Lord Kitchener single comes from the calypso, story-telling tradition. It was played on some radio stations at the time, which is a little surprising when you listen to the rich double-entendres of the song, obviously really about a doctor trying to give an injection:

I push it in, she pull it out
I push it back, she start to shout
Dr Kitch, It's terrible
I can't stand the size of your needle.

NHS appointments with Dr Kitch are reputedly hard to get….

Tonight You're Gonna Fall In Love With Me

THE SHIRELLES

PYE INTERNATIONAL 7N 252233

Maximum respect is due to The Shirelles for kick-starting the girl group pop genre back in 1960. As other groups made their mark they continued with a run of fabulous and influential songs such as 'Boys', 'Dedicated To The One I Love', 'Soldier Boy' and 'Baby It's You', which affected everyone from the Beatles down. By 1963, they had flagged a little, but came back with a bang with this lovely shuffle rhythm song with its oh-so-sexy lead voice that was just impossible to resist.

It seems strange now that there wasn't a rush of covers of this Toni Wine/Art Kornfeld song, although Manfred Mann (exhibiting good commercial taste again) grabbed their next one, 'Sha-La-La'.

Tell Him
THE EXCITERS
UNITED ARTISTS UP 1011

While The Exciters had the US hit, it was Billie Davis, one of the hottest-looking ladies of the Sixties, who had the UK one. However, The Exciters' version was an absolute cracker with its powerful lead from Brenda Reid. She, along with the guy in the group and sometime husband Herb Rooney, kept a version of The Exciters working for several years.

Other group members were Lillian Walker and Carol Johnson – it was Lillian who sung the song at the Rhino Records box set launch party.

Herb Rooney acts as a kind of participant manager, having found the original quartet in New York's Queens borough and introduced them to the famed Jerry Leiber and Mike Stoller.

The song was written by NY writer/producer Bert Berns under his Bert Russell moniker, though the group's follow-up, the equally strong 'He's Got The Power', came to them from the Greenwich/Barry team, who also delivered 'Do Wah Diddy Diddy' to them before Manfred Mann got the big hit with it.

The group is also remembered for making one of the first colour promo films for their hit.

Push A Little Harder
THE NOVAS
RCA 1360

This one from The Novas is another rare girlie record and is almost certainly another group of session girls.

The lead singer is into setting the bar ever higher for her man to push, push, push ever harder if he really wants to impress her.

The record appeared as by The Avons in the US, but the company simply reversed the name in the UK to avoid confusion with the British group of the same name.

With 'Oh Gee Baby' on the flip, this is a genuine rarity, and, as with virtually all the girlie discs, it is distinguished by all-round quality.

The only complaint is that the lead voice and the back-up girls sit a tad too low in the mix, but you can't have everything…

Our Day Will Come
RUBY & THE ROMANTICS
LONDON HLR 9679

'Our Day Will Come' is a beautifully smooth number that's immediately memorable for all the right reasons. The quintet from Akron, Ohio was fronted by the sole female member Ruby Nash, whose voice carried the song so perfectly. It was their first UK issue – leading off nine singles, two EPs and two albums – and is certainly their best known. Their sound was timeless, and they broadly stuck to the formula on subsequent issues that included 'Hey There Lonely Boy' and 'When You're Young And In Love'.

While 'Our Day Will Come' was a US smash hit, for some reason it only paddled briefly in the lower reaches of our charts for a short time.

Not Me
ORLONS
CAMEO PARKWAY C 257

The Orlons were part of the stable of Philadelphia artists on the Cameo Parkway label that included Chubby Checker, Bobby Rydell, Dee Dee Sharp and The Tymes. Under the direction of the label bosses, a lot of material and production sounds were recycled, although The Orlons broadly managed to retain their distinct identity, the croaking frog bass voice of Stephen Caldwell as a counterpoint to the three girls.

They had a long run of pop novelty hits, of which 'Not Me' was the fourth after 'The Wah Watusi', 'Don't Hang Up' and 'South Street', the latter being the place 'where all the hippies meet'. 'Not Me' has echoes of the Gary US Bonds' hit 'New Orleans'. This is partially explained by one of the writers being Frank Guida, the architect of the so-called 'Norfolk' sound of Gary US Bonds, Jimmy Soul and sax man Gene Barge (aka Daddy Gee).

The Orlons had hits in their recognised style until 1965, and came up with their stunning soul stomper 'Spinnin' Top' in 1966.

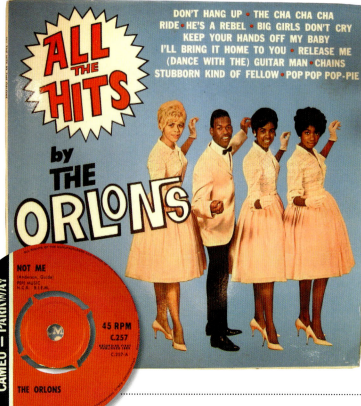

Um, Um, Um, Um, Um, Um
MAJOR LANCE
COLUMBIA DB 7205

Probably one of the few examples of speech filler titles, this Major Lance release, his third in the UK, introduced the smooth R&B work of Curtis Mayfield. Previously, his main song outlet had been for his group The Impressions.

Mayfield's 'The Monkey Time' had been Lance's first issue, and was a reasonably standard dance description song, but 'Um' immediately caught listeners' ears to find out what the lyrics were about. There was a man…and a bench…and he only seemed to 'Um' any responses, neatly avoiding the need for any extra chorus lines.

Mr Lance lost out with the UK hit through a Wayne Fontana & The Mindbenders cover, even though Major's was by far the better version.

He has retained the love of the Northern Soul fans who have since tempted him to tour on the strength of his continued popularity at clubs like The Torch.

Just One Look

DORIS TROY
LONDON HLK 8749

Doris Troy was good fun to be around, and put on a corking live show at Golders Green Refectory in North London when she toured to promote her original issue of her Northern classic 'I'll Do Anything'.

'Just One Look' came out a few years earlier, and was her first UK issue as an artist and writer under her real name of Payne.

She was a New Yorker who had begun her career singing backups for the likes of Chuck Jackson and Solomon Burke, before meeting Artie Ripp who produced her first hit. She eventually relocated to London, where she worked on some releases and back-up work for the Apple label, before eventually returning to New York in the Eighties to work in gospel fields.

Among her other credits were singing back-up vocals on Pink Floyd's *Dark Side of the Moon*, as well as working with the Rolling Stones, Kevin Ayers, Dusty Springfield, ex-Beatle George Harrison, Carly Simon and Nick Drake.

Not Too Young To Get Married

BOB-B-SOXX AND THE BLUE JEANS
LONDON HLU 9754

Bob-B-Soxx And The Blue Jeans were one of Phil Spector's studio creations as a counterpoint to The Crystals and their novelty version of 'Zip-A-Dee-Doo-Dah' had brought the oddball name into the public's consciousness.

For this cheerful doo-wop-rooted number, Phil had turned to Ellie Greenwich and Jeff Barry and launched a songwriting relationship that was to lead to 'Be My Baby', 'Baby I Love You' and 'River Deep Mountain High'.

This song was recorded back in November 1962, but was held back while Spector concentrated on building The Crystals; strangely, it wasn't included on the group's sole album in 1963.

Bob-B-Soxx was Bobby Sheen, who had worked on several occasions with Phil under a number of names, while The Blue Jeans were Darlene Love (who had provided the lead voice for the Crystals' breakthrough hits 'He's A Rebel' and 'He's Sure The Boy I Love') and Fanita James, though there are probably other voices in there as well. The record wasn't a hit of any size anywhere, which was a shame – on the flip, 'Annette', Spector himself takes the lead guitar role and falls into some la-la vocalisations near the end.

Phil Spector

For Phil Spector, 1963 was his first key year of really consistently big hits. Having had fits and starts since 1958 with The Teddy Bears, The Paris Sisters, Gene Pitney and many more, he established The Crystals as a fully hot act in the States, and had set up his own Philles label as an outlet for his own productions.

His growing empire was founded on a unique mixture of musical talent, an ability to recognise a hit song, to use the studio more fully than others, and sheer arrogance. He became the industry wunderkind as The Ronettes and Bob B Soxx were added to The Crystals and his sound increased to previously unheard richness.

Musically, he used the well-established New York Latino style of Leiber & Stoller with elements of doo-wop and Brill Building/Aldon Building girl group feels.

The absolute breakthrough happened when he returned to Los Angeles' Gold Star studio where he had cut The Teddy Bears some years before. There, he linked with arranger Jack Nitzsche, engineer Larry Levine, and a group of musicians who were younger and arguably more open-minded than their New York contemporaries.

Together the team went along with and helped to extend Spector's grandiose plans, and produced some of the most distinctive pop ever made.

With Phil's approach, the artists became subservient to the master plan, though they had to have voices that could cut through the massed sounds – singers such as Darlene Love, Ronnie Spector (nee Bennett), La La Brooks and eventually Tina Turner and Sonny Charles became key to making the whole thing work.

Perhaps Spector's most lasting effect was his approach to making the studio an integral part of the whole and elevating the position of producer to previously unknown heights. Before Spector, the role of producer had been a variable or nebulous one, but afterwards there was never any doubt as to the positive nature of the role.

A Fine Fine Boy
DARLENE LOVE
LONDON HLU 9815

Unusually for a Spector record, Darlene Love does a spoken introduction as a lead into what must be one of the fullest *Wall Of Sound* discs ever: this one has the lot with all the usual doubled, tripled and quadrupled bass, guitar and piano players with saxes and a glockenspiel on top. Even Darlene, blessed with some of the strongest pipes in the business, struggles to get above the mix at times, especially at the point when the title is sung, which may explain why it wasn't one of the biggest Spector hits.

However, it still leaves you breathless, and has a surprise at the end when everything stops briefly for the most memorable section as Darlene opines: "My boy, he's a fine, fine, superfine boy" before the final blast and fade.

Poor Ms Love never had her promised album from Spector back then, but as some sort of compensation she did have one when the 1981 nine-album vinyl box set *Wall Of Sound* was issued. This featured a collection of 13 of her best tracks, including this one plus other hits and rarities such as 'Run, Run, Run Runaway', 'Stumble And Fall' and her then more recent blaster with Phil called 'Lord If You're A Woman'. Sadly, the album was never issued separately from the box set, but is very well worth searching for.

Wait 'Til My Bobby Gets Home
BEVERLY JONES
HMV POP 1201

Love Hit Me
THE ORCHIDS
DECCA F 11785

Spector's reverberations were felt immediately in the record industry. Both in the UK and the US, producers and artists rushed to either cover the associated songs or to try to replicate the sound, and here are two UK records that represent both approaches.

Beverley Jones had already covered Spector's 'Why Do Lovers Break Each Other's Hearts', and was backed here by The Mike Sammes Singers – remembered principally for their residency on the Sing Something Simple BBC radio show. The producer doesn't attempt the Spector rumble, but settles for the Darlene Love US hit song and a reasonably standard British full arrangement, with Beverley providing a confident vocal lead.

By contrast, The Orchids went for the whole shebang and made a better fist of it than most. With co-production by the new kid on the block Shel Talmy, who wrote the song, the trio describe the thrills of a party-based romance.

The group of quite ordinary-looking Coventry schoolgirls even wore their school uniforms for the publicity photos, which probably didn't do them any long-term favours, even though they did get a performance in the pop film Just For Fun.

They managed three UK issues as The Orchids, followed by one as The Exceptions, and most unusually had a US-only release.

They are not the same Orchids who recorded 'That Boy Is Messing Up My Mind' as a US-only release the same year. All the British Orchids releases are rated highly by collectors, and any are worth searching for, especially the full-blooded 'Love Hit Me'.

" 'A Fine Fine Boy' was as close to pure R&B as Phil ever got. Many Of Phil's singles charted R&B, but I think he felt that most of his audience was white, though he produced black artists. We must have done the ending of that song 20 times, to the point where I sounded as if I'd just come in from the fields."
DARLENE LOVE

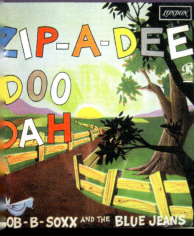

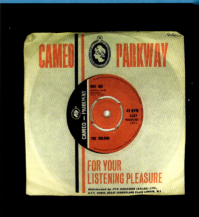

Nelson Mandela is sentenced to life imprisonment, Labour ends a decade of Conservative rule and Radio Caroline starts broadcasting from a ship in the Thames estuary

Beatlemania reaches America after their February performance to 70 million-plus viewers of the Ed Sullivan TV show, and by April they hold the top five places on the Billboard chart, with another seven places elsewhere in the Hot 100. Other British acts conquer America in their wake, wiping out many US acts and genres almost overnight, though by this point Motown has developed a recognisable house sound, and hits from Mary Wells, Martha & The Vandellas and finally The Supremes bring more recognition for the Detroit-based company.

In the UK rival gangs of Mods and rockers do battle amid seaside deckchairs, and just off the coast the pirate radio stations make pop music available all day long for the first time.

A Hard Day's Night becomes the summer's must-see film, just as the US involvement in the Vietnam War ratchets up considerably in the Gulf Of Tonkin.

The year ends with Sam Cooke being shot, Brian Wilson having a breakdown, and Phil Spector releasing his biggest hit, The Righteous Brothers' 'You've Lost That Lovin' Feelin'.

I Can't Get You Out Of My Mind
THE CONTRASTS
PARLOPHONE R 5095

It's Just A Little Bit Too Late
THE DRUIDS
PARLOPHONE R 5134

The Time It Takes
ALAN DEAN AND HIS PROBLEMS
DECCA F 11947

Head Over Heels
MIKE RABIN AND THE DEMONS
COLUMBIA DB 7350

With Beatlemania in full swing, groups seemed to be appearing everywhere. The high streets of Britain were suddenly full of dirty Commer vans adorned with lipsticked girls names, causing heads to turn to see if they were 'someone'. More often than not, it turned out to be 'Clinton Frunge and the Doorknockers' or some such, rather than anyone truly exciting, but everyone kept looking…

The major labels cottoned on to the potential market quickly, and hundreds of groups from around the country released two or three singles, some weren't bad and some shouldn't have bothered. These four are from the former category. All could have been hits, had it not been for the log jam above them.

The Contrasts, a five-piece from Huddersfield, had two Parlophone releases at the height of the boom. The first, 'I Can't Get You Out Of My Mind', was a solid beat group record – good song, good thumpy performance and good group vocals – but, strangely, it is only valued at a fiver today, cheap compared to many others.

The Druids were East London boys who, after playing a few dates in Hamburg, had a couple of issues on the same label. The first, a well-respected version of 'Long Tall Texan', got them known and built a fan base. This one should have seen them break through, because it is an immensely catchy and well-produced pop record, with great light-touch guitar work, and they had the benefit of an attractive pretty-boy front man known as Gearie Kenworthy. It had seemed as if all the required elements were in place…

Collectability increases with Alan Dean And His Problems, although they, too, only rated two boom-time issues. 'The Time It Takes' uses a prominent harmonica against a sparse walking beat arrangement, creating a most distinctive sound. This time the group was from Peterborough.

Completing our quartet of two-beat release champions are Mike Rabin And The Demons, whose 'Head Over Heels' weighs in as the most expensive for a collector now, with a price tag of £75. They were big city boys from Manchester who delivered a heavier maracas-filled head-down rocker that had some air play at the time, but still disappeared unjustifiably quickly. Mike Rabin spent some time as the vocalist with The Toggery Five, also from Manchester, a group that came close to a breakthrough as runners-up to the Bo Street Runners in Ready Steady Go's R&B group contest of 1964.

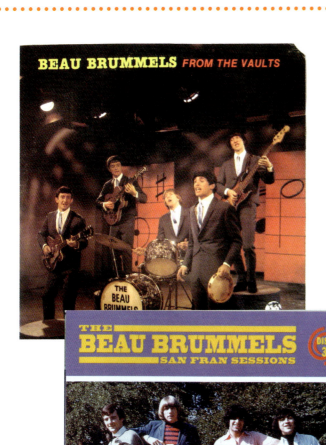

Laugh Laugh
THE BEAU BRUMMELS
PYE INTERNATIONAL 7N 25293

Having moved from its short-lived red-and-yellow label to the pink in-house colour, Pye International now served as an outlet for The Beau Brummels, a heavily Beatles-influenced group from San Francisco.

In the wake of The Beatles mega breakthrough in April 1964, when they not only held the top five places in the Billboard Hot 100 (notably on four different labels), but also had another seven singles elsewhere in the top 100 (Nos 31, 41, 46, 58, 65, 68 and 79, since you ask), similar hair, clothes and a British-sounding name was to become a well-trodden route for many US bands. It had a not-unexpected and immediate effect on US groups and record companies, who, in time-honoured fashion, performed some rapid bandwagon jumping.

The five-piece Beau Brummels turned out to be a very talented bunch, whose Ron Elliott wrote both sides of their first hit. Offering an early example of the softer acoustic-led beat sound that often characterised the US groups, they went on to have a string of excellent releases and several strong albums. Later, when they had dropped down to a quartet, they became early pioneers of country rock.

The group also enjoyed the rare privilege of being transformed into The Beau Brummelstones in an episode of The Flintstones – Betty and Wilma were seen drooling over the soundtrack of 'Laugh Laugh'.

The Beau Brummels. Look carefully, the red striped t-shirt got passed around!

"'Laugh Laugh'...I'd get too much gas from everybody. 'Too many chords' they'd say...The lyrics to it are just a situation I invented to get a song down...(but) it didn't really surprise me that we had a big hit!"

RON ELLIOTT

We Love You Beatles
THE CAREFREES ORIOLE CB 1916

As The Beatles swept all before them in the Billboard April 4 chart, one of the many Brit singles reached No 42. 'We Love You Beatles' needs little description musically as it is the simplest example of a mixture of cash-in and pure adoration that sums up this moment of Moptop madness. The Carefrees were a hastily assembled Liverpudlian studio aggregation, which apparently included John Stevens, Johnny Evans, Don Riddell, Barbara Kay, Betty Prescott and Lyn Cornell. Betty and Lyn were also Vernons Girls members before joining the Breakaways, soon to be Britain's premier group of female backing singers. Barbara Kay also had a variety of work, including some solo releases in 1965. Getting a US-only hit for a Brit record was an achievement then, and it's indicative of just how manic the time was.

What Have They Done To The Rain
THE SEARCHERS
PYE 7N 15739

Since the departure of lead singer Tony Jackson, The Searchers had developed a softer, more melodic approach, and had embraced the US-led sounds that were developing into folk rock. Taking broadly the same tack as Pete Seeger had with 'Where Have All The Flowers Gone', American writer Malvina Reynolds wrote 'What Have They Done To The Rain' amid growing worries of nuclear fallout. The Searchers produced a great, understated version of the song (Tony Hatch added strings to it), and it was very much in sympathy with the group's performance. Although it was a top 20 hit, it was not nearly as big as it deserved to be.

We'll Sing In The Sunshine
THE LANCASTRIANS
PYE 7N 15732

The Lancastrians were a quartet from Manchester who worked in much the same vein as SF's Beau Brummels – soft, harmonised vocals in a vague pop/folky crossover. Pye Records must have rated them as they funded six single attempts, of which this was their first.

'We'll Sing In The Sunshine' is a Shel Talmy-produced cover of Gale Garnett's US hit, and set the tone for the group's future work. Their next single was a Jay & The Americans cover, an attractive, gentle offering when those around them were getting quite noisy.

SEARCHERS: "What Have They Done To The Rain" (Pye). I think it needs a firmer beat. Don't know who the songwriter is but the story is very bizzare and melancoly. The lyric is great – sad, morbid, and I think it will appeal to people who like torch music. I think it could be a hit with enough exposure.
Marvin Gaye, Melody Maker, November 28, 1964

Sound was right for Searchers

TOP TIP

The Searchers
What Have They Done To The Rain; This Feeling Inside (Pye N15739)

TONY HATCH tells me: "I suddenly got the feeling about 'What Have They Done To The Rain' that it would sound marvellous with strings on it and the distinctive Searchers' sound. So I got The Searchers into the studio one day and taped their performance of the song. The next day they had to go back on tour, they were out of London when I took the strings into the studio and added them to the recording. The result, I feel, is in complete sympathy with their sound."

The group agree, I gather, and are happy with this, their first excursion amid the strings. "It happens to be one of our favourite songs," say the boys. "And we're glad to have been able to put it on disc at last."

MY VERDICT: I think Tony Hatch was wise to put the strings in the backing because the Searchers are not a true folk group and it would have been wrong to throw them into direct competition with the stars of that sector.

As it is they sing the folk number with gentle warmth and feeling for the importance of the lyric. The more numbers like this that can find their way into the pop scene the better it will be for the world, just for music but for the Group boys themselves penned the contrasting quick-beat B-deck.

Stage Door
TONY JACKSON
PYE 7N 15876

When Tony Jackson left The Searchers, he initially stayed with the sort of material that the fan base knew him for, and had three Pye releases before trying another tack with this splendid piece of Goffin/ King-penned up-town pop.

New York Broadway influences are all over the record – piano lines contrasting with distinct percussion and heavy bass in a cavernous production. This was Jackson's last for Pye. He moved to CBS, releasing a further four singles before giving up. All of his releases are very collectable.

My Baby Left Me
DAVE BERRY
DECCA F 11803

Sheffield-born Berry had a strange ambition: to be in TV shows, but almost without letting himself be seen. He achieved this admirably, peeking from behind gloved hands or turned-up collars, or simply hiding behind various stage props.

He had a top 20 hit with his first release, a good cover of Chuck Berry's 'Memphis Tennessee', before turning to Arthur Crudup's Elvis-recorded classic 'My Baby Left Me' for the follow-up. Surprisingly, it only scraped into the top 40, but stands as one of the best UK R&B covers, helped to a great extent by Mike Smith's crisp production and Jimmy Page's blistering guitar work on the track.

Dave's own group, The Cruisers, are credited on the 'Hoochie Coochie Man' B side, which is leaden in comparison to the fine top side. Dave ended up adopting a more pop-based image with hits such as 'The Crying Game' and 'Little Things', but this record alone is a fine one to be remembered for.

Motown

From Motown's earliest days in 1959, the company was working towards a recognisable 'house' style in the Snakepit – the affectionate name for the famed Studio A at West Grand Blvd in Detroit. The earlier records had followed the accepted patterns of R&B records of the time and had not attempted much more than to support the artist and the song. However, by 1963-64, Motown was beginning to build records around bass and guitar riffs, such as the three bass and six guitar note repeats on The Temptations' 'My Girl', played respectively by James Jamerson and Robert White, that totally mesmerise the listener before David Ruffin even sings a note. Motown always believed in simple riffs to hook listeners from the start, another being Marv Tarplin's wonderful intro to 'Tracks Of My Tears'.

The first Motown band from 1959 to 1963 had been led by pianist Joe Hunter, and they perfected the loose but effective feel on early cuts from Martha & The Vandellas, The Marvelettes, Mary Wells and the first hits from Marvin Gaye, who was a Motown session drummer himself.

As Joe Hunter gave way to Earl Van Dyke, the Funk Brothers, as they have become known, really hit their groove with the whole feel tightening up. Often Motown arrangers would build on the bass and guitar, and use piano and tambourine for internal rhythms. Saxes and other horns would tend to be held back to join later and build fullness after the first verse and chorus, and vibes would sometimes double with piano to get an altogether richer sound. Everything was anchored by the tight drumming of either Benny 'Papa Zita' Benjamin, Uriel Jones or Richard 'Pistol' Allen.

By 1964, the Motown machine was well in gear, and the strictly-run approach the company had to recording was enabling them to record a mass of products around the clock. Every angle was covered, from the dance steps, the vocal arranger, the deportment coach, the writer/ production team right down to the groups of kids that the company would let in once a week to give their views on the latest singles.

A competitive but co-operative air filled the house. This extended to the out-front artists who, although they would join in with background voices, would seek to outdo each other for attention from the owner Berry Gordy and key writer/producers such as Smokey Robinson and the newly emerging Holland/ Dozier/Holland who were just begining their incredible run of hits.

Nothing like Motown is ever likely to happen again in terms of the consistent quality of the product, and the way the company achieved and maintained their position in the market.

The Motown studio preserved at the museum.

As Long As I Know He's Mine
THE MARVELETTES
STATESIDE SS 251

Too Many Fish In The Sea
THE MARVELETTES
STATESIDE SS 369

Without The One You Love
THE FOUR TOPS
STATESIDE SS 371

He Was Really Sayin' Somethin'
THE VELVELETTES
STATESIDE SS 387

This is a selection from the Stateside label's Motown output in Britain at a time when the Detroit recordings were still known only to a few collectors. In truth, any fan will be able to list a different four, as the releases at this key stage were all special.

The Marvelettes, Motown's first big girl group, had peaked early with their million-selling 'Please Mr Postman', but didn't managed to retain that position, especially when The Supremes finally broke through.

The distinctive 'As Long As I Know He's Mine', with its bass-led intro and cute vocals, features on one of the early Motown compilations, *A Collection of Big Hits Vol 2*. Later in the year, they released the more fully formed 'Too Many Fish In The Sea', remarkable for its strong vocal line interplay on top of what had become the recognisable Detroit sound.

Originally a five-piece at the Postman stage, the group settled as a trio of Gladys Horton, Katherine Anderson and Wanda Young after Georgeanna Tillman and Juanita Grant left. More personnel changes occurred, including occasional group member Florence Ballard helping out, but enduring success eluded them despite a series of fine records.

The Four Tops took a long time to get going. Formed in 1954, they were seen as a jazzy supper club unit by Motown before Holland/Dozier/Holland took them on board. They were part of the subtler end of Motown, with 'Without The One You Love' following just after 'Baby I Need Your

Lovin''. It is similarly constructed, the group singing in unison on the chorus, and the lead voice of Levi Stubbs being somewhat restrained compared to what would happen later. The Tops were renowned for their harmonic vocals, arranged by group member Laurence 'Grass' Payton. The four of them, Payton, Stubbs, Abdul 'Duke' Fakir and Renaldo 'Obie' Benson, stayed together as an unchanged line-up until the deaths of first Payton and then Benson.

The Velvelettes were, by contrast, more 'in-your-face'. The group, which came to Detroit from upstate Flint, included two pairs of sisters: Millie and Cal Gill and Norma and Bertha Barbee, who have remained close to this day.

Working with producer Norman Whitfield, the group made a trio of classic Motown singles: 'Needle In A Haystack', 'These Things Will Keep Me Lovin' You', and 'He Was Really Sayin' Somethin''. Each one was cute and riff-laden, the latter full of hooks after a jerky piano-led intro.

The girls' stand-out vocal break of 'Bop Bop Sookie Do Wah', one of the best-loved Motown vocal hooks, acts as a great break alongside the sassy answer lines in the verses. Personnel changes took their toll on the group by marring consistency, but, without doubt, they deserved a really major hit that sadly never came.

I'll Never Stop Loving You

TOMMY REGAN
COLPIX PX 725

It's neo-doo-wop throwback time! Tommy Regan takes the film song and re-constructs it with the help of the un-credited Marcels in this highly collectable one-off single. Never before had Sammy Cahn's work been turned into such a teen item.

It's a fast arrangement with a bass voice providing the intro and further interjections. The record has an obscure Greenfield/Keller/ Orlando Aldon Building song on the flip: 'This Time I'm Losing You'.

The Rag Dolls were originally conceived as a studio-only group

Society Girl
THE RAG DOLLS
CAMEO PARKWAY P 921

Dusty
THE RAG DOLLS
STATESIDE SS 398

Originally conceived by producer Bob Crewe as a studio-only female version of his Four Seasons, The Rag Dolls proved popular enough to warrant an act to go on the road for promotion. The recorded lead voice was Jean Thomas, who made a great job of the 'poor little rich girl up in her penthouse' scenario of 'Society Girl', which was Crewe's answer disc to his own produced 'Rag Doll' hit. The record was an East Coast US hit, and 'Dusty' was written as the follow-up. All of Crewe's usual cohorts were involved, and it used a full-on Four Seasons bells 'n' whistles arrangement. Both are great pop records that show off Jean's lead voice.

She was always kept busy doing backgrounds for other artists, including Lesley Gore, Neil Diamond, Andy Kim, as well as all-time greats such as Ella Fitzgerald, Sarah Vaughn and Barbra Streisand.

ORIGINAL ALBUM FRONT

(Just Like) Romeo & Juliet
THE REFLECTIONS
STATESIDE SS 294

The Reflections were a five-piece vocal group on the Detroit-based Golden World (later swallowed up by Motown Records), consisting of tenor Phil Castrodale, baritone Raymond Steinberg, lead singer Tony 'Spaghetti' Micale, second tenor Danny Bennie and bass John Dean. It is easy to tell they came from a mixture of backgrounds – in fact, Bennie was from Strathclyde in Scotland. Together they made some wonderful vocal group/pop soul crossover records, '(Just Like) Romeo & Juliet' being their biggest US hit, landing them an American album and a rare, collectable UK EP release. It was a bouncy, hand-clappy, up-tempo song that stayed in your mind after just one play, and was memorable enough to attract a British cover from Peter's Faces.

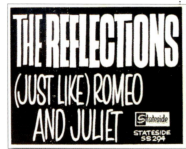

Goin' Out Of My Head
LITTLE ANTHONY AND THE IMPERIALS
UNITED ARTISTS UP 1073

Probably best known for their 1958 hit 'Tears On My Pillow', Little Anthony and The Imperials had a long career that lasted well into the Seventies. The Fifties hit group had parted company with Anthony Gourdine in the early Sixties, but reunited with him as their lead singer for the 1964 US hit song 'I'm On The Outside Looking In'. 'Goin' Out Of My Head' was the follow up to this and was even better, reaching No 6 on Billboard's pop chart. It became a standard with many covers and had subsequent appearances on soundtracks and karaoke machines around the world. Producer/writer Teddy Randazzo combined with the group to lay down a great slab of NY uptown soul with a spacious arrangement that used cavernous drums and a Burt Bacharach feel. This partnership continued to produce genre classics, including the Northern Soul stomper 'Gonna Fix You Good' in 1966, and what is essentially a sunshine music great with 'I'm Hyponitized' in 1969, in which the group sound very much like The Critters. Surprising but true!

I Want You To Meet My Baby
EYDIE GORME CBS AAG 215

Eydie Gorme continued her sidestep into the pop market with a perky Barry Mann/Cynthia Weil song.

It is not clear whether Eydie is double/triple tracked here, or whether there are some remarkably similar-sounding back-up girls with her, but she (or they) power through the song. The repeated middle section is unusually strong, with a change of pace and feel culminating in an instrumental drop-out for all but the drums, which is particularly effective.

Whenever A Teenager Cries
REPARATA & THE DELRONS
STATESIDE SS 382

Wow Wow Wee
(He's The Boy For Me)
THE ANGELS
PHILIPS BF 1312

Mixed-Up, Shook-Up Girl
PATTY & THE EMBLEMS
STATESIDE SS 322

Plenty of good girl groups were still around, despite the Beatles onslaught, and the way many were recorded gradually took them towards pop soul.

The Reparata & The Delrons disc was the first of a long list of fine and varied records made by the group. Here, they have an effective and melodic song from Ernie Maresca, which is built on simplicity and well-placed handclaps behind Mary 'Reparata' Aiese's lead vocal.

The twists and turns of group membership are too tangled to record here, but, suffice to they, they had trimmed down from a quartet to a trio when this first song was a hit for them in the US, and the only continuing member of the trio that later had a hit with 'Captain Of Your Ship' was Reparata. On the strength of 'Whenever A Teenager Cries' they put out a US-only first album. Its cover was notable for using the world's worst wigs and some substantial, unflattering party dresses.

The Angels had had a girl group classic with 'My Boyfriend's Back', and 'Wow Wow Wee (He's The Boy For Me)' followed shortly after. At that time, the group comprised two sisters, Barbara and Jiggs Allbut, and lead singer Peggy Santiglia, whose strong voice also graced records by The Beach Nuts, Dusk and Jessica James & The Outlaws. Driven along by a busy drummer, the girls are sure they've found the right fella on this teen tale. Saxes and handclaps add to the rich sound on this Feldman/Goldstein/Gottehrer production.

Patty & The Emblems emerged briefly from the US Herald label, the home of good R&B and doo-wop. Their only UK issue, 'Mixed-Up Shook-Up Girl' (not the same as the song with the same title recorded later by Willie De Ville), was a good step towards a danceable soul sound, with a fairly advanced production job for the day, making it an attractive find for Northern collectors.

Too Young To Go Steady
ANDEE SILVER
HMV POP 1297

It's endlessly interesting to compare US and UK examples of the girlie genre. Most collectors would agree the US led the field with cute or sassy singles, which sometimes suffered in translation when covered by Brit girls. However, by 1964, UK producers had settled on often heavily orchestrated productions where the supporting brass was given more prominence than it had on US counterparts.

Andee Silver's 'Too Young To Go Steady' was the first of five singles she cut for HMV, Fontana and Decca between 1964 and 1970, when she had an obscure album release called *A Handful Of Silver*.

On this single, she works the time-honoured theme of youthful frustration so often enjoyed by the under 16s (that's the theory anyway). It's a convincing take on the scenario, with just the right amount of self-pity coming through, though secretly you can imagine she was really a suitably pampered princess.

The Goldebriars with Curt Boettcher on the left.

Sea Of Tears THE GOLDEBRIARS COLUMBIA DB 7384

The first years of the Sixties had seen an upsurge in folk music. Attention was split between the socially and politically conscious work of Pete Seeger (whose roots lay in The Weavers and The Almanac Singers), Buffy St Marie, and Dylan, and the more entertainment-based smart groups like The Highwaymen, The Kingston Trio, The Countrymen and many others. While there was some crossover, they essentially attracted different audiences. With the accompanying press and media attention, many folk-orientated groups were able to get record deals, The Goldebriars being one example. They had a couple of album releases on the Epic label in the US. One single, 'Sea Of Tears', from their second album *Straight Ahead*, crossed the Atlantic and stands as testament to a most interesting group.

The group was made up of sisters Sheri and Dottie Holmberg, Ron Neilson (who apparently didn't sing) and Curt Boettcher, who went on to become one of the most collectable cult producer/singer figures of the later Sixties through his work with The Millennium, The Ballroom and others.

'Sea Of Tears' stands out on the album as a plain marker towards his soft vocal arrangements of later years, with delightful circular vocal harmonies floating around a central theme that never quite develops.

The recording is way ahead of its time, predating The Mamas and Papas and The 5th Dimension, who went on to work in a broadly similar vein, with Boettcher later using many of the recording elements that he learnt with the Goldebriars.

Baby Don't Go
SONNY AND CHER
REPRISE R 20309

This was the twosome's first UK release, which was (not surprisingly) re-promoted on the strength of 'I Got You Babe'. Sonny had been a sort of odd-job record business chap around Los Angeles, learning most of his skills as Phil Spector's gofer. The early records that he turned out for his duo with Cher, or for their various individual releases, benefited from his links with the studios and the key LA session players, and this easy jog-along song was attractive enough for everyone to realise that Cher was a strong enough focus to co-front a record, instead of keeping her in the background vocal mix as Spector had. Almost a hit on its own with the later re-release, it is testament to how the pair's personal partnership came through on record.

If All You Think
M.F.Q.
WARNER BROS WB 147

This was the B side of a song called 'The Love Of A Clown', and is the more interesting of the two. The Modern Folk Quartet, to give them their full name, had previously had a 1963 album release in Britain that depicted them as a straight-looking US folk band, but by the time they recorded this single they had embraced Beatle influences and had thoroughly made them their own.

The groups members, Chip Douglas, Jerry Yester, Cyrus Farrer and Henry Diltz, were an interesting lot. All later had success in different ways before re-uniting to make some absolutely splendid harmony recordings in the Eighties: Douglas went to The Turtles for a while, Yester spent time in The Lovin' Spoonful as Zally's replacement, and Diltz became known as one of rock's best photographers.

The feel of 'If All You Think' sets the template for The Association, who were to arrive a year later. It is interesting to note that Jerry Yester's brother Jim was a founder member of The Association, and may have heard his brother's effective definition of the later group's sound from this outing.

Red Bird Records

In serious Sixties record collecting circles, the London American label has long stood supreme in terms of desirability, owing to the huge amount of rare and quality material that saw the light of day in the UK through its output. More recently, EMI's Stateside label, originally modelled on the London label, has received collector attention from its wealth of vocal groups and earlier soul/pop crossover issues. The Red Bird label, though of much shorter duration with around 100 US issues, is now attracting increased attention from girl group and soul collectors.

The label was owned and overseen by Jerry Leiber and Mike Stoller, and was effectively an extension of their earlier Daisy and Tiger imprints. The pair acted as

executive producers, handing over the day-to-day creativity to the younger hotshots such as George 'Shadow' Morton and the Ellie Greenwich/Jeff Barry partnership. Hits flowed almost immediately with Morton's work with the Shangri-Las, and Ellie and Jeff's with The Dixie Cups, The Jelly Beans and The Butterflys.

Other collectable names cropped up as licensed in tracks, such as Roddie Joy, Bessie Banks, The (US) Poets and The Tradewinds. The music, though best-known for being out-and-out pop, was more of a mixture, varying from the surfy rock of The Rockaways' 'Top Down Time' to the Deep Soul of Bessie Banks' 'Go Now', by way of Righteous Brothers' soundalikes Kane and Abel. Almost every issue ranks high in collectable interest to collector groups.

Leiber and Stoller were, at this stage, involved in various business arrangements with some of New York's most colourful and potentially dubious record business characters in the form of George Goldner and Morris Levy. To this day, Jerry and Mike have never told the whole story behind the sudden sell-out of their interests in the label. "We got bored after a couple of years. That's the official story," said Jerry Leiber in an interview in 2001. They apparently weren't greatly enamoured with some of the more lightweight product that was released: understandable, given their fine R&B backgrounds. Nevertheless, the label's output in all its variety is beloved by collectors.

I Wanna Love Him So Bad
THE JELLY BEANS
PYE INTERNATIONAL 7N 25252

People Say
THE DIXIE CUPS
RED BIRD RB10 006

Goodnight Baby
THE BUTTERFLYS
RED BIRD RB10 009

Iko Iko
THE DIXIE CUPS
RED BIRD RB10 024

These fine pop records from The Jelly Beans, The Dixie Cups and The Butterflys represent the lighter girl group side of Red Bird and the involvement of writers/producers Greenwich and Barry. All were US hits.

The Dixie Cups sold well in the UK, especially with their first hit 'Chapel Of Love', which had been recorded by both the Ronettes and The Crystals without being released by Phil Spector. The Dixie Cups' sound was simplicity itself, with minimal backing tracks and sweet vocals, and their 'Chapel'-soundalike follow-up 'People Say' was nearly a UK hit.

'Iko Iko' emerged almost as a studio throwaway – their producers caught the three girls singing an old school playground chant. Realising how catchy it was, it was recorded with mainly percussive backing and is a fondly remembered track of theirs, which was later revived by The Belle Stars. The three girls, Barbara Ann Hawkins, Joan Marie Johnson and Rosa Lee Hawkins became disillusioned with the business after mysteriously disappearing royalties, and returned to New Orleans after a brief (but largely unsuccessful) move to ABC Records. Barbara and Rosa

**The Jelly Beans,
Maxine Herbert,
Alma Brewer,
Elyse Herbert and
Charles Thomas**

**Jeff and Ellie
with the
Dixie Cups.**

revived the act occasionally thereafter.

The Jelly Beans, Maxine Herbert, Alma Brewer, Elyse Herbert and Charles Thomas, had their easy-going hit released on Pye International just before Red Bird became an imprint in its own right in the UK. They disappeared even more quickly than The Dixie Cups, after only two singles, although they did re-appear briefly in the mid-Seventies with a one-off single released in Britain on the Right On label. A Red Bird album was recorded but never released at the time, and appeared as part of the various Red Bird Story vinyl or CD compilations of more recent times.

Producer Steve Venet brought The Butterflys to Red Bird, who were thought to have previously recorded as The Buttons. It's possible that Ellie Greenwich could be somewhere in the vocal mix of the record. Their ranks also included ex-Crystal Mary Thomas. They made two fine records for the label, but sadly only this one found a UK release. The other was a slower version of The Crystals' 'I Wonder.'

THE JELLYBEANS: I Wanna Love Him So Bad (Trio, BMI) (2:40) – Modern reading of boy next door story done in medium tempo, Detroit style. Flip: "So Long" (Trio, BMI) (2:00). **Red Bird 10-003**

The Boy From New York City
THE AD LIBS
RED BIRD RB10 102

My Life
ORPHEUS
RED BIRD RB10 041

Go Now
BESSIE BANKS
RED BIRD BC 106

This trio, of incredibly different issues, represents the more varied end of Red Bird. The wonderful Ad Libs had a string of issues on a variety of labels, each quite different, but managed to retain a magic for collectors. The group, from Newark, NJ, comprised Mary Ann Thomas (no relation to The Butterflys' Mary Thomas), Hugh Harris, Norman Donnegan, Dave Watt and Danny Austin.

'The Boy From New York City' is probably one of the best-known songs in this book, having been regularly covered over the years (for example, by Darts), but the Ad Libs' version remains the definitive one.

The male group members act as the Greek chorus to Mary Ann, who carries the song as she tells of her new bloke. After Watt's goofy bass intro, the repeated 'Ooo Wah, Ooo Wah Come On Kitty' refrain hooks us from very early on. It became a comparatively rare example of a record that has a balance of importance between the lead and the varied backing vocals.

'My Life' from Orpheus has a memorable descending guitar figure throughout the song. Featuring a prominent tambourine, it is effectively a folk rock record before the term was coined, strengthened by the 'protest' lyric. It is an angst-ridden tirade against an unspecified 'they', who will not run his life: he is going to wear what he likes, and do and say what he likes, and it is delivered in a Barry McGuire-type snarl. It could be inter-generation, or it could be anti-Government, or it could be simply a hissy and petulant winge. Whichever, it is certainly one on its own and quite different from other Red Bird outputs.

The wonderful original of 'Go Now' by Bessie Banks is also quite different. Issued about a year before the Moody Blues' cover, it is a slow and heartfelt plea – raw emotion in record form. The backing group includes Dee Dee Warwick.

Dave Godin loved the Bessie Banks disc so much that it became an early re-issue on his own later Soul City label.

THE AD LIBS: The Boy From New York (Trio, BMI) (2:50) – New group on Red Bird's new subsid label. The sound is tested and proved with with the usual commercial fare to br expected from L & S. Flip: "Kicked Around" (Trio, BMI) (1:47). **Blue Cat 102**

"'Go Now' is easily one of the most beautiful, dramatic and overpowering records ever to emerge...one wonders if she is going to make it to the end of the recording without crying."

DAVE GODIN, RHYTHM & SOUL, 1966

Soulful Dress
SUGAR PIE DESANTO
PYE INTERNATIONAL 7N 25249

I Can't Stand It
SOUL SISTERS
SUE WI 312

Get Your Hat
DON & DEWEY
LONDON HL 9897

With a growing interest in black US R&B (starting to be called soul), certain records were heard in clubs everywhere. This trio were good dance records with arresting vocal delivery, putting them head and shoulders above much of the chart material of the day. The Mods knew it, and so did many of the artists and record business people still working today.

Sugar Pie, Don & Dewey and the Soul Sisters were the real deal. The sheer power of the large ladies in Soul Sisters duo could shake the stage and the audience. They belted out the powerhouse 'I Can't Stand It' and other R&B favourites to the backing of Elton John's Bluesology, a group that consistently did the honours for a variety of visiting American acts.

Let It Be Me (Je T'Appartiens)
BETTY EVERETT & JERRY BUTLER
STATESIDE SS 339

The emerging soul output in 1964 had other acceptable forms, and this combination of Jerry Butler and Betty Everett represents the smoother side of what was still well-rooted in the East Coast orchestrated traditions. The pair's voices combine well on the Everly Brothers hit, breathing a new and soulful feel into the song while still retaining its simpler pop essence. Both Jerry and Betty have extensive catalogues of solo work elsewhere, all worthy of extensive attention.

Dancing Silhouettes
JACKIE DE SHANNON
LIBERTY LIB 10165

This is a lesser-known Jackie de Shannon B Side, which she wrote with partner Sharon Sheeley (Eddie Cochran's girlfriend at the time of his death). The song reverses the roles in Del Shannon's 'Two Silhouettes', as Jackie is unable to sleep, and just happens to go for a night walk past the boyfriend's house precisely at the moment when he is in a close dance clinch with another. Shock! How could this be? Well, no good usually comes to those who venture out in their nighties as moviegoers know well. Jackie's record builds nicely until, by the instrumental break, it has almost become like a Spector production.

Jackie De Shannon (real name Sharon Lee Myers) supported The Beatles on their first tour of the US and her backing band included Ry Cooder. She also wrote 'Don't Doubt Yourself Babe' for the first album by The Byrds. She also wrote with Jimmy Page during a visit to the UK in 1965.

Joy Ride
THE ROADSTERS
STATESIDE SS 293

Drag
RONNIE & THE
DEL-AIRES
CORAL Q 72473

California Sun
THE RIVIERAS
PYE INTERNATIONAL 7N 25237

Hot Rod USA
THE RIP CHORDS
CBS AAG 202

RONNIE AND THE DEL-AIRES: Drag; Just Wigglin' 'n' Wobblin' (Coral Q 72473). Two items from the film "The Horror At Party Beach" Topside, Drag, opens with the snarl of exhaust pipes.

Over on the West Coast, the surf and drag race craze had become a vocal phenomenon in terms of the hits generated.

The Roadsters' disc is a one-off rarity on both sides of the pond, probably generated for inclusion in the Horror Of Party Beach film, sub-titled the First Horror Monster Musical. The Roadsters are closest in sound to Ronny & The Daytonas of 'GTO' fame.

The B side, also from the film, was called 'Drag', which brings us nicely to Ronnie & The Del-Aires, whose version of the same song ('Drag') was included in the film with them performing it. It's a tougher version than the Roadsters', and is just as rare.

By contrast, The Rivieras are reasonably well-known, and the song is easy to find on compilations, if not on original disc. Their reedy organ-led song was a US top ten hit, which received a fair amount of radio play in Britain without being a hit. The record was more-or-less a home-made affair for the six-piece group, the nucleus of which was singer Marty Fortson, guitarist Doug Gean and organist Otto Nuss. The only other songs of theirs to make waves were 'Let's Have A Party' and 'Little Donna'.

The Rip Chords had enjoyed a small hit with 'Here I Stand' followed by a massive one with 'Hey Little Cobra'. The follow-up (of which 'Hot Rod USA' was the B side) was 'Three Window Coupe', which extended their established car theme. By this point, their recording activities were being directed by future Beach Boy Bruce

Johnston and soon-to-be Byrds producer Terry Melcher.

That 'Hot Rod USA' was relegated to be the B side of 'Three Window Coupe' is unbelievable – it is one of the finest examples of the drag vocal genre, and stands proudly alongside the best of Brian Wilson or Jan Berry's output of the time. The song even concurs with the lyric: "The whole thing started back in '63, Jan & Dean, The Beach Boys and me." It represents an initial peak in the vocal and production abilities of Bruce and Terry.

The Del-Aires

Frankie Avalon, Dick Dale and Annette

WEIRD ATOMIC BEASTS...
WHO LIVE OFF HUMAN BLOOD!

THE FIRST HORROR MONSTER MUSICAL!

THE HORROR OF PARTY BEACH

FANTASTIC!!! | HORRIFYING!!! | WEIRD!!!

Please Don't Leave Me
THE CINDERELLAS
COLPIX PX 11026

They're Jealous Of Me
EARL-JEAN
COLPIX PX 748

As two later examples of New York's Dimension Records output, these tracks highlight how quickly the production feel improved in a short time. The Cinderellas were The Cookies under another name, and Earl-Jean was a member of the same group. Both sides of each record are fabulous.

'Don't Ever Leave Me' is a much bigger sound than most of the Cookies discs, the more involved arrangement possibly being brought about by a bigger budget on the back of a string of hits.

Earl-Jean's song was the B side of 'Randy', in itself a very commercial outing. Here, her soft vocals purr seductively enough to melt the heart of most listeners. A wonderfully melodic Goffin/King song, many were hooked by the end of the first verse and chorus.

Goin' Places
THE ORLONS
CAMEO PARKWAY C 332

While the A side, 'Knock! Knock! (Who's There?)', was in the well-trusted traditional Orlons' hit territory, this B side took them in a new direction towards pop soul, via a reasonably typical Bob Crewe stompy production sound. It's an easy mid-pacer with handclaps, and, being The Orlons, we await a bass voice interjection that never comes – although Steve Caldwell is there in the vocal mix and emerges slightly towards the end.

Shirley Brickley, Marlene Davis and Rosetta Hightower had become one of the best vocal group blends, and it is sad that their later work for the Cameo label in the US didn't do as well as their earlier work. Unlike many of their contemporaries, the group didn't stay in music or hit the oldies circuit: Rosetta moved to England, Steve went into education work in Philadelphia, Marlene became an IT expert, and unfortunately Shirley died all too early.

Spanish Harlem
SOUNDS INCORPORATED
COLUMBIA DB 7321

Instrumental versions of great songs don't always work well, but this one does. Sounds Incorporated was everyone's backing group of choice on package tours, but they were a popular act in their own right.

This re-working of 'Spanish Harlem' is taken at a slightly faster pace than Ben E King's original, and is effectively a sampler of their talents. Leading off with an interestingly toned guitar with answering flute, they bring in gently droning saxes on the second verse. The flute then takes a verse before a single sax takes the same bridge line as on the vocal version, and the guitars return to take the whole thing to fade. Beautifully constructed and played – hats off to them!

She Was My Baby
THE SHOUTS
REACT EA 001

The first, and possibly only, release on the React label was well-produced by Pat Meehan, whose name appears later in the Sixties in connection with groups such as Pesky Gee.

Who The Shouts were is not known, though aural evidence points to a black group. The tale is a familiar one: his baby has gone off with his (former) best buddy, and even the local gypsy woman can't seem to help him. Despite this wretched luck, the whole thing is really quite jolly with a jog-along beat, light guitar break and lively choruses. Certainly a good record for the time.

Blowing In The Wind
STAN GETZ
VERVE VS 520

Hidden away as the B side of The Girl From Ipenema, this really deserved topside status, as Getz effortlessly interprets the new kid on the block. While the strings are a little syrupy and intrusive at times, the sax playing is, as you would expect from a master like Getz, absolutely marvellous.

Now We're Thru
THE POETS DECCA F 11995

All I Want Is My Baby
BOBBY JAMESON
DECCA F 12032

Young Love
BO AND PEEP DECCA F 11968

So Much In Love
THE MIGHTY AVENGERS
DECCA F 11962

The common link between these four records Is that Andrew Loog Oldham, whose stock was high with Decca Records owing to his already successful management of The Rolling Stones, produced them all. Although The Stones had taken time to become established, Oldham had hit on the marketing idea of making them the surly antithesis of The Beatles, with the odd added extras of talent and energy. It all worked a treat.

From early on, Oldham had been interested in production, and had invited his then-idol Phil Spector along to Regent Sound Studio in London's Denmark Street, where the Stones recorded all their early work. Spector influences are all over both the Poets and the Bobby Jameson discs, as both marry beat influences with big drums and plenty of echo.

The Poets' disc, which was a smallish but now largely forgotten hit, was written by the central axis of the group: vocalist George Gallagher, co-vocalist Hume Paton and guitarist Tony Myles. Other members at this stage were bassist John Dawson and drummer Alan Weir, but many personnel changes overtook the Glasgow band before they disbanded in the late Sixties. Their later singles are particularly collectable though.

Bobby Jameson was a wandering American who pitched up in London and met The Stones crowd. Keith Richards is credited as co-writer with Oldham and musical director on 'All I Want Is My Baby'. This was his first Decca single after one on London, but despite it being a good single with tempo changes and a full falsetto-led mid section and a lot of publicity, fame wasn't beckoning.

Bo and Peep's was a manic, almost surfy-styled remake of the old Tab Hunter hit. For years, collectors were under the impression that it was The Stones having a laugh, but was actually a piece of devilment largely concocted by Oldham and madman-about-town Kim Fowley (who takes the lead 'vocal' – for want of a better phrase – on the flip 'The Rise Of The Brighton Surf', which takes the rise out of 'The House Of The Rising Sun'). The top side, however, was a full-on commercial, if slightly over-produced, bit of fun, and received several radio plays.

Goodbye Dolly (Gray)
THE MASSED ALBERTS
PARLOPHONE R 5159

It's not too big a stretch to say that without the cheerful insanity of folks like the Goons and The Massed Alberts, we would not have had the Pythons, Bonzos, Grimms, or any of the particularly British acts that followed in their wake.

The vocalist here is Professor Bruce Lacey, who was a friend and contemporary of Spike Milligan with much the same oblique outlook on life. Bruce lived with his first six children and wife Pat in the Mock Tudor parade of houses in North London's Durnsford Road, a few doors away from Ashley Hutchings, one of the co-founders of Fairport Convention. The Lacey house was always full of noise, activity and wonder, a fact that became immediately apparent when passing the full-sized stuffed camel in the hallway to encounter the various humanoid machines deeper within. Ashley had befriended him, which explains the 'Mr Lacey' song on Fairport's second album. Bruce was not always everyone's cup of tea – an actress walked out on him from an oddball production of his at London's famed Royal Court theatre. Bruce simply replaced her with a robotic device with a tape recorded in its chest to speak her lines, topped off with an enormous pair of red lips, but it kept breaking down in performance, necessitating Bruce going on to do running repairs.

This record was one of his many collaborations with the Alberts and features a re-visiting of the old World War One song with an increasingly manic jazz band. The intro promises that, while singing the song, Bruce will also be doing such things as sword swallowing and fire-eating. The crazy thing is, he may well have done just that…

Little Latin Lupe Lu

THE KINGSMEN
PYE INTERNATIONAL
7N 25262

Forever known for their excessively raggedy-round-the-edges version of 'Louie Louie', The Kingsmen did make some pretty decent records. Never pretending to be something they were not, they cut a version of the-then standard 'Little Latin Lupe Lu' (written by Brother Phil Medley), which had been popularised in the States by the Righteous Brothers before they got to Phil Spector.

This version is a big sound, driven largely by loud drums and tambourine, with seemingly scant attention paid to needles going into the red in the control room. The whole thing has a raw, live feel to it that works really well. The group's leader was singer/sax player Lynn Easton (who memorably comes back in at the wrong point after the break on the issued 'Louie Louie'), lead guitarist Mike Mitchell, bassist Norm Sundholm, organist Barry Curtis and drummer Dick Peterson. They appear to have hailed from Portland, Oregon.

I Wonder THE CRYSTALS LONDON HLU 9852

This is one of the most collectable Crystals' issues because the song was never issued in the US at the time. Phil Spector had announced that their next issue was to be 'Little Boy', but then changed his mind and put this one out a few weeks later, with 'Little Boy' on its flip. Having two vocal tracks on a Spector record was unusual (previous ones often had throw-away instrumental B sides to avoid deflecting attention from the main song), but here are two corkers for the price of one.

'I Wonder' is often sited as being among collectors' favourite Spector sides, and it is easy to see why. Firstly, it is a really strong and melodic Spector/Greenwich/Barry song, and, secondly, it is probably the peak of the full *Wall Of Sound*, with everything thrown into the mix, leaving just enough room for high-soaring strings to be saved for the break. Interestingly, this one had been recorded at New York's Mirasound Studio back in November 1963, rather than Spector's usual Gold Star Studio in LA, but was held until March 1964 when it made an all-too-brief appearance in the UK chart at No 36 for one week only. It was one of LaLa Brooks' very best leads for the group.

Don Julian & THE LARKS
THE JERK – The MONEY Recordings

KENT

The Jerk
THE LARKS
PYE INTERNATIONAL 7N 25284

The Larks were a three-piece group based in Los Angeles led by 'Jerk'-writer Don Julian, who had been privileged enough to have taken music lessons from Joe 'Honeydripper' Liggins. A top ten US hit took the group overnight to hot act status, commanding much-increased fees, and launched them onto a seemingly endless list of dance songs: 'The East Coast Jerk', 'Soul Jerk', 'The Roman', 'The Slauson Shuffle', 'The Philly Dog', 'The Skate' and 'The Duck'. They at least covered their bases!

Their high-pitched vocal delivery fitted in with a recording style that has subsequently been termed 'floater', and which was used by other acts of the day such as The Astors on Stax and The Radiants on Chess.

Citation of Achievement
1964
"The Jerk"
Cash Songs Publishing Co.
1065 East Vernon Ave.
Los Angeles 11, Calif

THE
SWINGING LARKS
HAVE DONE IT AGAIN.
COME BACK BABY
MONEY #127
1065 E. VERNON AVE., LOS ANGELES, CALIF.
MONEY RECORDS
ADems 1-9188

The Crusher
THE NOVAS
LONDON HLU 9940

Novelty 'dance' songs abounded in the Sixties, but this song took it to extremes with a growl of a voice so rough that the poor man probably wasn't able to speak for a week after the recording. Lyrically, it appears to concern a group of wrestlers referred to as 'turkeynecks' who are being extolled to do 'The Crusher' and 'The Eye-Gouge'. Everybody's doing it, don't you know?

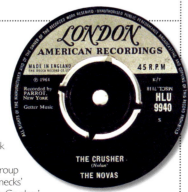

Georgie Fame

At the time when The Flamingo Club in the lower reaches of London's Wardour Street was the very hippest place to go, Georgie Fame and His Blue Flames were without doubt THE band to see there. His highly talented players filled the small stage with a sound big enough and powerful enough to get the whole place moving, and Georgie directed it all from his hunched position over the organ. Their Flamingo-based R&B album proved to be one of the key staging posts of hip listening at that stage.

Georgie obviously had a breadth of musical taste, and by 1964-65 had branched out to follow more of a pop/jazz solo career that gave him huge hits with 'Get Away' and 'Yeh Yeh' to name but two. Drawing from country, R&B, soul and sometimes even comedic influences, he continued a classy path that included a tie-up with Alan Price from The Animals.

It was as a result of trying to get one of Fame's records played on the radio (no one would do it) that Ronan O'Rahilly ended up creating his own station - Radio Caroline - to do so.

GEORGIE FAME
funny how time slips away

85

Cross My Heart
THE EXOTICS DECCA F 11850

The Exotics were possibly from Liverpool, and different from another similarly named group later in the Sixties. 'Cross My Heart' is a delightfully infectious slab of happy mid-tempo Blue Beat that is impossible to keep still to. It appears to have been their only release, which is a shame because they were a lot of fun. This copy, according to its sleeve, was previously owned by one Ian Westmorland – good taste, Ian!

Shang A Doo Lang
ADRIENNE POSTER
DECCA F 11864

When this track was included in the Decca CD collection *The Girls' Scene*, the notes referred to the track as "the most overtly Spectorish" that Andrew Loog Oldham had cut. And indeed it is. The Jagger/Richard song is given a gentle glockenspiel intro before the full force of the track explodes into a blast of *Wall Of Sound*, the like of which has rarely been heard outside Gold Star or Mirasound studios.

Maybe there is a good reason for this – Bobby Graham's fascinating book The Session Man (Broom Horse, 2004) has a chapter devoted to this session (Bobby was one of the best-know session drummers of the Sixties, and his own 'Skin Deep' record can be found elsewhere in this book). His memories of this session at Olympic Sound in London's Carlton Street indicate how secretive it appeared to be at the time: "A session was booked…without even the usual clue as to what sort of session it was to be. A number of the musicians asked, but each was told the same thing, which was – nothing. The upshot was that it was a secret. There was a frisson of excitement."

Once all the players were in place, the artist was revealed as Adrienne Poster, and the word was that the session was to be co-produced by Andrew Oldham and Phil Spector, with arrangements from Charles Blackwell. Oldham was his normal busy self at the session, giving out ideas to the players, but Spector did not make himself known to them. Bobby recalls: "I looked up and saw this figure wearing a cloak; that was Phil Spector's sartorial hallmark of the time and I was pretty sure it was him. Any doubts I had were removed when the session got under way." Spector's musical influence was soon apparent with the doubling of two pianists on

one piano, and a "thunderous echo" applied to his drums. He also heard an American voice directing things in the control room.

The question remains, then, as to whether it was an official, but uncredited, co-production, or whether it was Spector just dropping in to help out his pal. Either way, it is a fascinating, and previously undocumented, musical event. As Bobby says: "It was a very interesting experience but weird, really weird."

**Adrienne Poster:
Spectorish**

Here She Comes
THE TYMES
CAMEO PARKWAY P 924

It's just a simple and joyous song: he's got a new girl, and here she comes, walking down the street. The Tymes move away from their smooth ballads and into pop soul territory with an irresistible song that works with handclaps, punctuating high group vocals, and occasional, but well-placed, vibes notes. Glorious in its simplicity, it's hardly surprising that this is by far and away the most sought-after Tymes disc for Northern dancers.

IF ALL YOU THINK
(Yester)

M.F.Q.

WB
147

USA No.
5481

Motown Historical Museum

TEEN BEAT

Number 4 JANUARY ISSUE

12 PAGES MONTHLY

ONE SHILLING

BEATLES · TREMELOES · PACEMAKERS · SEARCHERS · BILLY J. · HOLLIES

LONDON
AMERICAN RECORDINGS
DEMONSTRATION SAMPLE NOT FOR SALE
MADE IN ENGLAND

45 RPM

Recorded by SPECIALTY
Hollywood

Venice Music

1969 OSIN
HL
9897

RECORDING FIRST
PUBLISHED 1964

GET YOUR HAT
(Harris, Terry, Jr.)
DON AND DEWEY

PYE
INTERNATIONAL

45 RPM

THE BEAU
BRUMMELS

7N.25293

LAUGH, LAUGH
(Ron Elliott)
COPYRIGHT CONTROL
An Autumn, U.S.A. Recording

MADE IN GT BRITAIN

Stateside
45 R.P.M.

Recorded in
U.S.A. by
20th Century
Records

Sunno
Mus. Co.

RECORDING FIRST
PUBLISHED 1964
(45-KR-4283)

SOLD IN U.K. SUBJECT TO
RESALE PRICE CONDITIONS,
SEE PRICE LISTS

SS-293

JOY RIDE
(from the film "Horror at Party Beach")
(Wilfred Holcombe—Edward Earl)
THE ROADSTERS

E.M.I. RECORDS LIMITED

PARLOPHONE

rave

THE FRANK LOOK AT TODAY'S POP WORLD · 64 PAGES

NO.4
MONTHLY
2s 6d

SCOOP!
BEATLES
SECRETS

DAVE CLARK
WITH THE
WAY-OUT
ONES!

PHILIPS PHILIPS 45 RPM

vocalion

immediate IMMEDIATE IMMEDIATE IMMEDIATE

RCA

Something is definitely happening... Lyndon Johnson launches the 'Great Society', Dylan goes electric and 50,00 0 troops head for Vietnam

FROM THE 'HANG ON SLOOPY' TEAM, ANOTHER GREAT DANCE HIT
LICENSED TO SELL...
'CARA-LIN'
The Strangeloves
IMMEDIATE IM007

NEW RELEASES
IMMEDIATE

BUT YOU'RE MINE

The Who

MOHAIR SAM
Written & Composed by DALLAS FRAZIER
★★★
RECORDED BY
Charlie Rich
ON PHILIPS
MUSIC CO. LTD...

45 R.P.M.
POP 1475
MEEKSVILLE SOUND

TUDOR RECORDS - ABC CINEMA - MUSWELL HILL
EVERY NEW RELEASE FOR WEEK ENDING 19th December, 1965

Kim Weston

Stevie Wonder

Doris Troy

THE TRACKER

SIR DOUGLAS QUINTET

KENNY BERNARD & THE WRANGLERS

America recovers from the Beatles' invasion by unleashing The Byrds, who adapted Dylan's growing song popularity into a more easily digested pop form, unleashing the more meaningful lyrics of folk rock onto the market.

Singles sales remain huge as the beat boom continues, and many well-crafted American recordings are issued in the UK, only to disappear amid the homegrown product.

The London American label is beginning to decline as other labels enter the game. Motown continues to make inroads, helped by EMI giving the company its own label and by the Sound Of Motown TV show hosted by Dusty Springfield. Ready Steady Go and Top Of The Pops are both essential viewing for all music fans, and London is fully swinging with mini skirts, Twiggy and Sassoon cuts. The Beatles release *Rubber Soul*, described by Brian Wilson as: 'A whole album of good stuff'...

Home Of The Brave
BONNIE & THE TREASURES
LONDON HLU 9998

As an issue on the Phil Spector offshoot US label Phi-Dan, this has all the hallmarks of a Spector production, but appears to have been produced by Phil's protégé Jerry Riopelle. For years, people thought this was Ronnie Spector in disguise, but it was sung by a young white lass known as Charlotte O'Hara.

In 'Home Of The Brave', the song is the key element, and it attracted a rival version by Jody Miller in the US. Jody won the chart battle, reaching No25 on Billboard, while Bonnie stalled at No77. Here in the UK, Peanut (aka Katie Kissoon) released another good version.

Bonnie soon issued another corker in the States called 'Close Your Eyes', but sadly that one never made it to British shores.

I Want That Boy
THE CHANTELLES
PARLOPHONE R 5271

This is a strong example of a British production that holds its own against American ones. The Chantelles lay claim to the chap of their dreams in most strident terms – the strong lead and backing voices on the up-tempo song power onwards with full orchestration from start to finish. This was the first of six singles managed by the group under this name between 1965 and 1967. Previously, they had been known as the Lana Sisters, a three-piece London trio that once included a young Dusty Springfield, and the Fifties-styled sister act morphed into a mini-skirted, white-booted, mascara-daubed sassy group. 'I Want That Boy' was a cover of a really obscure disc by Sadina.

He Knows I Love Him Too Much
GLO MACARI
PICCADILLY 7N 35218

This is another strong British girl record with a very good Goffin/King song.

Out In The Sun (Hey-O)
THE BEACH-NUTS
LONDON HL 9988

On the subject of one-off records, here is another brainchild from the NY-based Feldman, Goldstein and Gottehrer team. Using the vocal talents of Peggy Santiglia from the Angels, Jean Thomas from the Rag Dolls, and presumably themselves, the production and writing team construct a cute question-and-answer song based around going to the beach. As simple as you like, but, put together with a light touch using steel band highlights, it found universal appeal with the repeated Hey-O chorus. Had it been around today, it would have made it onto the football terraces as a celebratory 'we're going up' chant.

Phil Spector had cut a slower, breathy version earlier with The Paris Sisters, but the Ivor Raymonde-directed arrangement shows what Spector should have done with the song. Despite Glo's family owning one of the West End's key music shops, this was her only release here, though it was rated high enough to warrant a US release on Capitol Records.

Hey Baby
THE HI-LITES
LONDON HL 9967

One song that has made it on to the football terraces is 'Hey Baby', which was originally a No2 UK hit for Bruce Channel back in 1962. The Hi-Lites turned the song into a big thumpy, stompy number years (nay, decades) before DJ Otzi did it. The vocal group version is enlivened by the addition of a Brian Wilson-styled falsetto surfing wail on the verses.

Thou Shalt Not Steal
GLENDA COLLINS
HMV POP 1475

Glenda Collins' powerful voice sits well on top of this Joe Meek production of the John D Loudermilk song that had been a US hit for Dick and DeeDee. Aural evidence suggest that The Outlaws provide backing here, as there are some very distinctive guitar licks that sound typical of Richie Blackmore. She got airplay with this, but it didn't quite make it.

GLENDA COLLINS: Thou Shalt Not Steal; Been Invited to A Party (HMV POP 1475). A very bright treatment given to the old John D. Loudermilk number. Plenty of high pitched guitars and thumping drums combine well with the voice.

I Do
THE MARVELOS
HMV POP 1433

I'm A Happy Man
THE JIVE FIVE
UNITED ARTISTS UP 1106

At The Discothèque
CHUBBY CHECKER
CAMEO PARKWAY P 949

By 1965, soul (previously known as R&B) came in many forms, and these three issues were at the more commercial end of the spectrum.

The least well-known of the trio, The Marvelos, were a six-piece act who had mainly met at school in Chicago (don't confuse them with the LA-based Marvellos, who had a hit with 'We Go Together'). Melvin Mason was the usual lead singer, with brothers Johnny and Frank Paden (bass and tenor respectively), Willie Stephenson (tenor), Andrew Thomas (another tenor), and guitarist Henry Bardwell. The group wrote 'I Do', and the majority of the songs on the album. This song is built on high and distinctive brass lines and has a strong tenor Do-Do-Do hook vocal line, but sadly it was rarely heard in Britain.

The Jive Five were better known, having already had a couple of isolated UK releases in their earlier doo-wop incarnation. The group was built around lead singer Eugene Pitt, who took the role of singer/manager. Pitt's fine voice glides over the rest of the group on an easy mid-tempo fingerpopper that re-established the group in the US charts. He produced a good tie-in album, which blended the group's doo-wop roots with Sixties pop soul sensibilities. The line-up at this stage was Pitt with Webster Harris (first tenor), Casey Spencer (second tenor), Norman Johnson (bass, but not the same one as General Johnson), and the all-male Beatrice Best as the baritone. Horace Ott handled the arrangements at Beltone Recording in NYC.

Chubby Checker had pretty well exhausted the dance record route by 1965, and took a most acceptable turn into this classic early Northern Soul fave. Great lyrics captured the feel of the new club phenomenon of discotheques in this perfectly balanced record, which featured a more restrained Chubby. He came to the UK to promote it, but it still didn't take off to become the massive hit it deserved to be.

May The Bird Of Paradise Fly Up Your Nose

"LITTLE" JIMMY DICKENS
CBS 201969

There should always be room for a little bit of absurdity to stop us taking things too seriously, so let's turn to "Little" Jimmy Dickens for some lyrical nonsense. As if the title line isn't strange enough, the next line is: 'May an elephant caress your tootsie toes' (although it may not be 'tootsie', as the words are somewhat garbled at that point). However, tootsie fits the standard of the surrounding style! It's a cheerful country music format with a convoluted storyline, which, silly or not, took it to No 15 on Billboard.

Hole In The Wall

THE PACKERS
PYE INTERNATIONAL 7N 25343

Baby I'm Yours

BARBARA LEWIS
ATLANTIC AT 4031

Had you gone to one of the new-fangled discotheques around London at the time, you may well have encountered these two. The Packers' instrumental bears a by-line of 'Pure Soul Music USA', and reveals the writers names as 'Cropper, Jackson, Jones and Nathan', most of which are immediately recognisable as members of Booker T and The MGs.

The story goes like this: a Los Angeles R&B disc jockey known as The Magnificent Montague (aka 'Nathan' on the writing credits) had promoted a gig at the 5/4 Ballroom with Stax artists such as Wilson Pickett, Rufus Thomas, Carla Thomas, William Bell, The Astors, and, of course, the MGs to back them all. A day or two after the gig, Montague convinced the MGs to help him cut a demo based around a riff the three MG members had created. Steve Cropper (guitar), Al Jackson (drums), and Booker T Jones (piano) were joined by Packy Axton on sax, Leon Heywood on organ, Earl Grant on bass, and The Magnificent Montague himself on congas, who duly paid everyone demo fees. A while later, somewhat cheekily and much to the surprise of the MGs, the record emerged with dubbed-on party noises on Montague's own Pure Soul label and turned out to be a fair-sized hit.

Barbara Lewis, from Salem in Michigan, had a hit with 'Hello Stranger'. Although signed to the NY Atlantic label, she mostly recorded in Chicago. 'Baby I'm Yours' was one of her best, and was a smooth and seductive come-to-bed song that few could resist. Sadly, Barbara had left the music industry before the end of the decade.

> **BARBARA LEWIS: Baby I'm yours; I say Love (Atlantic AT 4031).** Marvellous. Strings and chorus herald Barbara's pungent voice, with a lot of charm in the performance. A mid-tempo ballad with fair melody, strong words. Not her best... but streets ahead of many others.

Genzene (What Have I Done)

THE SHANGAANS
COLUMBIA DB 7551

Not too many groups of the period used chopi piano, kalimba and tribal drums on a regular basis, but the South African Shangaans did. Very popular in their home territory they came to London to try their luck with a couple of singles and an

The Lurch
TED CASSIDY
CAPITOL CL 15423

Sticking with absurdity a while longer, we must add the phrase 'cash-in' to this one.

West Coast producer Gary Paxton saw the possibilities of a novelty hit in the form of a dance record at a time when the TV show The Addams Family was at its peak. The character of the gaunt-faced butler, Lurch, was played by actor Ted Cassidy, whose deep tones of "You rang…" and his immovable blank look was one of the key parts of the show.

In 'The Lurch', a female chorus begs our hero to teach them the new Lurch dance, and Ted provides all the expected deep interjections and groans as he shows them. The imagination boggles as to what the dance may have entailed – what a shame it was before the advent of an accompanying video, which would have revealed all. Perhaps Thing and Cousin It could have joined…no, enough!

'Genzene is more of an obvious stab at the pop market than their album that contains several strong instrumental pieces, and the record is a strikingly good one.'

album. Grahame Beggs, Alain Woolf, Mark Berry, Bill Muller and Glen Muller played a whole host of instruments between them, and all of them join in at times on a variety of African percussion.

'Genzene' is more of an obvious stab at the pop market than their album, which contains several strong instrumental pieces. The record is a strikingly good one. The production of both the backing and vocals is warm and well balanced, with just enough of an African influence to make it sound different. A little organ motif comes through now and again, and the strong chorus is made more noticeable by one of the group adding several perfectly in-time chuckles towards the end. Genzene, by the way, is a girl who they are trying to apologise to…

Incense
THE ANGLOS
BRIT WI 1004

Long thought to feature an uncredited Stevie Winwood lead vocal, this was the first of several UK releases of this exciting song. If you google the title and group name you'll find some conflicting accounts as to the history of the recording: some claim a New York-based group performed for producer Jimmy Miller, while others say it was a London session that Miller had with Winwood. Most recent consensus seems to detach any Winwood involvement, even though it does sound remarkably like him, but ultimately it doesn't matter because it is an absolutely cracking record that deserves to be heard regularly by all. This is the first and rarest issue of three in the Sixties.

Feel A Whole Lot Better
THE BYRDS CBS 201796

The Byrds cut over a dozen Dylan songs in their career, and to some extent will always be associated with him. Their follow-up to 'Mr Tambourine Man' was indeed another slab of Bob's work, 'All I Really Want To Do'.

However, tucked away on the B side was this wonderful Gene Clark song, that showed that the group had a very fine writer in their ranks. As witness to its lasting appeal, this song has appeared in modern acts' set lists.

Clark's future proved not to be with The Byrds and he was an early leaver, though he did re-join briefly some years later. Instead, he set off on a erratic but rewarding path of solo work and collaborations, almost any of which ought to be within people's collections. 'Feel A Whole Lot Better' was the perfect marriage of reasonably simple words on top of a great melody, where everything fitted together perfectly.

Liar, Liar
THE CASTAWAYS LONDON HL 10003

This is a prime example of what was fast becoming known as US garage band rock. If the arrival of The Beatles in the US had had its most profound effect on existing musicians, then the slightly later arrival of The Stones probably had its greatest effect on the young kids who were starting out. This caused a proliferation of the so-called garage bands, later celebrated with the well-known Pebbles series of albums.

The Castaways (no relation to Tony Rivers' Essex lot) appeared on the US Soma label out of Minneapolis with this song based on the 'Liar Liar, Pants on Fire' playground chant. It is built on a reedy organ riff and high vocals, which largely obscure the lyrics. Nevertheless, it is immediately memorable, making this a long-standing collectable record.

Sins Of The Family
PF SLOAN RCA 1482

Is This What I Was Made For
THE IGUANAS
RCA 1484

Child Of Our Times
BARRY MCGUIRE RCA 1493

One of the first established pop industry men to see the potential of folk rock was Lou Adler, who had started up in the Fifties with his partner Herb Alpert and had ended up managing Jan & Dean. He set up Dunhill Records in Los Angeles with new partners Jay Lasker and Bobby Roberts, and employed the young Phil Sloan and Steve Barri as in-house writers and producers. Success came quickly for the pair, who had previously worked under the name The Fantastic Baggys, when they produced one of the best vocal surf albums ever.

Sloan adapted easily to writing on political and social concerns, resulting in the massive

I Ain't Gonna Eat Out My Heart Anymore
THE YOUNG RASCALS
ATLANTIC AT 4059

The first issue by the Young Rascals was a snarly, garagey-sounding affair, though it was written by professionals and recorded by Atlantic. The writers were Lori Burton and Pam Sawyer, whose names grace many a fine song; Lori Burton's own *Breakout* album effectively acts as a sampler of their songwriting talents. This was quite a departure for Atlantic at the time. In hindsight, it can be seen as one of the label's first moves into the rock world, which later served them so well in the Sixties and early Seventies. It's not easy to discern the blue-eyed soul of some of the Rascals' later work here, but it is certainly a striking start on the 'choose now girl, or you're gonna lose me' theme that they rapidly capitalised on, with the altogether lighter follow-up 'Good Lovin''.

Folk Rock Arrives

The dual influences of Bob Dylan's songs and the effect of The Beatles came together on January 20 1965 when producer Terry Melcher took Jim (later Roger) McGuinn into Columbia's Hollywood studio to record a version of 'Mr Tambourine Man'. The Byrds themselves had already recorded their own version, but it was thought to be less than perfect with its almost militaristic drumming, so Melcher has assembled four experienced session players (Jerry Cole on rhythm guitar, Larry Knetchel on bass, Leon Russell on electric piano, and Hal Blaine on drums) to join Jim, who played the electric 12-string guitar that was to become his trademark.

Melcher's production poured a good dollop of California cream onto Dylan's song, and at a stroke invented the pop genre of Folk Rock, US styled. Seeing the huge sales, there was an immediate collective whoop of joy from all the pop producers

who had seen surf and girl groups get comparatively pushed aside by The Beatles. Here was something they could adapt to, so, by the summer, a large number of well-crafted records replicating the Byrds jangle followed, either through Dylan covers or productions and songs in a broadly similar vein. Much of this work erupted on the West Coast, solidifying what had already begun to happen through Phil Spector: the first shift of emphasis away from New York as the recognised centre of the US pop industry.

As with the surf and girl genres, the records that emerged were of a consistently high standard, many becoming big US hits, and some also hit in Britain… However, many fine records were missed over here in the UK. Some acts, like The Turtles, Jan & Dean and The Beau Brummels, made none too subtle shifts in their repertoire to join the others, while other new acts arrived with the sound in place, like the Leaves and their version of Dylan's Love Minus Zero. The movement meant that writers were looking to move away from traditional pop areas, towards material that might be considered more meaningful.

Although this first wave of folk rockers did not often produce earth-shatteringly wonderful songs, they did prove to be a major stepping stone towards later rock and pop making room for the more thoughtful singer/songwriters of the Seventies. But, as pop folk it was a most satisfying explosion…

worldwide hit 'Eve of Destruction' fronted by ex-Christy Minstrel Barry McGuire.

Sloan and Barri were prolific, and their excess songs were put out on an album under Sloan's own name, from which the 'Sins Of The Family' single was taken. It received radio play everywhere and even led to a trip to Britain for Phil to perform the song on Ready Steady Go. He played guitar on all the sessions, and drew from the regular crowd of session players so often led by Hal Blaine, which in turn led to a recognisable Dunhill house style that is evident on all three of these.

Sins tells of the dangers of parents transferring their own problems down a generation, which at the time was not an easy or usual subject for the pop market.

The Iguanas' 'This Is What I Was Made For' is lyrically much more familiar, dealing in standard relationship issues, but with the full Dunhill folk rock sound. There has always been some debate as to whether the group was an existing one, and consensus seems to be that they were, albeit one that spent most of their time in studios under various names. It's more than likely that both Sloan and Barri are in there in the mix.

'Child Of Our Times' was the little-known follow-up to 'Eve Of Destruction', and is a good double-sided record from Barry McGuire with a very strong song, 'Upon A Painted Ocean', on the flip. Keeping with the

concerned themes, this one looks at difficult youth as the product of societal ills, although it was maybe a step too far for most record buyers after the frightening and apocalyptic views expressed in his hit.

For You Babe
THE SPOKESMEN
BRUNSWICK 05941

With answer discs still a popular route for producers to follow, 'Eve Of Destruction' was too great a target to ignore, and the challenge was taken up by the experienced team of John Madara, David White and Ray Gilmore, whose names will be well known to the small print readers in our midst.

They simply turned the negativity of the hit song into, arguably unwarranted, positivity with 'The Dawn Of Correction'. They managed to replicate the Dunhill sound in New York with equivalent

session men (Messrs Wisner, Chester, Saltzman, Butler, Bell, Martin, Gorgoni, Kaplan etc), and even managed a whole album on the strength of sales. On the flip of 'Dawn' was the song 'For You Babe', which is quite funny as it contains the couplet:

'If you were hungry, I would feed you,
If you needed to be needed, I would need you'

Wonderful stuff, and nearly as good as the unbelievable over-blown album notes that proclaimed that the group 'represent the voice of

a generation that has endured many and frequent changes, a generation that hovers on the dawn of a new and better tomorrow.' Hmm...

It's All Over Now Baby Blue
LEROY VAN DYKE
WARNER BROS WB 5650

Daddy You Been On My Mind
JOAN BAEZ **FONTANA TF 604**

Can You Please Crawl Out Your Window?
THE VACELS
PYE INTERNATIONAL 7N 25330

It Ain't Me Babe
JOE & EDDIE **VOCALION VN 9250**

Following hits from The Byrds and The Turtles, acts everywhere quickly looked for Dylan songs to cover. Leroy Van Dyke, who was well established with previous country styled hits 'The Auctioneer' and 'Walk On By', grabbed the 'Baby Blue' song, which The Byrds had recorded

We Didn't Ask To Be Brought Here
BOBBY DARIN
ATLANTIC AT 4046

Another existing star to try folk rock was Bobby Darin. He had always had an eye for pop trends, and had co-written the Rip Chords' 'Hot Rod USA' (included earlier). Here, he has written about a younger generation's viewpoint in terms of the state of the world. The production captures the folk rock sound and feel perfectly, but, unfortunately left record shops around the land observing: 'They didn't ask for it to be bought here.'

You Were On My Mind
WE FIVE
PYE INTERNATIONAL 7N 25314

Let's Get Together
WE FIVE
PYE INTERNATIONAL 7N 25346

One act that was intelligent enough to begin to look elsewhere for decent material was We Five – four chaps and one lady who had gathered in San Francisco and caught the ear of Trident productions there.

Three Californians, Mike Stewart, Pete Fullerton and Beverly Bivens, linked with Hawaiian Bob Jones and Jerry Burgan from Kansas to form what was mostly an acoustic band in which all the members sang and played instruments. For their first US hit they found a great song by Sylvia Fricker, of the Ian & Sylvia Canadian duo. However, their chance of a British hit was washed away by the cover by Crispian St Peters, which went all the way to No2 in the UK. Undaunted, they carried on, and found 'Let's Get Together' from local SF writer Chet Powers (aka Dino Valente), a song that became a real pop standard. It was representative of the hippie love ideal, and has been covered by many artists including Fairport Convention, The Youngbloods, and Brian Wilson's bandleader Jeff Foskett. However, We Five's version may well have been the first cover of the memorable song – unless, of course, you know better…

but not released.

The song was also covered by Joan Baez, but Leroy's version was faster and poppier and it received a good deal of play on UK radio programmes, boosted at this time by the off-shore pirate stations.

Baez, of course, had much more right than most to sing Dylan's songs, because the pair had spent so much time together, often sharing stages or political platforms.

On the flip of Joan's 'Baby Blue' cover was her version of 'Daddy You Been On My Mind', which is one of Dylan's earlier gently rolling country songs. Joan sings it sweetly, allowing the quality of the song to carry the recording, leading many to wonder why there weren't more covers of it.

The Vacels was a one-off release for Britain from the Kama Sutra label, and featured a muzzy but effective reading of one of Bob's weirder titles. The Vacels had previously had a US-only issue with 'You're My Baby (And Don't You Forget It)', so we can safely assume that Dylanesque folk rock was new territory for them.

Joe & Eddie had been around since the Fifties as a gospel-rooted duo based in Los Angeles. This cover, on the flip of 'Walking Down The Line', was a sideways – but effective – step for them.

Pied Piper
THE CHANGIN' TIMES
PHILIPS BF 1442

Crispian St Peters' manager must have been good at ferreting out decent US songs to cover, because he followed up the big hit 'You Were On My Mind' with a cover of this great little-known folk rock gem.

Some may have presumed they were a studio group, but this was actually the first of six US singles on Philips and Bell, but their only issue here.

The song has a great pop sound and is more obviously Byrds-inspired than Crispian's admittedly good cover, so should be of great interest to 'group' collectors of this era.

A Beginning From An End
JAN AND DEAN LIBERTY LIB 10225

Also filed away under the 'What did they think they were doing?' box, this amazing B side from Jan and Dean can be found on the pair's good, folky cover of 'Norwegian Wood'. With a sound and construction most akin to Dead Man's Curve, it is the story of the singer's girlfriend/wife who dies giving birth to their child – but it's all alright because the child looks and acts just like her!

Complete with middle 'talk' section and a big brass-filled production, this is Jan Berry excess all the way, and is now one of their rarer tracks…

Come Away Melinda
WENDY HUBER
PHILIPS BF 1446

The first half of the Sixties had been dominated by the Cold War, and, if 'Eve Of Destruction' frightened a few record buyers, this one terrified us.

It presents a sectionalised question-and-answer session between mother and daughter in an unspecified post-apocalyptic scenario, where the little girl is trying to make sense of the changes around her. Alternating between the voice of a six-year-old and the careworn and shattered tones of the adult survivor, Wendy Huber explains how it was 'before they had the war'.

Occasional finger cymbal notes punctuate the little girl voice, while strident backing adds weight to the adult voice. Really odd and unforgettable.

Can't You Hear My Heartbeat
GOLDIE AND THE GINGERBREADS
DECCA F 12070

Goldie and the Gingerbreads comprised four American ex-pat girls who sang and played their instruments, which was still quite unusual in 1965. The Animals' Alan Price had spotted them in New York, and had brought them to London to record. Vocalist Goldie Zelkowitz (later known as Genya Ravan), guitarist Carol MacDonald, drummer Ginger Panebianco and organist Margo Croccitto made up the group.

For their first single, Price chose a cute and catchy song (written by John Carter and Ken Lewis of The Ivy League) with a repeated 'Baby baby' cleverly integrated. The record hovered for some weeks, getting plenty of radio plays, but stubbornly refused to climb higher than No36 on Britain's official chart, although it made No28 on the NME chart.

But You're Mine
SONNY AND CHER
ATLANTIC AT 4047

Don't Talk To Strangers
THE BEAU BRUMMELS
PYE INTERNATIONAL 7N 25333

I Still Love You
THE VEJTABLES
PYE INTERNATIONAL 7N 25339

Try asking the pub quiz question: what was Sonny and Cher's follow-up to 'I Got You Babe'? and, it being a smallish hit, you will probably get blank looks all round.

'But You're Mine' is a more rounded sound from the pair with less stops and starts than the hit. There is a more obvious use of Sonny's Phil Spector time, as he tries to plug all the sound gaps with a rolling backwash of bells and assorted percussive noise. All in all, it stands up very well.

The Beau Brummels continued from 'Laugh Laugh' via another goodie 'Just A Little' to 'Don't Talk To Strangers', which is co-written by group member Ron Elliott. This track is one of their best, and it gives Sal Valentino's rich lead voice a wonderful opportunity to carry the song in the sections where the group harmonies drop out. Sal's leads caused friction within the group as he recalls: 'Sometimes Declan and Petersen would have problems…I guess he wanted us to sound more like The Beatles, more of a Declan sound than a Sal sound…The Beau Brummels were always way too serious. We should have lightened up a little bit.'

There was brief personnel crossover between the Beau Brummels and another San Francisco group, The Vejtables, when the latter's lead guitarist Reese Sheets was borrowed for a tour. The Vejtables had been signed up enthusiastically by the same local label Autumn, probably partly in response to their girl drummer Jan Errico. 'I Still Love You' showed that the group could compete on the jingle jangle guitars and heavy bass front as they delivered a Beatlesque song written by young Ms Errico.

They didn't last much more than a year, which is a shame as they had obviously taken so much trouble with their hair and stage wear of matching leather jerkins and spotty shirts, though Jan was allowed to wear her purple trouser suit.

The Water Is Over My Head
THE ROCKIN' BERRIES
PYE 7N 35270

'The Water Is Over My Head' (on *Volume One, Look At The Sunshine*, of the *Ripples* CD series), is one of the Rockin' Berries most convincing covers.

The Tokens had recorded this strong Al Kooper/ Irwin Levine song in the US, as had a number of others, but the Berries can certainly claim to have produced one of the best, if not the best, version. Lead singer Geoff Turton (aka Jefferson) had perfected a mid-Atlantic singing voice, while the group's production values with Pye became even higher.

Dark Shadows and Empty Hallways
TAMMY ST JOHN
PYE 7N 15948

This wonderfully dramatic cityscape story from Tammy St John is the third delve into the *Ripples* series, this time from *Volume Four, Uptown Girls and Big City Boys*. It came from an obscure Wand label original by Diane and Annita, but Tammy's version is the one that makes the cinematic song really memorable.

It is a huge and cavernous New York-styled production with quieter gaps and added Spector flourishes, over which Tammy exhibits a wide vocal range. An East Londoner from Hornchurch, she cut this tour de force when she was, amazingly, only 14 or 15. She went on to tackle another strong cover: The Chiffons' 'Nobody Knows What's Going On In My Mind But Me'.

Around The Corner

THE DUPREES
CBS 201803

The Duprees don't usually figure high on vocal group collectors' lists because much of their material verged close to the middle of the road when they were with the US Coed label. However, this was the first track they cut for Columbia and is a big New York sound based on the Drifters and Jay and The Americans records.

With production from Artie Ripp on a Teddy Randazzo co-written song, the group sing the material as if they were born to it, their strident vocals letting rip. A good song, good arrangement and good production all added up to a US No91 hit, but zilch over here.

Their personnel changes are too tricky to document here, but for this number they changed their lead voice from Joey Vann to Mike Kelly. They recorded four more in a similar vein for Columbia, before returning to the blander material (aside from a well-loved dance track in 1970 called 'Check Yourself' that, for reasons best known to themselves, they decided to issue under the name of The Italian Asphalt And Pavement Company). What was Mamma putting in the pasta sauce?

New York's A Lonely Town

THE TRADE WINDS
RED BIRD RB10 020

THE TRADE WINDS: New York's a Lonely Town (Red Bird). If youe a surfer this is a scrummy disc. His folks moved to New York from California and his buddies warned him, but now there is a surfboard and nowhere to go — snow everywhere, and not a wave insight.

Absolutely ducky words and the tune is luscious.

AVAILABLE TOMORROW

The Trade Winds were initially a studio creation by Pete Andreoli and Vinnie Poncia, who we first met as members of The Videls back in 1960. This song was reviewed by Disc & Music Echo's Penny Valentine, who loved it, referring to the 'absolutely ducky words' and sad scenario of a West Coast surfer moving to snow-covered New York. It was a perfect record, with a really powerful melody and words, plus excellent vocal harmonies. In the States, the record was successful enough for them to assemble a road band for appearances.

The following two splendid Red Bird singles, 'The Girl From Greenwich Village' and 'Summertime Girl', didn't do nearly so well, and consequently didn't rate UK releases.

Shut 'Em Down In London Town

THE MAJORITY
DECCA F 12271

The Majority appear to have originated in Hull, and to have housed the talents of Roger France, Bob Lang, Ken Smith, Don Hill and Harry (or possibly Barry) Graham. They had a run of eight Decca singles, of which this is the B side of the second, so someone must have believed in them.

Round about this time, many British groups tried American surf and drag sounds with varying results, and very often the record companies would relegate their attempts to the B side.

The collectable top side, called 'A Little Bit Of Sunlight', came courtesy of Ray Davies of The Kinks, while their description of road racing around the capital, although an unlikely scenario, was probably one of the best UK attempts at the West Coast sound.

Little Surfer Girl
KENNY & DENY
DECCA F 12138

This extremely collectable one-off from Kenny and Deny is another West Coast-orientated B side and is a hard one to find.

Kenny was Kenny Rowe, who was soon after to join up with Tony Rivers and The Castaways, staying with them when they changed to Harmony Grass, and eventually ending up with Capability Brown in the early Seventies.

Deny was the ubiquitous Jimmy Page, who wrote and directed the surf song, which is probably closest in melody and feel to The Beach Boys' 'Farmer's Daughter'.

....

THE NITESHADES: Be My Guest; I Must Reveal (CBS 201763). From the film of the same name. New group from Stevenage (six-strong). They go for a Beach Boy surfin' sound and it's not bad, though not orignial. Fast-tempoed item, with falsetto background vocal touches. Could take, we suppose.

Be My Guest
THE NITESHADES
CBS 201763

The Niteshades were a six-piece from Stevenage who managed two singles for CBS before disappearing. 'Be My Guest' is a lively, vaguely surfy-sounding, Shel Talmy co-written song that was featured in a film of the same name. The group's vocal harmonies lift it well above the pack.

William 'Smokey' Robinson

During the taping of The Sound Of Motown TV special in 1965, the whole Motown tour put on their show. At that point Smokey's group The Miracles were considered the kingpins, and

they would close the show by leading the other acts in a massed version of their 'Mickey's Monkey' hit. At the rehearsals, it was clear just how important Smokey was to the whole operation on the floor of the studio. Berry Gordy was there in a smart black coat, pressing flesh and talking to music industry people, but Smokey was active. He cut a fine figure with his very attractive wife Claudette, who was no longer performing live shows then with The Miracles, but was along for the trip. Smokey was at the height of his writing at that point, having had hits with Mary Wells, who had skipped the Motown nest, and The Temptations, who were yet to reach their full recording heights. Berry Gordy had recognised his talents early on, but, in his turn, Smokey recognised the need for Berry to take control of as much of the company organisation as possible, with his famous statement "Why work for the man? Why not you be the man?" Berry made Smokey a vice-president of Motown, and ever

since Robinson has acknowledged their close relationship. He is best known for his Miracles' hits 'Tracks Of My Tears' and 'The Tears Of A Clown', and probably earns as many royalties from The Temptations' 'My Girl' and Mary Wells' 'My Guy'. His work is appreciated by everyone in the business from Bob Dylan to Brian Wilson.

Theme From "A Summer Place"
THE LETTERMEN
CAPITOL CL 15405

There was smooth, there was smoother, and then there was The Lettermen, standing proud as the ultimate all-American neat college boys, who were forever associated with the lettered sweaters they wore to underline their name. While never anywhere near hip, they somehow managed to stay (well, mostly) the right side of schmaltz.

'Theme From "A Summer Place"' had the advantage of being an already well-known decent melody from various instrumental versions. The Lettermen's harmonies sit well on it, and are enhanced with a well-placed glockenspiel amid the expected sweeping strings.

It was the sort of record that was used in films in the 'end of the midnight party on the beach scene,' when the young teens finally realise they are made for each other.

THE LETTERMEN: Theme from a Summer Place; Sealed With A Kiss (Capitol CL 15405). Highly stylised vocl harmonise with the high-pitched sequences dominating. Nicely drawn-out, and the song is good ... though perhaps too familiar, now.

Beach Boy
RONNY & THE DAYTONAS
STATESIDE SS 432

Tiger-A-Go-Go
BUZZ & BUCKY
STATESIDE SS 428

The beach and its associated shenanigans provided the focus for the teen exploitation movies that were filmed in the early Sixties following the success of the Gidgit series of flicks. This activity provided platforms for the West Coast writers and producers, from Brian Wilson down, to put out great vocal harmony records based on the surf sound.

These two, however, come from Nashville, hardly the surf capital of America, but are certainly up there with California in sound and lyrical content.

Ronny & The Daytonas centred around John 'Buck' Wilkin, who was the youthful voice of Ronny, supported by a decent cluster of local musicians, including Buzz Cason, and Bergen White.

'Beach Boy' was the fourth UK issue by the 'group' after the oft-heard first one 'GTO', and is a clever record with nifty switches in and out of falsetto lines on a song that glorifies beach life. It benefited from a strong B side in 'No Wheels', which finds our hero without a car for the summer.

Buzz and Bucky, using Wilkin's and Cason' nicknames, was made up of the same session crew on another West Coast ode to the post-beach night-time club scene centred then on the Whisky-A-Go-Go on 8901 Sunset Strip in West Hollywood.

The lyrics tell of the beach boys meeting some 'California Hippies' who take them along to the hippest scene in town. The Whisky, first known as a club called The Party, was originally opened as a records-only club in 1964. With the name change came the first live gigs from stars like Johnny Rivers, before the really famous years when the stage was taken by The Doors, The Who, Cream, The Kinks et al. The 'Go-Go' part of the name referred to the dancing girls primarily, and was soon franchised all over America. Along with the Miracles "Going To A-Go-Go', this great little Buzz and Bucky record was one of the first to pick up on that scene.

BUZZ AND BUCKY: Tiger-A-Go-Go; Bay City (Stateside SS 428). Story of a trip to San Francisco with almost a Beach Boy approach most of the way. It's got a good beat, nice backing, furious guitar and a sort of ultra-determined way with it. Not bad.

She's Just My Style
GARY LEWIS & THE PLAYBOYS
LIBERTY LIB 55846

Gary Lewis was the son of Jerry Lewis, a man whose 'comedian' description usually seemed to confuse people – perhaps he didn't translate too well. People were similarly bemused by what American buyers saw in Gary Lewis' earlier hits like 'This Diamond Ring' and 'Count Me In', although when 'She's Just My Style' came out, it was immediately ear-grabbing.

It is simply one of the best pop records of the year, cut presumably with many of the usual top crew of West Coast session players. The song is strong with an instantly memorable chorus, great ringing guitars and fine vocals throughout, which also sound as if they have come from session guys on the backgrounds. It was a cracking record in every way and did well in the States, but absolutely nothing in the UK.

GARY LEWIS and THE PLAYBOYS make a great sound with surfin'-type music on their latest "She's Just My Style." Contrasting vocals makes the disc original and very commercial.
****(Liberty)

The Little Girl I Once Knew
THE BEACH BOYS
CAPITOL CL 15425

There is a striking ringing guitar tone on this lesser-known gem from The Beach Boys. This was one of Brian Wilson's more experimental Beach Boys' issues as it contained several dead air breaks that radio DJs hated because it confused their audiences.

The song itself is good, with complicated group harmonies, yet it was never destined to be a hit for the group.

The song was re-visited in the early Eighties by the studio-based British accapella group Harmony Beach (Alan Carvell, Chris White, Rick De Jongh, Chris Thornton, Graham Dene and Bruce Venton) who between them produced two alternative versions: one broadly using the Beach Boys' arrangement, and another with extra vocals to cover the original gaps.

The Monkey's Uncle
ANNETTE
HMV POP 1447

The Beach Boys could also be found, uncredited, on this Annette single taken from the film of the same name; one of the many 'zany' Beach Movies of the time.

This particular flick revolved around some chap running about in a gorilla suit in chases featuring Harvey Lembeck's Eric Von Zipper character. Great fun all the way, it is structured much like an early Beach Boys song, even though Wilson didn't write it. The group's instrumental and vocal performance deserved co-crediting, though company contracts probably forbade it at the time. It is certainly the only time when full Beach Boys harmonies wrapped themselves around the word 'chimpanzee'. For years, Beach Boys fans would search this single out, until someone realised that it could be had on a six-track Disney EP, usually available in Woolworths for 29p!

(Here They Come) From All Over The World
JAN AND DEAN
LIBERTY 55766

You Really Know How To Hurt A Guy
JAN & DEAN
LIBERTY 55792

Liberty Records were very happy sticking with Jan and Dean, even if they couldn't decide consistently how to write the name on the labels (the artist names on all the entries in this book follow how they appear on the labels).

The duo were still selling solidly in the US, and had always got fair sales in the UK up to this point. From 'All Over The World' was conceived by Phil Sloan and Steve Barri (aka, at this point, The Fantastic Baggys) as the theme song for the TAMI televised show. It is a 'list' song that attempts to include the names of many of the key acts appearing on the show.

A big error came when The Rolling Stones from Liverpool were included (but this can be forgiven as British knowledge of American geography and artists' home towns at this stage was also hardly magnificent). The song is a goodly romp with the well-established Jan Berry production sound, but only reached No56 on Billboard.

Somewhat different, though, was Jan's next, which took Phil Spector's first Righteous Brothers productions as its reference point. 'You Really Know How to Hurt A Guy' was a heavy left turn for Jan, which reputedly had Dean Torrence walking out of the studio and pitching up with the Beach Boys down the hall and singing the lead on 'Barbara Ann' for them. Whether or not it was this actual occasion may be in doubt, but it's a good story with more than a grain of truth.

While 'Barbara Ann' was certainly a fun recording, 'You Really Know How To Hurt A Guy' was a fine piece of work too. Jan had an acknowledged and genuine talent for orchestration, which he used extensively here on a song he wrote with Roger Christian (co-writer with Brian Wilson on several occasions) and his girlfriend Jill Gibson, who was later to briefly join the Mamas and Papas as a replacement for Michelle Philips.

The song was slower and less obviously youth orientated than the usual Jan and Dean fare, so was consequently ignored by some of their fans. However, it still managed to reach No27 on Billboard, indicating that it was potentially a good direction for them to follow.

It remains one of Jan's finest and, had he not suffered his terrible crash not long after, indicates how he could have been a major player in the *Pet Sounds*-influenced world of 1966.

Give Us Your Blessings
THE SHANGRI-LAS
RED BIRD RB10 030

Right Now And Not Later
THE SHANGRI-LAS
RED BIRD RB10 036

Sailor Boy
THE CHIFFONS
STATESIDE SS 332

My Place
THE CRYSTALS
UNITED ARTISTS UP 1110

Here is ample proof of the continuing class of girl-group records. The Shangri-Las, forever known for seagulls and motorbikes, embarked on one of their last slabs of teen angst with 'Give Us Your Blessings'.

It's heartbreak all the way as Mary and Jimmy are forced to run away because her mom and pop refuse to sanction their union...then, thunder, rain, tears...a missed Detour sign...and tragedy, told with a mixture of talkie sections and strong choruses, with that inevitable piano still banging away in the background. The

disc climbed to No29 on Billboard.

'Right Now And Not Later' is a total contrast as the girls take on full Motown-influenced pop on a song built on a bed of bass and vibes before the full force of cod Motown back-ups hits. It's all done with the Noo Yawk voice atop everything, and is a splendid record that should have been a big hit, but even in the States it only hung around for a couple of weeks at No99.

The Chiffons' Judy Craig never sounded sexier than on 'Sailor Boy'. It's a song that re-treads the 'Now we're parted' storyline that was set up earlier by The Shirelles on 'Soldier Boy', but this one has the benefit of being a Gerry Goffin/Russ Titelman song. Titelman's name (spelt in a bewildering different number of ways) is one that crops up as co-writer on some of the very best-loved Sixties records: The Cookies' 'I Never Dreamed', The Inspirations' (or Lesley Gore or The Chiffons) 'What Am I Gonna Do (Hey Baby)', Glen Campbell's 'Guess I'm Dumb', and The Honeybees' 'She Don't Deserve You'. His melodies have an elegance to them that allows his songs to be re-interpreted in many ways and still sound wonderful.

The Crystals had left Phil Spector by this time and had joined United Artists. With a full Charlie Calello arrangement of brass, string guitar and big, big drums, the description could make it sound Spectoresque, but this is, in fact, very decent uptown pop soul that draws from all the traditional elements of New York Sixties' record production.

For once, the backing voices are heard clearly, with the group doing fine doo-dooing lines behind the strong lead.

I Don't Want To Be Your Baby Anymore
THE POPSICLES VOGUE V9243

The Sh-Down Down Song
THE GINGER-SNAPS
RCA 1483

Cold, Cold Winter
JEAN AND THE STATESIDES
COLUMBIA DB 7439

With girl groups still providing an outlet for quality songs, here are three more rarities. The Popsicles was almost certainly a one-off double-tracked Ellie Greenwich release, with two great sides (the B side was 'Baby I Miss You') that may have originally been put down as demos.

The Ginger-Snaps featured another great commercial Sloan/Barri song, one of the few they cut with female singers. Taking its name from the vocal background lines, it was a minor US hit, but disappeared over here.

Jean and The Statesides (a group of girls from Chester, featuring the voice of Jean Hughes, who seemed to specialise on decent covers of well-chosen US material for their three collectable Columbia issues) chose to cover a Pixies Three US original, producing a really strong version that to many ears improves on the original.

Candy
THE ASTORS
ATLANTIC AT 4037

As Motown was starting to take off in Britain, we were becoming aware of a US company who were developing a recognisable 'house' style. The Stax label, based in Memphis, was at this stage distributed and marketed under the Atlantic banner, and it had an altogether earthier sound compared to Motown.

The Astors' 'Candy' was striking, yet the record sounded slightly imperfect, as if all the elements weren't quite so tightly locked together (which Motown managed every time). It was the slight feeling of imperfection that was attractive – the looser-sounding brass, the rougher and less-tutored vocals, and the general flow of the simple song. It had what is now often called 'floater' vocals – ie vocals usually approaching high tenor/falsetto range that somehow sat on top of the mix rather than amid it. It was one of those songs that was played back-to-back for hours.

The group, named after The Astor Hotel in Times Square, originally comprised lead Curtis Johnson, tenors Richard Harris, Richard Griffin and Elihue Stanback, and baritone Sam Jones.

'Candy' was almost surreptitiously recorded by ex-Mar-Key Packy Axton when Stax owner Jim Stewart was out of town, and it took the group to No63 on the Billboard pop chart and as high as No12 on the R&B chart.

It's Growing
THE TEMPTATIONS
TAMLA MOTOWN TMG 504

I'll Always Love You
THE DETROIT SPINNERS
TAMLA MOTOWN TMG 523

My Girl Has Gone
THE MIRACLES
TAMLA MOTOWN TMG 540

Tamla Motown developed so well that EMI granted Berry Gordy's wish for them to be issued under a catch-all imprint in Britain. The earliest batch of issues reflected the variety of acts on the label, and the more obscure issues are now incredibly collectable in both promo or stock copy form.

'It's Growing' was the eloquent follow-up to 'My Girl', and was another fine example of Smokey Robinson's poetic writing and strong Temptations harmonies behind a distinctive lead. This was the classic Tempts line-up of David Ruffin, Otis Williams, Paul Williams, Melvyn Franklin and Eddie Kendricks, and it was included on The Sound Of Motown TV special that was filmed during the Motown British tour of 1965. (Also included in the Sounds Of Motown show were The Miracles, who sung 'You Really Got A Hold On Me', the 'everyone up and dance' show-closer 'Mickey's Monkey', and the powerful 'Ooo Baby Baby', which was their latest at that point.)

All the Tempts were slim, tall and good looking, and when they began to move in their choreographed dance steps they looked absolutely awesome. They were the best movers there, with the possible exception of The Miracles' Bobby Rogers, who was surprisingly nimble for a big fellow.

'I'll Always Love You' seems to represent all that was good about Motown production values. It is a strong Stevenson/Hunter song, has a good group vocal performance, and all the 'Snakepit' (Motown's Studio A in Detroit) elements fully in place. The mid-tempo melody and chorus was rated highly by Motown aficionados. The Detroit Spinners, known without the 'Detroit' in the States, were so-called to avoid confusion with The Liverpool-based folk group Spinners. As if anyone ever would have...

The slightly lesser-known 'My Girl Has Gone' is further proof of the newer classy ballad sound that Smokey was developing with the group. It's almost a whole group composition rather than purely a Smokey song, the background vocals being strongly featured. Like so many Miracles' records, it was built around a Marv Tarplin introductory guitar figure.

Neighbour Neighbour
THE ADLIBS
FONTANA TF 584

Before confusion creeps in, this group is not the same as the Ad-Libs of Boy From New York City fame. Despite the line on the record attributing it as a Vee Jay Recording (which could fix it to Chicago or somewhere US East Coast) this was a British band who performed the song on a TV show at the time. Aimed at the Mod club-goers, it featured congas, organ and punctuating brass behind a rough lead voice that was not too dissimilar to Georgie Fame. They were a largish group of perhaps seven or so members, and the quite collectable record stands up extremely well today as a danceable sound.

Johnny My Boy
THE ADLIBS
CONTEMPO- RARIES CS 9029

This one is a bit of a cheat. This offering from the US group wasn't released in the UK until it came out as a B side to 'Boy From New York City' in 1975. It was, however, a bone-fide 1965 release in the States on the Red Bird subsidiary label Blue Cat (BC 123), and was simply one song/performance that was so good that to miss it out would have been unforgivable.

Similar to The Astors''Candy', it has a lovely loose and almost unfinished feel to it. This time around it has a male lead, presumably Hugh Harris, who has one of those 'cracked' voices like the wonderful General Johnson.

The whole thing tumbles along in a rolling mid-tempo fashion – the group commenting on the lead's seeming misery and trying to help him out of his slough of despond and see things in a better light.

I'm So Thankful
THE IKETTES **POLYDOR BM 56506**

When not on duty with Ike Turner, The Ikettes were sometimes marketed as a group in their own right, though the various line-ups are notoriously difficult to document. The version of the group that cut this Motown-rooted sexy mid-tempo song was a three-piece that recorded six singles and one album for the US Modern label with the stable line-up of Venetta Fields, Robbie Montgomery and Jessie Smith. Marc Gordon and Frank Wilson, both Motown West Coast staffers, wrote this song.

The group slide seductively through the number – Ike Turner distinctly chose the group members for their beauty and sexiness, and to experience them on tour with the complete Ike and Tina Revue was virtually a male rite of passage at the time.

A Little Bit Of Soap
THE EXCITERS
LONDON HLZ 10018

After their initial hit period on United Artists, and a few good singles on Roulette, The Exciters moved to the new Bang label and this was their first release.

It is an easy and attractive re-make of the old Jarmels No12 US hit of 1961 that took them to No58 on Billboard, and marked their last US hit of any size. The record's intro is reminiscent of the Ben E King/Spanish Harlem NY feel of a few years earlier, but then Brenda Reid's strident tones take over to let us realise why a decent remake was valid.

Take Me For A Little While
EVIE SANDS
RED BIRD BC 118

This record from Red Bird's Blue Cat subsidiary was the first UK release from the very collectable and talented Evie Sands. The song was written by Trade Martin and was chosen to launch Evie in the States as part of a new deal with Blue Cat. However, someone got hold of a copy of her version and whisked it over to Chess Records, who copied it with their artist Jackie Ross. Heavy phone calls were made and that version was eventually taken off the market, but the cream of the early sales had been skimmed off and Evie's version suffered, even though it performed well in some East Coast markets.

As with so many of Evie's other issues, she had chosen to go with an outstanding song, but it was destined to be one that few British ears would hear until it became a regular inclusion on various Red Bird compilations from the Seventies onwards.

"I liked the song first time I heard it played (on the piano) and loved the record we made – and still do. It's one of my faves, but we were upstaged. I picked up a copy of Billboard and there on the page after the cover was a full-page ad for Jackie Ross. It said 'Destined to Be No1!' At first I thought it must be another song with the same title, but then we heard it and they had copied our version completely." **EVIE SANDS**

"I was happy to see 'Skin Deep' come out, but I think it only sold about eight copies, and I had five of those. So now I know where at least one of those other three went!" **BOBBY GRAHAM**

Skin Deep
BOBBIE GRAHAM
FONTANA TF 521

The ex-Outlaws skin basher had been kept busy playing sessions since leaving the group, and this was one of two solo outings that apparently also feature Jimmy Page, although there is no distinct aural evidence on the A side here.

A huge brass fanfare leads into a driving instrumental with regular drum breaks of a few bars. Half way through, Graham takes over with a variety of drum patterns before a final building brass crescendo to round things off.

'Skin Deep' was a tune of the great Louis Bellson's that Bobby had learnt some years before. He had included it in stage work along with a duet devised with Johnnie Sawyer from the Teddy Foster Orchestra. Drum records had been very saleable earlier in the Sixties with the likes of Sandy Nelson and The Surfaris, so this was a bit of an anachronism in 1965, but it still sounds an incredibly powerful arrangement that it is not dated. The unusual flip title that he co-wrote with Jimmy Page – 'Zoom Widge and Wag' – refers to nicknames for his wife, daughter and dog. Not many people know that…

Harlem Shuffle
BOB AND EARL
SUE WI 374

This ultimate club disc from Bob Relf and Earl Nelson starts with a fanfare. The 'Bob' in this pair was subject to variation. The first one was Bobby Day of Rockin' Robin fame, and then came Bob Relf who cut this famous disc, before he was supplanted by Bobby Garrett.

The 'Earl' seems to have stayed fixed, though he also worked as Jackie Lee, and had several much-loved dance records, such as 'The Duck', on the collectable US Mirwood label.

If any one record sums up the mid-Sixties' club scene, it's this classic.

Get Out Of My Life, Woman
LEE DORSEY
STATESIDE SS485

Lee Dorsey had a string of UK releases that were always club favourites, and this one has since been sited as a stepping stone to rap, with its stripped-down drum and bass-heavy backing track.

The song was one of several, including 'Holy Cow' and 'Working In A Coal Mine', that the great New Orleans piano player Allen Toussaint wrote for Dorsey. It helped to revive his career after an early Sixties dip.

Dorsey, a former boxer who had worked as 'Kid Chocolate', always maintained other interests in car businesses up to his all-too-early death in 1986.

Ten Commandments Of Man
PRINCE BUSTER **BLUE BEAT BB 334**

Heart Of Stone
DERRICK & NAOMI & BABA BROOKS GROUP **SKA BEAT**
JB 185

As the music of Britain's West Indian communities became better known, the term Blue Beat gave way to the newer Ska alternative, and heroes like Prince Buster led the way to cross-over sales. Here, Buster lets his woman know the rules in a way far from any of today's political correctness – he can do what he likes, and she must accept it, and if she moans she'll incur his wrath.

More of an equal partnership is evident with Derrick and Naomi, who seem content with each other taking alternate verses and Baba Brooks' Group jogging along behind them. Records like these paved the way…

Jenny Take A Ride
MITCH RYDER & THE DETROIT WHEELS **STATESIDE SS 481**

This full pounder from Mitch Ryder was a million miles from Lee Dorsey's sparse soul. Co-written and produced by Four Seasons' man Bob Crewe, it is a powerhouse recording driven by organ, guitars and handclaps. The song is an amalgam of Little Richard's 'Jenny Jenny' and the old standard 'CC Rider', which explains Richard's name on the writing credits (Penniman mis-spelt as Tenninan). Productionwise, the record was a tour-de-force, and is often seen as the template for Bruce Springsteen's band.

Down In The Boondocks
BILLY JOE ROYAL
CBS 201802

Produced and written by Joe South, this record introduced Britain to a new word. The Boondocks refers to the poor side of town, or the other side of the tracks, from where poor Billy Joe hails, and from where he gazes up to the big house on the hill.

The heartbreak tale is told to a classic 1, 1-2 pop rhythm that extends into a nifty percussive break before the key change. Great stuff.

This is Billy Joe's best-known performance of a string of UK issues, that even included an album in 1966 called *Introducing Billy Joe Royal* – which was a tad late, perhaps, as his first single came out in 1962.

My Name Is Mud
EDDIE RAMBEAU
STATESIDE SS 448

Eddie Rambeau's third of six UK single releases on Stateside is an example of Bob Crewe's more restrained production work. Pennsylvanian-born Eddie had enjoyed a big US hit with a very decent cover of Unit 4 Plus 2's 'Concrete And Clay', and on the subsequent US album Eddie included this one.

He was a good writer, with credits to his name that included Diane Renay's 'Navy Blue' and Shirley Matthews' 'Big Town Boy', plus titles for The Four Seasons, The Orlons and Dee Dee Sharp.

"MY NAME IS MUD", huh? Well, all I can say is that when Bob Crewe came to both Bud Rehak and myself with that title we almost fell on the floor from laughter. We both knew he wanted a good follow up to 'Concrete And Clay' so I guess 'MUD' was the next best choice. I would have preferred BRICKS, I suppose. So all three of us sat down to write it and, to be honest with you, I was never pleased with it being my 'Concrete and Clay' follow-up...however, there was no arguing with Bob Crewe."

EDDIE RAMBEAU

Wish I Didn't Love Him
MIA LEWIS DECCA F 12117

Mia Lewis had five releases on Decca and Parlophone between 1965 and 1967, none of which made any impression on sales figures, although this first one certainly deserved to.

Produced by the ubiquitous Larry Page, it features a restrained arrangement from Alan Moorhouse befitting of the sad mood of the title. As well as Mai's fine vocal, the quality and melody of the song makes this one stand out. Unlike many of her contemporaries it seems that Mia did not follow the cover version route, preferring to try original songs by British writers.

She Just Satisfies
JIMMY PAGE
FONTANA TF 533

Quite what prompted this one-off solo single is probably lost in the mists of time. It's a strong record built on an attacking and repeated guitar riff over which Jimmy adds a raw vocal; with the addition of a harmonica break it is in the Stones/Pretty Things/Kinks territory.

It sounds quite a rushed job, which probably adds to its charm for collectors – after all, had it been better sung and produced it might have sold and not been so collectable now.

Page was in demand as a session player and he was producer Shel Talmy's favoured guitarist and featured on both early Kinks and Who recordings. Session credits included Marianne Faithfull's 'As Tears Go By', The Nashville Teens 'Tobacco Road', and Van Morrison's 'Here Come The Night'.

In 1965 he was hired by Andrew Loog Oldham as house producer for Immediate Records which gave him the chance to play on sessions with Nico, Eric Clapton, John Mayall and Chris Farlowe among others.

Jimmy Page is his early Denmark Street session days.

Beyond The Rising Sun
MARC BOLAN DECCA F 12288

As the B side of Bolan's rare first single The Wizard, this is not very well known to people other than hardcore Marc fans, and the record itself is one of the rare cases where stock copies are valued higher than demos.

As with Mr Dwight (above right) much of Marc's phrasing is already intact on this orientally flavoured song, but probably of even more interest to collectors is the fact that he was already dealing with the lyrical content that was to propel him to stardom a few years later – 'Beyond The Rising Sun' includes a unicorn among other fanciful imagery.

Come Back Baby
BLUESOLOGY FONTANA TF 594

This mini-section of 'before they were famous' features two 1965 singles from Elton John's Bluesology group. Then plain old Reg Dwight, he was usually more involved with the band, backing up a variety of visiting B list US soul stars; Bluesology always seemed to be a permanent fixture on the club circuit.

This one is a good first issue, with Reg's piano and voice being allowed full rein on the attractive mid-tempo song. Close listening reveals that much of his later vocal phrasing was already in place in these early days.

I'll Do Anything (He Wants Me To Do)
DORIS TROY
CAMEO PARKWAY C 101

Bluesology backed Doris Troy on her promo dates for this wonderful release. The song was laden with commercial hooks, and Doris was right on the button vocally with this up-tempo pop soul dancer.

It received an airing on Ready Steady Go at the Wembley Park studios, and she played several London dates including the Golders Green Refectory, a small sweaty room below the North London Freehouse where Jimi Hendrix could be found in early 1967.

This was one of the earlier records to be fully picked up on the Northern Soul scene, indicating some pretty damn good taste before later excesses crept in. The quality and demand for the record is underlined by the fact that it had two re-releases: on Toast in 1968, and on Mojo in 1971.

You Turned My Bitter Into Sweet
MARY LOVE
KING KG 1024

A very collectable name on the Northern scene is Mary Love, and this is the first and rarest of her UK issues on the small King label.

Originally released in the States, when the record emerged on the Modern label, the other side, 'I'm In Your Hands', was chosen as the A side. Marc Gordon and Frank Wilson, two Motown staffers who were well able to replicate the feel of Supremes' recordings with her, oversaw 'Love on the West Coast'. While both sides are commercial, it is easy to see how 'You Turned My Bitter Into Sweet', with its trademark handclaps, became so popular and sought-after here in Britain.

A more recent CD compilation of Love's material.

Thank You Baby
GRAHAM BONNEY
COLUMBIA DB 8111

'Thank You Ruby' was co-written and co-arranged by Beach Boy Bruce Johnston, and was the fifth of 14 singles he had out on Columbia between 1965 and 1970.

The song, also recorded later by Johnston himself, features the sort of soft vocals that were to become associated with Sunshine Pop, making Graham and Bruce somewhat ahead of the game here. Bonney, from Essex, was once with the Riot Squad and toured Germany (where he later emigrated) with The Trends.

His other remembered song is 'Super Girl', which was a near hit and provided the title for his only album in 1966.

Bonney was the ultimate Carnaby Street man.

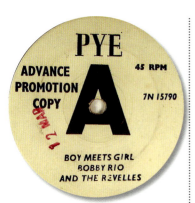

Boy Meets Girl
BOBBY RIO AND THE REVELLES
PYE 7N 15790

This later Joe Meek production shows a good deal of restraint from the producer as he concentrates on the overall brightness and immediacy of the record rather than any gimmicky sounds. It works very well, and allows Rio and the group to make the comparatively simple song into much more.

This was the first of three singles the group made with Meek in 1965, before Rio went solo the following year with a cover of The Four Tops' 'Ask The Lonely'.

Are You There (With Another Girl)
DIONNE WARWICK
PYE INTERNATIONAL 7N 25338

Quite why all Dionne Warwick records weren't immediate top five entries remains a bit of a mystery. Here she is with another Bacharach/David number that oozes class in every department, including the fine piano-led arrangement. It has one of the best opening lines ever: 'I hear the music coming out of your radio…", and Dionne's voice effortlessly swoops and dives around the lyric showing the full extent of her range. Nothing more needs to be said.

Under The Boardwalk
THE MARIONETTES
PARLOPHONE R 5300

The Kind Of Boy You Can't Forget
LITTLE FRANKIE
COLUMBIA DB 7490

Some covers of good American originals make painful listening, but here are two examples that, while they may not out-strip the originals by The Drifters and The Raindrops respectively, are certainly decent versions that bring something a bit different to the songs.

The Marionettes were a black London two boy/two girl group comprising Lance King and Pauline Sibbles, both from India, and Jerry and Katie Kissoon. Katie was already building a name for herself on the London session scene under a variety of names including Peanut.

Their version on 'Under The Boardwalk' was the second of five singles. They do justice to the song, which, of course, has retained its quality through hundreds of attempts on it…

although there was Bruce Willis…

Little Frankie takes Ellie Greenwich and Jeff Barry's song head-on with the perspective of a young bratty teen. Although she gives a thoroughly nasal delivery, she pulls off the song as if it was written for her; a bit like Lesley Gore's kid sister.

Although only around 16 at the time (sounding younger), Frankie was a show-biz veteran, having already been in The Chimes, featuring Denise on Decca in 1963/4 where she was Denise. A second single was issued by Little Frankie and The Country Gentlemen, before she covered 'It Doesn't Matter Anymore' when she was produced by a young Graham Gouldman.

Not The Lovin' Kind
DINO DESI & BILLY
REPRISE R 23047

Ok, admittedly they had a bit of an advantage in the States: Dino was Dean Martin's son, Desi was Lucille Ball's, and Billy was a pal who also came from an advantaged background. They were in their early teens when they gathered to audition for Frank Sinatra for his Reprise label. They set up their then sparse equipment to sing a couple of songs for Frank and proud poppa Dean. Pretty soon they became the darlings of the US teen mags, with this jangly folk-rocky single making No25 on Billboard late October 1965. They bravely tackled Dylan's Chimes Of Freedom on the flip.

Dino Martin went on to marry actress Olivia Hussey, but tragically died in a plane crash in 1987 near Palm Springs. Billy Hinsche, brother-in-law to Carl Wilson of the Beach Boys, sung on 'Heroes And Villains' and 'Darlin'' before joining the Beach Boys touring band for many years, where he notably handled the Wipe Out rap. He is a regular visitor to Britain as an attendee and supporter of Beach Boys' fan conventions.

"What I love about this song is the Jim (nee Roger) McGuinn-influenced jingle jangle 12-string guitar riff that opens the song and is prevalent throughout. The lyrics are also very clever and wry. To this day, it is one of my favourite songs to perform in concert."

BILLY HINSCHE

Early Morning Rain
PETER PAUL & MARY
WARNER BROS. WB 5659

The popular US trio, who had been in the forefront of popularising Bob Dylan's songs both here and in the States, moved on to the-then much less well-known writer Gordon Lightfoot. The Canadian writer, from Ontario, was just starting to attract covers from fellow Canadians Ian And Sylvia, but was still some way off his best-remembered album years in the Seventies.

'Early Morning Rain' was melodic with memorable lyrical imagery that used the potential freedom of an airport as a metaphor for frustration. Peter, Paul and Mary are their usual professional selves, and deliver the song to perfection.

Jackson C Frank
BLUES RUN THE GAME
COLUMBIA DB 7795

Jackson C Frank was born in Buffalo, New York State, but in the mid-Sixties could be found around the folk clubs in London's Soho and going out with fellow folkie Sandy Denny.

'Blues Run The Game' is loosely based on his trip to England aboard the Queen Elizabeth. Once here, he linked with not only Denny, but also other notables on the scene: Paul Simon, Al Stewart and Bert Jansch.

Columbia issued this one single, taken from his very fine self-titled album. Denny later regularly included the song 'You Never Wanted Me' (from the same album) in Fairport Convention live sets when she joined them before their second album.

'Blues Run The Game' was taken back to New York by Paul Simon, where he recorded it with Art Garfunkel as part of the *Sounds Of Silence* session four days before Christmas 1965.

Immediate Records

Immediate Records was formed by the ever busy, creative and ambitious Andrew Loog Oldham with partner Tony Calder. Unmistakably modelled on his sonic idol Phil Spector's US label Philles, Oldham set out to make Immediate the new, hot independent UK label to fit with everything that was hip and happening in London at that time.

While Spector had his 'Tomorrow's Sound Today' by-line for Philles, Oldham's for Immediate was even more fanciful: 'Happy To Be Part Of The Industry Of Human Happiness'. Like John Lewis, Oldham was never knowingly undersold. The 84 singles that were released between August 1965 and October 1969, if not actually of American origin, certainly lent heavily at first on US sounds and trends. Starting with a (suitably) immediate hit with their first release, 'Hang On Sloopy' from The McCoys, the label then went for over 30 issues before a second major hit with Chris Farlowe's 'Out Of Time'. In between, however, came a string of never-less-than-interesting singles by largely unknown names, many of which featured involvement from everywhere-man Jimmy Page. Another big one came with PP Arnold's 'First Cut Is The Deepest', before the label settled in with a series of fabulous hit issues from The Small Faces. Oldham's taste and production talents were well represented on the rarities chosen to close the choices for 1965.

happy to be a part of the industry of human happiness

IMMEDIATE

IMMEDIATE

I'm Not Saying
NICO
IMMEDIATE IM 003

Andrew Oldham produced this one-off oddity from the distinctly unusual Nico. With a pretty elaborate string arrangement reminiscent of Bob Lind's hits, Oldham effectively shifts attention away from the fact that Nico's obvious Teutonic charms didn't fully extend to her singing. Despite this, it remains a strangely compelling record that is collectable partly through the lady's imminent connections with the Velvet Underground.

The striking looking Nico.

Bells of Rhymney
THE FIFTH AVENUE
IMMEDIATE IM 002

There is Byrdsian jangle aplenty on this Pete Seeger co-written song about a mining disaster. 'The Bells of Rhymney' is a cover of the song that appeared on the first Byrds album, so, for The Fifth Avenue, it was a case of: 'If you're not going to put it out as a single, then we will.'

The Fifth Avenue was actually a duo: Denny (Denver) Gerrard and Kenny Rowe, who later joined Tony Rivers and The Castaways while Gerrard went to be part of Warm Sounds. Jimmy Page produced it.

Moondreams
LES FLEUR DE LYS
IMMEDIATE IM 020

This is another Jimmy Page production, which in some ways anticipates the flowery psych sounds that were to arrive 18 months later.

The Buddy Holly song 'Moondreams' takes in a few time shifts as it progresses on its merry way, and is the first of several very collectable records made by the group in its various guises for Immediate, Polydor and Atlantic.

Personnel changes are far too complicated to attempt here; suffice it to say that various members, including Gordon Haskell, went on to a wide variety of work with many acts during the Sixties and later.

At the time of this release they were a clean-looking four-piece with a distinct penchant for frilly-fronted shirts.

She Belongs To Me
THE MASTERMINDS
IMMEDIATE IM 005

Covering Dylan songs was the thing to do in 1965, and here is a British cover that was enhanced greatly by a distinctive wandering and descending guitar line that remains nicely high in the mix.

The singer adopts a suitably Dylanesque drawl, which was very much the order of the day for such covers. The group was from Liverpool, and is thought to have included Joey Molland, later of Badfinger, Doug Meakin and George Cassidy.

They went on to become the Fruit Eating Bears…well, someone had to…

The Monkey Time
The Golden Apples Of The Sun **IMMEDIATE IM 010**

Although there is only one main voice audible, accompanied by what sounds like session players, The Golden Apples Of The Sun could have been a real group as they were apparently co-managed by Oldham and Sixties lensman and gad-about David Bailey.

This is a strange marriage, with what sounds like a folk rock track for a cover of the Curtis Mayfield-written hit for Major Lance, but bizarrely it works, probably down to the feel and quality of the song. The lead voice handles it all pretty well, and it wouldn't have been too out of place in a club setting then.

Cara-Lyn
THE STRANGELOVES
IMMEDIATE IM 007

It's the Feldman, Goldstein and Gottehrer New York production team again…they keep cropping up, mainly because they did make some marvellous records that sounded unlike anyone else's.

This time, they are with their Strangeloves identity, banging away on African drums and, clearly Jewish men already of certain years, looking faintly ridiculous in their zebra waistcoats and tight leather trousers. Nevertheless, they knew how to construct great-sounding pop records, and 'Cara-Lyn' is simple and unforgettable, with production values that throw all the right things to the top of the mix.

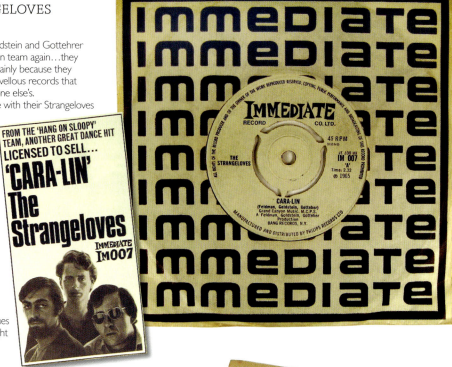

You Can't Buy My Love
BARBARA LYNN
IMMEDIATE IM 011

Like the Strangeloves record, this was another release that Immediate licensed in from a US label, in this case Jamie of Philadelphia. However, most of her early recording had been done at Cosimo's famous New Orleans studio where artists such as Irma Thomas recorded.

Barbara Lynn was one of the few women who looked right with a guitar in 1965.

Barbara had become known through her powerful 1962 hit 'You'll Lose a Good Thing' and her later 'Oh Baby (We Got A Good Thing Going)', with the latter getting a good Rolling Stones cover on 'Out Of Our Heads'. On this less-well-known outing, Barbara is in total control, working well off two or three backing girls on a fast-paced organ-led number that appears to have been an R&B response to the similarly titled Beatles hit of the previous year.

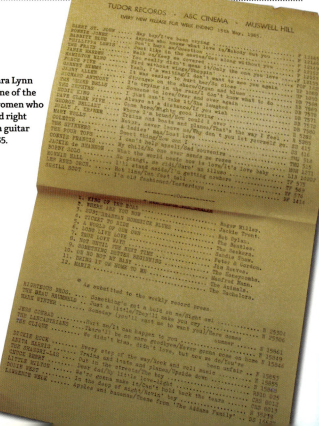

reprise:

45 RPM

R.23047

DINO, DESI & BILLY

NOT THE LOVIN' KIND
(Lee Hazlewood)
MECOLICO

fontana

TF 584

45

MONO

A

NEIGHBOUR NEIGHBOUR
(A. Valier)
THE ADLIBS
A Vee-Jay Recording

THE BYRDS
NEVER BEFORE

BiG BEAT
THE POP 'N' ROMANCE MAGAZINE

LIBERTY

THIS RECORD MUST BE PLAYED AT 45 RPM

PYE PICCADILLY PYE JAZZ PICCADILLY PYE INTERNATIONAL PICCADILLY PYE JAZZ PICCADILLY PYE INTER

WE FIVE

LET'S GET TOGETHER

DISTRIBUTED BY
PYE RECORDS (SALES) LTD., A.T.V. HOUSE.
GT. CUMBERLAND PLACE, LONDON, W.1.

LONDON
AMERICAN RECORDINGS

45 R.P.M.

HL 9988

OUT IN THE SUN (HEY-O)
(Feldman, Goldstein, Gottehrer)
THE BEACH-NUTS

ANNETTE Sings
GOLDEN SURFIN' HITS
SIDEWALK SURFIN'
SURFER'S STOMP
SURFIN' U.S.A.
SURFER BOY
SURF CITY
SURFIN' SAFARI
RIDE THE WILD SURF
BALBOA BLUE
BOY TO LOVE
JUST STRICTLY SURFIN'
NO ONE COULD BE PROUDER

and just for fun
"THE MONKEY'S UNCLE"

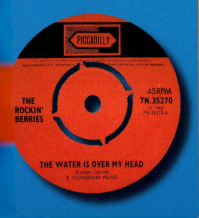

PICCADILLY

45RPM

7N.35270

THE ROCKIN' BERRIES

THE WATER IS OVER MY HEAD
(Kuoper-Levine)
A SCHROEDER MUSIC

DECCA

45 RPM

F.12271

SHUT 'EM DOWN IN LONDON TOWN
(Ford, Thomson)
THE MAJORITY
Music Director: David Whitaker
Production: Jim Economides

Red Bird

45 RPM

RB10 036

RIGHT NOW AND NOT LATER
(Moseley, Bateman, Hollon)
THE SHANGRI-LAS
A Kama Sutra Production

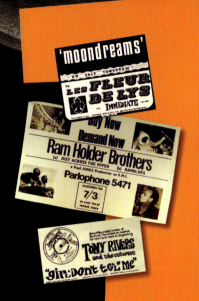

England wins the World Cup at Wembley, Mao Zedung launches the cutural revolution and The Monkees' tv show is launched in the US

The year is dominated by The Beach Boys' Pet Sounds and the Beatles' response with Revolver and its ground-breaking 'Tomorrow Never Knows', drawing much more focus onto the album as an entity rather than two hits and ten filler tracks. New forms of rock music and concerts are starting up in San Francisco with bands like The Grateful Dead, whilst anti-war and civil rights protest movements gather force. The Supremes and The Four Tops cement Motown's position, and the Stax label continues to grow. Phil Spector sulks as Ike & Tina Turner's 'River Deep Mountain High' fails to repeat its British success in the States, and Bob Dylan begins a two year withdrawal after his motorbike accident. Good Vibrations is released to top charts everywhere as the most expensive single ever made. New acts include The Doors, The Velvet Underground, The Troggs and Cream, and The Animals' bassist Chas Chandler brings Jimi Hendrix over to London.

Ram Holder brothers

Dusty Springf...

Episode Six

Phil Spector

Caroline No
BRIAN WILSON
CAPITOL CL 15438

The emergence of this first solo release from Brian Wilson indicated some interesting thinking on someone's part...but whose has never been clear.

One scenario has Capitol Records testing the waters to see if there was a market for Brian under his own name rather than the Beach Boys, which could potentially had led to Pet Sounds (on which the song also appeared) being issued as a solo album. If the company was uncertain about the album with its departure from regular Beach Boys' sound and imagery, this could have been a course to take had the single been a big seller. Alternatively, did Brian fancy a solo shot himself, or had he picked up on some vibes of uncertainty from Capitol; It's well documented that there were some from within the band at the time. Or was it simply that this particular song was so very much Brain rather than a group recording. Either way, despite the obvious qualities of the work, it was an odd choice in 1966 as the first part of Pet Sounds to emerge.

Don't worry about searching out this individual track, just get the whole album if you haven't already.

Guess I'm Dumb
DANI SHERIDAN
PLANET PLF 106

In 1965, Brian Wilson had been experimenting with some of the instrumental sounds and feels that were to make *Pet Sounds* ground breaking, and careful listening to his recording of the track for Glen Campbell's US release of 'Guess I'm Dumb' reveals many instrumental blends that would re-occur later. There was also ample evidence of Burt Bacharach's influence creeping in, with some of the themes of 'Walk On By' being recycled.

Producer Shel Talmy took the bold step of covering the song with the unknown Dani Sheridan, and came up with a very decent recording of a song that is a difficult one to sing. Trivia buffs will need to know that Dani's daughter now plays the ever lustful Edie Britt in Desperate Housewives.

Ready Steady
THE CLOCKWORK ORANGES **EMBER EMB S 227**

Another four-piece group, personnel unknown, drew inspiration from the Beach Boys and married it to beat group sensibilities. The obvious West Coast influence comes in part from producer Jim Economides, who had worked as an engineer/producer at the Capitol Tower in Los Angeles from the Dick Dale days. He had developed a somewhat dubious reputation there and had washed up for a while in Britain during this period. This song's choruses owe more than a little to 'I Get Around,' and is thus quite a rarity for Beach Boys' collectors.

Farmer's Daughter
THE SUMMER SET
COLUMBIA DB 8004

The Summer Set were a very competent vocal harmony unit. On the occasion that they supported Tony Rivers and The Castaways at one of the Marquee's Surfin' nights, they were a four-piece group, fronted by a chap called Dave.

They produced an impressively full harmonic blend for various Beach Boys covers, and this BB cover proves their talents. Picking a scarcely known Brian Wilson song from the Beach Boys' second album *Surfin' USA* was quite a bold move, but it showed that they recognised the song for what it was: one of Brian's first steps towards a richer and more emotional approach for his band. 'The Summer Set' more than did the number justice.

Summer Of Last Year
THE PYRAMID
DERAM DM 111

The Deram label, formed by Decca Records to make them seem hipper in the mid-Sixties, quickly gained a good reputation for interesting and adventurous records, such as this one-off release from the originally Scunthorpe-based three-piece group, which has two excellent sides of original songs.

Though rooted in West Coast harmony and the emerging Sunshine Pop, they were certainly no copyists, and created an identity of their own. Denny Cordell (who was about to take the newly arrived Brooklyn boy Tony Visconti under his wing to set him off on his multi-activity role in British pop), produced the sides for The Pyramid

The group was made up of Steve Hiatt (who wrote both sides), Al Jackson and Ian Macdonald. Ian was to soon become Ian (then Iain) Matthews and join Fairport Convention, before forging his own route through the music business with a superb voice and musical taste that was first found on 'Summer Of Last Year' and the flipside 'Summer Evening'.

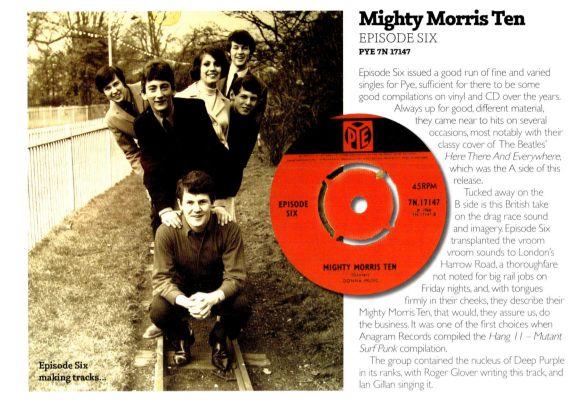

Episode Six
making tracks...

Mighty Morris Ten
EPISODE SIX
PYE 7N 17147

Episode Six issued a good run of fine and varied singles for Pye, sufficient for there to be some good compilations on vinyl and CD over the years. Always up for good, different material, they came near to hits on several occasions, most notably with their classy cover of The Beatles' *Here There And Everywhere*, which was the A side of this release.

Tucked away on the B side is this British take on the drag race sound and imagery. Episode Six transplanted the vroom vroom sounds to London's Harrow Road, a thoroughfare not noted for big rail jobs on Friday nights, and, with tongues firmly in their cheeks, they describe their Mighty Morris Ten, that would, they assure us, do the business. It was one of the first choices when Anagram Records compiled the *Hang 11 – Mutant Surf Punk* compilation.

The group contained the nucleus of Deep Purple in its ranks, with Roger Glover writing this track, and Ian Gillan singing it.

Here Today
THE ROBB STORME GROUP
COLUMBIA DB 7993

By 1966, it was almost as acceptable to cover songs from Beach Boys' albums as Beatles' one, and 'Here Today' was one of the most immediately accessible tracks from the *Pet Sounds* album.

This release was recorded at Landsdowne Studios in London, and produced by Monty Babson. The five-piece Luton group were the regular back-up musicians for Paul and Barry Ryan, and their members comprised lead vocalist Robb, guitarist Tony Ollard, bass Lew Collins, piano/sax Jim St Pier and drummer Wilson Malone.

As well as arranging this one, Malone went on to join The Orange Bicycle and to start Morgan Blue Town Productions.

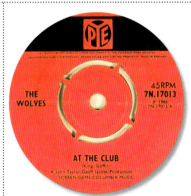

At The Club
THE WOLVES
PYE 7N 17013

This group came down to London from Wolverhampton, and had released a couple of singles before this one.

Recording Goffin/King songs was always a guarantee of quality material, and this Drifters number is no exception. The Wolves turn in a bright and breezy version, at a slightly faster pace than the original, adding tambourine and organ to boost the arrangement. It was used as the opening track to *Ripples Vol 4*.

(You're My) Soul And Inspiration

THE RIGHTEOUS BROTHERS
VERVE VS 535

All Strung Out

NINO TEMPO & APRIL STEVENS
LONDON HLU 10084

Two men who had no problems re-creating the full-blooded Spector Wall of Sound were Bill Medley and Nino Tempo, both of whom had spent hours in the studio with the man himself: Medley as one half of the Righteous Brothers, and Tempo as a contributing musician and one of Spector's closest friends.

By 1966, Bill Medley and Bobby Hatfield had fallen out with Spector, so Bill, who had produced their earlier work and even some of their Philles albums, set about the task of maintaining their sound on his own. '(You're My) Soul And Inspiration' was his first attempt, and magnificent it was too, as the pair took the strong Barry Mann/Cynthia Weil song straight to the top of the US charts. Strangely though, it only briefly crept into our top 40, making it one of the great lost hits.

Tempo once again teamed up with his sister April Stevens, who he had enjoyed several hits with earlier in the decade, and produced one of the strongest releases of the year.

Nino wrote 'All Strung Out' with fellow Spector sideman Jerry Riopell (aka Riopelle) with the Righteous Brothers in mind, and when they didn't want it, he just said: 'Right, I'll do it myself.'

He did it so well that he landed a sizable US hit (No26) with a very decent follow-up album that contained another slab of Spectorian might, 'The Habit Of Lovin' You Baby.'

Just You

THURSDAY'S CHILDREN
PICCADILLY – 7N 35276

Replicating the Spector sound in British studios was never easy, but this single (one of two from Thursday's Children) nailed it pretty darned well.

The brother-and-sister-duo from London took the Sonny Bono song from the first Sonny and Cher album and made it their own.

Phil Cordell was likely to have been on the production side, so hats off to all involved here. It can be found on *Ripples Vol 7, Rainbows.*

The Coldest Night Of The Year

APRIL STEVENS & NINO TEMPO
ATLANTIC 584048

Soon after 'All Strung Out', Nino and April reverted to something akin to the breathy vocals of their earlier work, while remaining every bit as effective. However, despite another marvellous Mann/Weil song, the pair once again failed to catch fresh British interest with 'The Coldest Night Of The Year,' despite their move to Atlantic being supported by a new album.

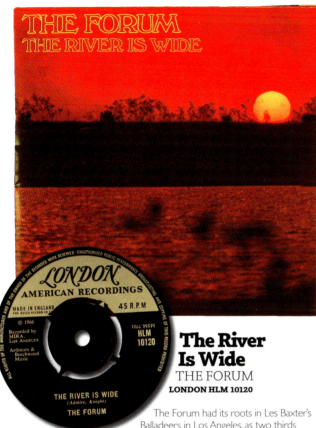

The River Is Wide
THE FORUM
LONDON HLM 10120

The Forum had its roots in Les Baxter's Balladeers in Los Angeles, as two thirds of the group, Phil Campos and Riselle Bain, had sung with them. Rene Nole joined them, and the trio cut this powerful, almost over-produced song, which went to No45 in the States. It was a big, bold full production in The Righteous Brothers' style.

The group enjoyed their hit for only a short time before Riselle left to go solo and Phil and Rene got together personally and professionally.

> " We used to go crazy when we heard The River Is Wide on the radio. We used to stop the car and start screaming whenever it was played. It was a pretty big hit in LA. It took days and days to get the vocals right."
> **RISELLE BAIN**

Andrea
THE SUNRAYS
CAPITOL CL 15433

Pollyanna
THE CLASSICS
CAPITOL CL 15470

A Lovely Way To Say Goodnight
THE FOUR EVERS
CBS 202549

Many vocal groups were still taking their cues from the Beach Boys and The Four Seasons, two of the US acts to survive the onslaught of UK acts in the so-called British Invasion of the American charts from February 1964 onwards.

The father of the Beach Boys' three Wilson brothers, Murry Wilson, had been sacked by his sons from his managerial duties and was determined to prove he could find success with another similar band. He chose an existing second-rank surf band, The Sunrays, led by the talented Rick Henn, and took them to Capitol where they got an immediate hit with the comparatively well-known 'I Live For The Sun'. 'Andrea' was the follow-up and in many ways is even better: Beach Boy-like vocally, but very much a song with a different feel.

The Classics' 'Pollyanna' is a full-on catchy East Coast Seasons-inspired song written by Joe South, with another good song, 'Cry Baby', on the flip. While this one was issued in the UK following its No106 showing on Billboard, its follow-up 'Little Darlin'' missed the cut because it didn't sell well in the States.

The Four Evers only UK release was another cracking double-sider, with the equally strong 'The Girl I Wanna Bring Home' on the B side.

The Four Seasons influences were even stronger than in The Classics, in that they were arranged and produced by sometime Seasons' arranger/member Charlie Calello, and the group had also recorded material written by their friend Bob Gaudio from the Seasons. The group were Joey DiBenedetto, Steve Tudanger, Johnny Cipriani and Nick Zagami. Their links with the Seasons came after they met producer Bob Crewe.

This was one of their later records, after several of consistently high quality on the Smash label, and they even made one for Red Bird before folding as a regular group.

Baby Don't You Do It
THE POETS
IMMEDIATE IM 024

So Much In Love
CHARLES DICKENS
IMMEDIATE IM 025

Goldie
HEADLINES
IMMEDIATE IM 026

Girl Don't Tell Me
TONY RIVERS AND THE CASTAWAYS
IMMEDIATE IM 027

You Baby
THE TURTLES
IMMEDIATE IM 031

Circles
THE FLEUR DE LYS
IMMEDIATE IM 032

GOLDIE: Going Back; Headlines (Immediate IM 026). Goffin-King song and Goldie's first with Andrew Oldham. Delayed instrumental intro, piano, then some first-rate singing from Goldie. There's a softly haunting appeal quality in her voice, lots of style and "presence". And it builds well, too . . . builds into a Fifty sure-thing. She phrases with bluesy enthusiasm. Flip is an Oldham original, also commended. TOP FIFTY TIP.

the golden surfin'sounds of American West Coast re-created for the first time in England by
TONY RIVERS
and the castaways
"girl don't tell me"

Immediate began 1966 as they had finished 1965 – with a fine stream of releases, these six coming before mid-March.

The Poets were (at this stage) Scots George Gallagher, Hume Paton, Fraser Watson, John Dawson and Alan Weir. They had picked a Holland/Dozier/Holland song from Marvin Gaye's output to try on the UK market. It was produced, let it be whispered, by Paul Raven (aka Gadd, Gary Glitter), and was popular with the Mod crowd at the time.

The name Charles Dickens was an alter-ego for London photographer David Anthony, and Oldham produced him on this Los Angeles-influenced remake of a song that had nearly made it for The Mighty Avengers. Despite a strong record that blatantly stole from the Beach Boys' 'California Girls', Dickens/Anthony went back to his lens work.

'Goldie's Headlines' was an Oldham penned and produced soul-type song hidden away on the flip of her version of 'Going Back'. Using every current soul riff, they made a danceable recording that certainly deserved a better fate than a B side.

Tony Rivers and The Castaways had transferred to Immediate from Columbia after a string of misses, and worked with Andrew Oldham on this power

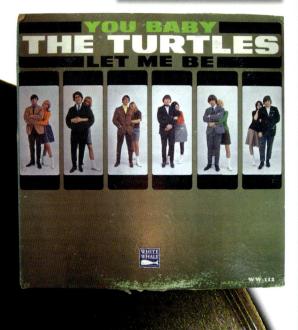

YOU BABY
THE TURTLES
LET ME BE
WHITE WHALE
WW-112

> **'Girl Don't Tell Me' was given to us to record by Andrew Oldham, having just signed to Brian Epstein's management. First thing he did was pull an EMI scheduled recording we'd made of 'Nowhere Man' (probably a No1 or top ten record had it been released). Anyway, we were now being produced by Mr Oldham, who had just acquired Sea Of Tunes publishing. He was looking for people to cover Brian Wilson songs. Hence us. Great song. Oldham asked us to do a Beach Boys on it, but I thought I'd use the ideas we often used live on stage – in other words, voices taking the parts that instruments would often take on records, which is how the 'ba bah ba bah ba babadah bah' bits came about. The other voice parts on our version were fairly straightforward Beach Boys 'signature' oohs. We/he, didn't get the balance of voices on the disc that I would have liked (an important part under-balanced can wreck the particular section). Ah well, it's still my favourite Castaways record (not the one with the strange pitch shift at the start). It was NOT my idea for the Walk Like A Man bit at the end; Andrew's idea on the session, I think."**
> **Tony Rivers**

version of a Beach Boys' album track. They wove in many new vocal lines and the single was pushed hard with ads and radio plays, but it only just scraped into the top 50. It is now the hardest of the group's singles to find.

The Turtles emerged at the forefront of the Folk Rock boom with their hit take on Dylan's 'It Ain't Me Babe'. This was their only Immediate release, and was a great Phil Sloan/Steve Barri song that had appeared on the first Mamas and Papas album. It was a natural choice for the talented ex-surf band Turtles, as was the rare B side 'Wanderin' Kind', another great slab of folk rock. When this one didn't sell, Oldham passed on future Turtles issues, and they went to the London label…bad decision.

The Pete Townsend song 'Circles' was grabbed by The Fleur De Lys, who worked with young producer Glyn Johns to make what is now considered a classic of the psych pop genre, explaining the current £500 price tag.

The group had split since their 'Moondreams' single a few months before, and this appears to have been recorded by a new line-up of Keith Guster, Gordon Haskell, Pete Shears and Phil Sawyer (a version of the originals co-existed).

The other change was to their prefix, which changed from 'Les' to 'The' for this track.

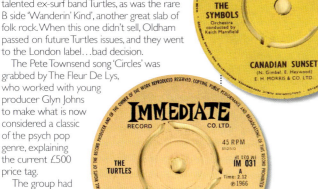

Let Me Be
THE TURTLES
**PYE INTERNATIONAL
7N 25341**

Before we leave The Turtles, 'Let Me Be' was their follow-up to their first US top ten hit, 'It Ain't Me Babe'. Written by PF Sloan, it was a plea for self direction rather than rule imposed from above…from parents, society etc. It maintained their breakthrough position, and showed how much of a commercial sound they had already developed.

Previously known as The Crossfires, a surf/frat party band, at this stage they included Mark Volman and Howard Kaylan (later to be known with Zappa as Flo and Eddie), Al Nichol, Jim Tucker, Chuck Portz and Don Murray.

A year or two later, after a few personnel changes, they hit their stride in Britain with hits such as 'Happy Together', 'She'd Rather Be With Me' and 'Elenore'.

Canadian Sunset
THE SYMBOLS
PRESIDENT PT 113

East London's The Symbols had the sense to cover The Four Evers' 'Lovely Way To Say Goodnight' in 1968, but, a couple of years before, they had released 'Canadian Sunset' on the new President label. 'Canadian Sunset' was an oft-recorded song that had already appeared in a variety of guises, but this time it arrived in stompy Newbeats harmony soul form. People often wonder why so many UK harmony bands hailed from the East London/Essex area, and perhaps it is because of their proximity to the pirate stations and better Radio Luxembourg reception. Whatever the reason, there has always been an Essex harmony mafia of interlinked bands, and The Symbols were as involved as any.

Johnny Milton, Chaz Wade, Mickey Clarke and Sean Corrigan produced excellent interpretations of US harmony pop and a couple of good Ronettes covers, including their near-hit 'The Best Part Of Breakin' Up' and 'Do I Love You'. Mickey Clarke went on to find fame with the Rubettes in the Seventies, and was part of the harmony gang (along with fellow mafioso such as Tony and Anthony Rivers, Tony Harding and Mickey Keen) who greeted Brian Wilson when he surprised everyone with an appearance at the 1988 Beach Boys Fan Club Convention.

Hide And Seek
THE SHEEP
STATESIDE SS 493

Our old friends Feldman, Goldstein and Gottehrer return for what could be a final appearance in this book, this time under the guise of The Sheep. They take the Bunker Hill 1962 hit song 'Hide And Seek', and crank it up in their well-formed Strangeloves drum-soaked approach to the Nth degree, producing one of the loudest and thumpiest sounds ever committed to wax. It climbed to No58 in the States, but probably sold only ten or so copies in Britain as no-one would have dared to play it for fear of the needles crashing out of their housings way past the red. Quite magnificent in its excess.

Magic Town
THE VOGUES
KING KG 1035

As The Sheep meandered up the US charts, this song leapfrogged them to reach No21 on Billboard.

It's a Mann/Weil song again and is a Drifters-throwback scenario of walking the streets on the Big Apple. The verses are lower and sonorous before the choruses build into higher ranges, and the group's lead voice, reminiscent of Jay Black of Jay And The Americans, soars above the others.

Unlike the group's other issues this emerged on the small King label based in London's Stamford Hill as part of R&B Discs Ltd. They had previously been on London, where they released the wonderfully poppy 'You're The One' and 'Five O'Clock World', but decided to settle for middle-of-the-road material, aside from their souly dancer 'That's The Tune', which sadly never emerged in Britain at the time.

The four group members were from Pittsburgh: lead Bill Burkette, baritone Don Miller; first tenor Hugh Geyer and second tenor Chuck Blasko.

Let's Call It A Day Girl
THE RAZOR'S EDGE
STATESIDE SS 532

Quite who this lot were is not really known, though on the aural evidence, and the inclusion of Irwin Levine as a co-writer on both sides, suggests a New York recording.

It struggled uncertainly up the US charts to stall at No77, which was a shame as it is a jolly vocal group performance that anticipated the sound of The Buckinghams' 'Kind Of A Drag' single, which was to top the US Hot 100 about six months later.

While it is not possible to track down much information about them, it would be safe to assume that a) they had an album called *Let's Call It A Day Girl*, b) there could well have been a follow-up single in which they may have got back together, and c) this sold in minute quantities in Britain despite its qualities, thus ensuring that nothing else from the group reached these shores.

The Batman Theme
THE MARKETTS
WARNER BROS. WB 5696

Guitar instrumentals took a long time to fade after such a strong following in the early years of the Sixties (for many they never did) and this Marketts' recording of Neil Hefti's Batman Theme was a real rarity at the time because it had a picture sleeve.

The non-too-serious Batman show had become incredibly popular on both side of the Atlantic, and all manner of cash-ins appeared, trying to pinch some of the caped crusaders magic. This one was trailing an album called *The Marketts Interpret The Batman Show* (Holy mouthful, Batman!), which was about to be released.

Dick Glasser's production of the particular session players masquerading as The Marketts was strong, with the addition of organ, brass and a female chorus to the group's more usual guitar-based work.

Little Bitty Pretty One
THURSTON HARRIS & THE SHARPS
SUE WI 4016

Fat's Shake 'Em Up PT. 1
CLAUDE 'FATS' GREENE ORCH.
ISLAND WI 290

Barefootin'
ROBERT PARKER
ISLAND WI 286

Meanwhile, back at the clubs, there was a steadily increasing awareness of the more obscure R&B releases, especially if they were danceable. The Thurston Harris record was a re-issue of a very collectable song that first came out in Britain in 1957 on Vogue Records. The instantly recognisable, half-sung, half-hummed intro helped to make this a club classic.

Thurston Harris was an ex-member of The Lamplighters and had worked around LA, mostly taking leads on their recordings for the Federal label. Members of The Sharps were also in the group, and when they adopted their new name they label-hopped for a while, taking in Vik, Jamie, Chess and Combo before a brief spell on Aladdin, where Little Bitty Pretty One re-united them with Thurston. The Sharps then became The Crenshaws for a short time before settling on The Rivingtons for their Liberty Records heyday.

No attempt will be made here to name the members of Claude Greene's Orchestra, though from the writing credits it is reasonable to assume that it included a Mr Galloway and a Mr Hodges. The record is a happy melding of calypso and early ska influences, and tells of Fats' strutting exploits at a dance.

Robert Parker was a native of New Orleans, where he played sax on a variety of recordings for the likes of Professor Longhair, Irma Thomas and Ernie K-Doe. 'Barefootin'' found him trying out singing, and gave him his biggest hit, with only 'Tip-Toe' coming anywhere near to the infectiousness of this still-popular dancer.

It's interesting to wonder how many copies of these three sold away from London and the South East.

Soul Searching

It is virtually impossible to pinpoint with any accuracy when the use of the term soul began. It certainly wasn't in common currency in the early years of the sixties, but by now, 1966, it had crept into descriptions in terms of it being a genre of music. The word was used with reasonable regularity by Ray Charles in the Fifties to describe his approach to singing certain songs, and Sam Cooke uses it in 'Shake' in 1964, but the gradual shift from what were called R&B records to 'soul' records developed over a three-to-four-year period from around 1963.

By the time it had settled as a commonly used descriptor, the form it took was already varied. Many artists and producers were rushing to integrate Motown influences into reasonably straight and, usually, white pop.

Other, usually black, artists were pushing on from the earlier dance and girl group genres, and Motown itself was continually pushing its own boundaries. Then, from the Southern States of the US, came the richer, earthier sounds of Memphis and beyond as the Stax label really found its feet and its signature sound.

Soul thus developed at different levels, from the ultra light-hearted to the downright emotionally charged soul bearing of what was subsequently called Deep Soul. New Orleans star Irma Thomas firmly stated recently that 'Soul' was not an adjective describing a genre, but a noun referring to a deep feeling.

Soul developed and so did the breadth of styles. There was blue-eyed soul, brown-eyed soul, Memphis soul, funk and Motown to name just five. One of the notable features was the number of female soul performers in the Sixties charts including Diana Ross, Dionne Warwick and Aretha Franklin.

Of the male performers that defined the Sixties James Brown, Otis Redding and Marvin Gaye stand out. Brown, is credited with inventing funk, which was heavily influenced by psychedelic rock. Redding gave a face to the Muscle Shoals sound and Marvin Gaye developed the art of the soulful ballad.

It's Too Late
BOBBY GOLDSBORO
UNITED ARTISTS UP 1128

Why Can't You Bring Me Home
JAY & THE AMERICANS
UNITED ARTISTS UP 1129

It's That Time Of The Year
LEN BARRY
BRUNSWICK 05962

May My Heart Be Cast Into Stone
THE TOYS
STATESIDE SS 502

Baby Toys
THE TOYS
STATESIDE SS 539

The common factor with these issues is that they all took their arrangements and instrumentation from Motown, even though the vocal deliveries varied from act to act.

Bobby Goldsboro and Jay & The Americans are the least obviously influenced, but each has a vibe and tempo that distinguishes them from their previous releases, evidenced by both records having found favour on UK dance floors at various times.

Len Barry came from the Dovells dance-based vocal group on Cameo Parkway, so was always aware of the need to fill floors. He hit big with '1-2-3' and 'Like A Baby', and 'It's That Time of The Year' continued the obvious Motown groove, though it failed to sell well as the others. Barry was produced by Messrs White and Madara, whose pedigree stretched way back via The Spokesman to Danny and The Juniors in Dave White's case, so their commercial ear was assured.

The Toys had broken through with the delightful 'Lovers' Concerto', and went on to issue many fine records without much further success. 'Baby Toys' came from a version by the US group The Victorians (not the LA girl group, but a male one formed by Nick Massi after he left the Four Seasons). Producers Sandy Linzer and Denny Randell's names were added to the credits here by dint of a new, somewhat different, introductory section

that was not found on the Victorians' faster-paced original. Once the main vocal section gets going, The Toys handle it well as a pop/Motown crossover, but, despite its class, it stalled at No76 in the US.

'May My Heart Be Cast Into Stone' was more distinctly Supremes-influenced, and Charlie Calello's arrangement leaves us in no doubt where they were heading.

A Lover's Concerto
MRS MILLER **CAPITOL CL 15444**

Using what sounds suspiciously like the original backing track, the unlikely named Alexis K De Azevedo produced Mrs Miller on her unique version of the Toys' huge hit. Mrs Miller looked like the archetypal American granny, but somehow got to make this single and a couple of albums for Capitol. Probably seen as oblique humour, how anyone actually heard her in the first place remains a mystery!

She warbles her way through, breaking out into doop-doops in one section, and later evokes jaw-dropping disbelief when she attempts to jump octaves. Impossible to listen to with a straight face, this is one of the funniest records ever made, whether it was intentional or not.

Then there was her whistling on 'Downtown' on the flip…

Stop Her On Sight (SOS)
EDWIN STARR
POLYDOR BM 56702

While 'Stop Her On Sight (SOS)' has since been classed as a Motown record, and was included on that label's compilations, this original issue was a Golden World release – across town from Motown.

Motown's Berry Gordy later bought Golden World, partly to cut down local competition, and it moved under the overall Hitsville umbrella. It was a Motown record in all but name anyway, as it was cut using the usual crew of Motown musicians in one of their famed moonlighting trips after hours.

Starr is in fine form as he works up all the right hooks with the girlie chorus.

Zig-Zagging
THE THREE CAPS **ATLANTIC 584043**

The Three Caps had previously been known as The Capitols, and they had hit with the ever-popular 'Cool Jerk'. This was the B side to the follow-up 'I Got To Handle It', although some believe it should have been the topside.

It is another urgent manic dancer; the group's high tenor voices almost scatting the title.

She Blew A Good Thing
THE AMERICAN POETS
LONDON HLC 10037

The American Poets were in the same predicament as the Detroit Spinners: they had to add on an explanatory part to their name to avoid confusion with British groups.

This slightly laid back, mid-tempo, New York dancer was a classic from day one, even though hardly anyone bought it – hence its high price today.

The song tells how the girl messed up her best chance with the guy, rather than the scenario that is sometimes suggested! Vocals, instrumentation and production by Juggy Murray are perfect. Juggy co-wrote the song (or reportedly re-jigged it) with the group's lead singer Ronnie Lewis. The group was from Brooklyn.

The Boogaloo Party
THE FLAMINGOS
PHILIPS BF 1483

This was a later version of the famed doo-wop group, which had decided to grab the feel of 1966 black music with this pulsating dancer.

A pounding and urgent backing track is topped by layers of vocal lines that provide hooks at every turn. With the bass in the red all the way, the track leads off with congas. A third of the way in, a tough sax drone comes in to build the track. Quite fabulous.

A Little Lovin' Sometimes
ALEXANDER PATTON
CAPITOL CL 15461

Alexander Patton's only UK release was an example of a perfectly formed mid-Sixties dance record, though it was a mid-tempo groove.

All the right elements are in place and well balanced, with a female group adding to the title line.

At the time, it probably sold only a couple of hundred copies, if that.

Picture Me Gone
EVIE SANDS
CAMEO PARKWAY C 413

This is somewhat of an oddity in the Evie Sands catalogue, who is more often found in reflective moods on crafted and thoughtful songs.

This, however, is a barn-storming stomper, which has become a major fave with collectors, resulting in a current price tag of £200-plus for a DJ copy.

Evie recalls: 'It's lovely that people like this recording so much. I was quite surprised a few years ago to find it was a Northern Soul favourite. I guess that it's really unlike the rest of my material, but, as a singer, on any given day I can enjoy all kinds of things. I enjoyed that challenge, though it was not really where I wanted to focus. A copy of 'Picture Me Gone' recently sold on the Internet for $271! I did love what Motown was doing at the time.'

Can't Satisfy
THE IMPRESSIONS
HMV POP 1545

Huge numbers of groups and producers set out to make Motown soundalikes, but few were as prestigious as The Impressions, led by the hugely talented Curtis Mayfield, who wrote this song.

Despite his own wonderful talents, he chose to let arranger and producer Johnny Pate lead them on what was effectively a re-tread of the Isley Brothers' 'This Old Heart Of Mine'. Collectors didn't mind, of course, as they got another great slab of the same sort of sound, and US buyers took it to No65 on the pop chart.

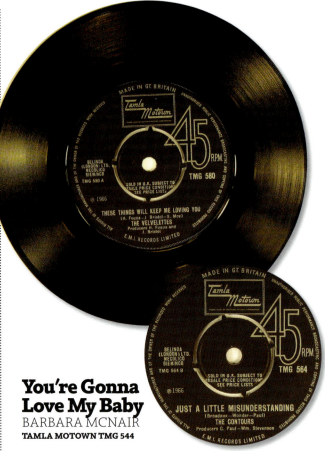

You're Gonna Love My Baby
BARBARA MCNAIR
TAMLA MOTOWN TMG 544

Just A Little Misunderstanding
THE CONTOURS **TAMLA MOTOWN TMG 564**

These Things Will Keep Me Loving You
THE VELVELETTES **TAMLA MOTOWN TMG 580**

These three are representative of Motown's variety and consistent class.

Barbara McNair, an already well-known actress, joined the company for a while, and cut this slinky and gorgeously melodic song 'You're Gonna Love My Baby'.

The Contours had been with Motown from early on, but their initial successes with dance songs (such as 'Do You Love Me') never quite got the attention it deserved from the company. 'Just A Little Misunderstanding', along with its equally good flip 'Determination', has long been a favourite with aficionados who love its typically strong and insistent beat.

The Velvelettes another group who were kept in the shadows, but continued to turn out great records. This song was co-written by the veteran Harvey Fuqua (ex-Moonglows mainman) who worked it up for the girls with Johnny Bristol and Sylvia Moy.

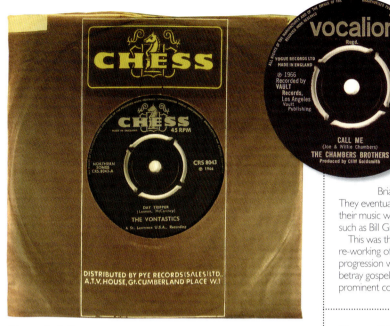

Day Tripper

THE VONTASTICS CHESS CRS 8043

Chess records, in Chicago, had been very active since their blues heyday, and, by developing their own house band, arrangers and producers, were fast trying to catch up some of the ground lost to Motown.

However, this one from The Vontastics was leased in from the small St Lawrence label. Various groups had tried re-working Beatles' songs, and this one was of the most radical and successful, though not in terms of sales.

Apart from the prominent bass, the rest (voices, guitars and horns) are trebly and insistent: the group even insert a 'Twist And Shout' vocal build half-way through. It made a one-week appearance on the US charts at No 100.

Searching For My Love

BOBBY MOORE AND THE RHYTHM ACES

CHESS CRS 8033

Another single to emerge on Chess in Britain was this lovely one from Bobby Moore. By all accounts, he led his group in a more benign way to some of the other band leaders of the time.

It is a reasonably simple song, but Moore's vocal lead and the answering choruses lift it into classic status.

It was on Chess' Checker subsidiary in the States, and, amazingly, the linked album of the same title came out in Britain as well. It was always a strong club spin in the Sixties, one that is immediately recalled by collectors.

Call Me

THE CHAMBERS BROTHERS
VOCALION VL 9276

Los Angeles had always had a thriving independent R&B scene, originally around the Central Avenue area, and the four local Chambers Brothers, Willie, George, Lester and Joe, linked up with white New Yorker Brian Keenan to form a R&B-based group. They eventually worked a crossover market by playing their music with a vaguely psychedelic twist at venues such as Bill Graham's Fillmore West ballroom.

This was their second issue in the UK, and is a re-working of the well-used 'Hang On Sloopy' chord progression with great call-and-response vocals that betray gospel influences. Rock instrumentation with a prominent cowbell supports it all.

Stay With Me

LORRAINE ELLISON
WARNER BROS. WB 5850

This unforgettable Lorraine Ellison record is perfect to illustrate how much deeper some singers could go. Dave Godin once suggested that his definition of Deep Soul is when the singer goes further out on a limb than might be expected – where they let go more than a little. 'Stay With Me' begins in a controlled fashion, and ends with Lorraine going into totally uncharted territory for both the song and her.

There is a good story behind how this happened: a huge 51-piece orchestra had been booked for a Frank Sinatra session, from which he had to pull out at almost the last minute. Producer Jerry Ragavoy was asked to make use of the musicians, who were being paid anyway, and took the almost-unknown Ellison into the studio with a set of pretty radical horn charts, which were far from the style of playing the musicians were expecting. Being professionals, they took it all on board, including the seemingly out-of-kilter horn sections.

This astounding performance was apparently achieved in only two takes, and Ragavoy elicits an emotional heart-searching performance from Lorraine comparable in power to that which Spector got from Tina Turner on 'River Deep Mountain High' after hours of beating her down. It is one of the most powerful, build-up songs ever recorded.

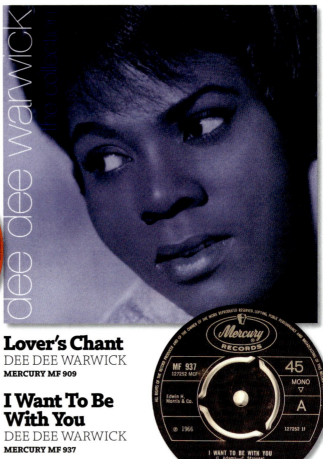

Patti's Prayer
PATTI LABELLE AND HER BELLES
ATLANTIC 584007

Take Me For A Little While
PATTI LABELLE & THE BLUEBELLS
ATLANTIC 584072

Another singer who could send shivers down your spine was Patti LaBelle. She could wow any audiences sensible enough to go and see her with The Bluebelles when they toured many of the small clubs in Britain in 1966, such as the famed Scene Club in Ham Yard. They always stayed to chat to fans after the show despite being emotionally and physically drained (both them and the audience).

Sarah Dash, Nona Hendryx and Cindy Birdsong gave wonderful support and looked suitably foxy, but there was no doubt that Patti's voice was the highlight.

'Patti's Prayer' and 'Take Me For A Little While' (the latter also recorded by Evie Sands) were probably too strong or too hardcore for the UK charts at the time, so the act remained a cult favourite.

Cindy joined the Supremes soon afterwards, bringing to an end a line-up that had survived for many years without a change. They didn't replace her, but went through a metamorphosis of their own when they became Labelle and discovered Bacofoil as stage costuming.

Lover's Chant
DEE DEE WARWICK
MERCURY MF 909

I Want To Be With You
DEE DEE WARWICK
MERCURY MF 937

Dee Dee Warwick, almost inevitably, was in sister Dionne's shadow, but for many fans it was Dee Dee's voice that excited.

'Lover's Chant' was written by Lorraine 'Stay With Me' Ellison and the song becomes an impassioned plea for attention both lyrically and through the arrangement from Horace Ott. Dee Dee pleads for her man, and who could refuse her on this showing.

The theme is continued with even more power on 'I Want To Be With You', and she catches our attention immediately with a high drawn-out shriek on the 'I'. Half-way through, the girlie chorus takes the lead on the verses, allowing Dee Dee to soar above them towards glorious climactic pleading on a genuinely dramatic record.

The B side – her version of 'Alfie' – is also wonderful. She is supported by a fine Ott arrangement with shimmering strings to provide what is, to many ears, the definitive reading of the song.

Sookie Sookie
DON COVAY
ATLANTIC AT 4078

James Brown wasn't the only guy on the as-yet untitled funk block. Covay, who had got his name around with 'See Saw', was getting down and dirty with this dancer; and it had all the hallmarks in place for the oncoming funk generation.

Grunts, basic lyrics, full horn lines and loose guitar lines all play their part towards building the whole. The peaks come with the repeated Sookie line where the instrumentation drops out. It showed much promise, which sadly remained largely unfulfilled for Don.

Whispers
JACKIE WILSON
CORAL Q 72487

This heavily Motown-influenced recording came just before Detroit's finest was about to enjoy a second coming in 1967 with 'Higher And Higher'.

Jackie builds the chorus in an impassioned performance and gives the track a distinctly Levi Stubbs/Four Tops feel (although with a higher register). This is one of those records that shows the extent to which Detroit had led the way towards the changes in Black American music.

Neighbour Neighbour
JIMMY HUGHES
ATLANTIC 584017

Willy Nilly
RUFUS THOMAS
ATLANTIC 584029

Never Like This Before
WILLIAM BELL
ATLANTIC 584076

The Atlantic label had fully cottoned on to soul being a hot-selling musical genre. As they changed from their black British label to the new red one, they were on top of their game with a good run of issues, which (except this first one) were leased in from the Fame label, coming from Stax in Memphis.

While the song 'Neighbour Neighbour' grabs an entry in this book with the Adlibs recording, Jimmy Hughes' original, which made US No66 in June, epitomises the feel of the soul club scene of that period. The R&B-flavoured base was still evident in most groups' approaches and the highly glossed pop soul hits were some way away from the feel of records demanded by the discerning club clientele.

Jimmy was born in Florence, Alabama, and was Percy Sledge's cousin, and had another Bubbling-under hit (No121) with 'Don't Lose Your Good Thing', in summer 1967.

Rufus Thomas' 'Willy Nilly' probably has one of the most distinctive Stax intros ever, using the same three bass notes that ushered in the Temptations' 'My Girl' – but with considerably more umph. Thomas shares the lines with the female singers, using his trademark lived-in growl to great effect as he attacks this simple song. One of its more memorable lines is the classic: 'The Boss with the red hot sauce knows how…'

William Bell's vocal delivery was more measured, as he based much of his breathing and phrasing on Otis Redding. 'Never Like This Before' also owes something to Sam And Dave in its production and arrangement – William was taking from the best there was. Bell released some great records over the years, although he seemed to remain in the second tier of artists in Memphis.

Ain't Love Good, Ain't Love Proud
JIMMY JAMES AND THE VAGABONDS
PICCADILLY 7N 35349

Meanwhile, back in the UK clubs that were playing Atlantic sounds, the best live act on the scene was Jimmy James and The Vagabonds. They were popular everywhere they played, especially in and around London, and were revered as total gods at the Birdcage Club in Portsmouth.

With the dual vocal attack of Jimmy James and Count Prince Miller, and more than solid back-up from Philip Chen (bass), Wallace Wilson (lead guitar), Carl Noel (organ), Milton James (baritone sax), Matt 'Fred' Fredericks (tenor sax) and Rupert Balgobin (drums), they could tear a place apart.

Soon after they reached London, they managed to get a slot on the Tonight TV show (Cliff Michelmore et al), but despite a series of great releases, including the very fine *New Religion* album, they never caught the power and sensuality of their live shows on record.

'Ain't Love Good, Ain't Love Proud' is indicative of their good taste in covers (which also included The Impressions, Tony Clarke, The Miracles and The Temptations), and

can take you back to the mega-sweaty shows led by 'Fat Boy' Jimmy James and The Count.

English Tea
ST LOUIS UNION
DECCA F 12386

After a vaguely Goon-like intro conversation, concluding with: 'There's not much going on round here', this oddball B side suddenly bursts into a driving club instrumental with heavy bass and organ. All-in-all, it is quite a hidden surprise on a follow-up record to St Louis Union's small hit cover of the Beatles''Girl'.

The group from Manchester included singer Tony Cassidy, lead guitarist Keith Miller, tenor sax man Alex Kirby, organist David Tomlinson, bass John Nicholls and drummer Dave Webb. It could be that this was more indicative of their sound than on 'Girl'. Either way, they dropped out of sight after one more, highly collectable, release on Decca with 'East Side Story'.

Hot Shot
THE BUENA VISTAS
STATESIDE SS 525

This (presumably) session-player recording offered another powerful club sound. It was arranged by Mike Terry, an ex-Motown sax player in the earlier house band led by the late Joe Hunter. By the mid-Sixties, Mike was jobbing around with some great arrangements and productions, including this, and some for the Platters on the Musicor label.

Hot Shot features heavy interplay between sax and trumpet against a bass and drum backbeat that breaks down here and there to interject what sounds like a Stax intro. The melody isn't too far from Len Barry's '1-2-3', making it a good club sound.

Crying My Heart Out
THE NEWBEATS
HICKORY 45-1387

Take equal measures of Motown instant-mix and Four Seasonings, add a splash of Land of 1000 Dances and you have this less-than-typical Nashville product from The Newbeats. They followed their foot-stomping trail of 'Bread And Butter', and gradually edged closer to Motown influences as and when they felt it safe to do so, to culminate in this string-punctuated dancer that was topped off with a generous ladle-full of Valli-esque screech.

In short, a fun record for all concerned.

She Ain't Lovin' You
THE DISTANT COUSINS
CBS 202352

Small print readers may anticipate another Four Seasons-linked item here by way of the writers and Bob Crewe's name as producer. Yet aside from the falsetto vocals and the end of the choruses, the song is more of a mix of the 'Hang On Sloopy' chords and some folk rock influences.

The two singers answer each other with the 'I Told You So' tale of both of them having lost the same girl. It's likely that The Distant Cousins were a Crewe studio concoction; Crewe houses the whole thing in a typically full production with every potential exit hole blocked with either percussion or vocals.

They had one more UK issue with Mr Sebastian, which was all about the Lovin' Spoonful main man.

DUSTY SPRINGFIELD

Dusty was Britain's brightest female star in the Sixties, bar none. While she possessed a voice that could adapt to many styles convincingly, it was her championing of early American soul that really marked her out and she helped to bring Martha & The Vandellas, Maxine Brown and some of the more soulful writings of Goffin and King to our attention.

Dusty auditions new back-singers...

Leaving the Springfields' happy easy country work, she was initially launched on the pure-pop, Spector-influenced route of 'I Only Want To Be With You' and 'Stay Awhile'. However, after her soulful reading of 'You Don't Have To Say You Love Me' it was obvious that her tastes lay deeper than pure pop stylings.

After that, there were sumptuous records such as 'Some Of Your Lovin'' and her version of 'Goin' Back', which stand as some of the best of the whole decade.

Delving into her albums, there are goodies aplenty to discover, that would be ripe for a rarities compilation to set alongside her many hits collections on the market.

It was no surprise that Dusty was the compere of the 1965 Sound Of Motown TV show, and sang a duet with Martha Reeves. She was nervous, but loved being with all the US stars she admired, excitedly chatting to everyone else as she waited to do her links. Many will remember her for her rich and infectious giggle. She was very special.

A classic Dusty live show.

The Great Airplane Strike

PAUL REVERE & THE RAIDERS FEATURING MARK
CBS 202411

Paul Revere and his gang of pretty boys were always going to be too American to make it really big on our shores, though many of their records were good.

This Terry Melcher production owes more than a little to the Stones. It powers along on a bed of fuzz guitar and maracas on a song made up of many verses, rather than the traditional verse/chorus format.

They are needed to tell the tale of the frustrating happenings of a journey thwarted by just about everything. Then, presumably when they are all exhausted anyway, the song is simply slowed down to nothing, rather than a complete stop or a fade.

A great sound all the way though, with a strong Jagger impression from front-man Mark Lindsay.

Cast Your Fate To The Wind
SHELBY FLINT **LONDON HLT 10068**

The Last Thing On My Mind THE WOMENFOLK **RCA 1522**

I Can't Grow Peaches On A Cherry Tree JUST US **CBS 202068**

What remained of folk music after Dylan's electrification and its commercialism with folk rock was a mixed bunch of sounds that usually kept melody pretty high on the agenda.

Vince Guaraldi's piano hit 'Cast Your Fate To The Winds', covered in the UK by Sounds Orchestral, was given a lovely vocal treatment by Shelby Flint in one of only two releases she had in Britain, the first being 'Angel On My Shoulder' back in 1961. She maintains the jazz qualities of the original while adding extra interest in the well-written lyrics for the tune.

The Womenfolk's vocals on Tom Paxton's 'The Last Thing On My Mind' were wonderfully warm. The five-piece group of Jean Amos, Leni Ashmore, Barbara Cooper, Judy Fine and Joyce James were well-schooled, having attended most of the key Californian colleges between them before forming the group. They played plenty of instruments, but usually stayed with guitars for TV shows on which, for some reason, they displayed a distressing need to wear matching tablecloths.

'Just Us' was a gentle and pretty production from the team of Chip Taylor and Al Gorgoni, and it appears to be that duo singing the song.

The record had a slow climb over some two months to reach No34 on the US charts before disappearing much more quickly. The name was revived in 1971 when 'Used To Be' made Billboard No103 on the Atlantic label.

Remember The Rain

BOB LIND
FONTANA TF 702

This follow-up to Lind's 'Elusive Butterfly' hit was once again was arranged by Jack Nitzsche, whose clever and distinctive use of strings lift each song.

There had been confusion at Lind's record company World Pacific as to which of his many great early songs to release as singles, 'Elusive Butterfly' initially being the last of four choices. By the time a follow-up was required there was confusion once again – DJ interest and sales being split between 'Remember The Rain' and its flip 'Truly Julie's Blues'. Consequently, the company took the unusual step of effectively killing both sides by quickly releasing another single, 'I Just Let It Take Me', far too early.

'Remember The Rain' has the same gossamer qualities of his 'Elusive Butterfly' hit, with intelligent lyrics that put it above most others at the time. Sadly it faded all too quickly from sight.

Come To Your Window

CHER
LIBERTY 12034

Cher's singles had previously been written either by Bob Dylan or her husband Sonny Bono, and the A side of this one, 'I Feel Something In The Air', is a Sonny song. However, hidden away on the flip is this Bob Lind song, which she handles as if it was written especially for her.

Cher had also cut a cover of 'Elusive Butterfly', which had been taken at a bit too much of a gallop, but this is another reflective and romantic Lind outing. It doesn't appear of either of his first two albums, nor to have been recorded by anyone else at the time.

Sonny Bono manages to cram a lot of bells and vaguely Spector-type sounds into the backing track, and somehow manages to get away with it without submerging Lind's song.

A Walk In The Black Forest (Our Walk Of Love)

SALENA JONES COLUMBIA DB 7818

Horst Jankowski's jaunty melody had already been a piano hit when this vocal version arrived. Salena Jones turns the bright tune into a sultry jazz trio number with some additional strings, completely changing the feel of the work. String, bass, drums and piano carry most of the arrangement, and help to make it a most distinctive recording.

Walkin' My Cat Named Dog

NORMA TANEGA
STATESIDE SS 496

A Street That Rhymes At Six A.M.

NORMA TANEGA
STATESIDE SS 520

Norma Tanega's breakthrough hit 'Walkin' My Cat Named Dog', with its distinctive harmonica line, made it to No22 in America, and even just scraped into the NME Top Twenty for a week at No19. However, the single's UK chances were spoilt by a rival version of the song from Barry McGuire that scraped into the NME chart for one week at No30.

Born in Vallejo, California, in 1939, Norma was an early singer/songwriter and a talented pianist and guitarist. 'A Street That Rhymes At Six A.M.' was her follow-up, which made only No129 on Billboard, and nowhere here.

The time-shifting song uses an unusual cello part with a bass, and appears to be about the need to look for new horizons: 'I'm looking for a new skyline.' Norma later moved to London and lived with Dusty Springfield for a lengthy period.

Tar And Cement
VERDELLE SMITH
CAPITOL CL 15456

Sometimes there is a record that is totally differently to all the other genres you usually enjoy; one that carries you along effortlessly without you quite realising why. This is a case in point.

It has a gorgeous melody that comes from an Italian song called 'Il Ragazzo Della Na Gluck', which Google translates as The Boy From The Na Gluck. Well-known American writer/producers Vance and Pockriss wisely wrote new words for the melody, coming up with, of all things, 'Tar and Cement'.

However, it is an effective song that puts a case for fighting the expansion of the urban sprawl. The country girl goes off to the big city leaving behind the meadows and wildlife, and experiences the loneliness of the city. When she eventually returns to the country, her haven has become covered with six-lane highways.

The arrangement begins the story quietly and sparingly, and gradually builds the backing with worm strings and the occasional little two-note slides.

Verdelle managed to climb to No38 on Billboard in August, but the record died a quick and most definite death here.

Probably the tar melted…

The Highway Code
THE MASTER SINGERS **PARLOPHONE R 5428**

The cat has just knocked over the 'unbelievable but true' box and, rather opportunely, out tumbles this 'song' that would have been of great use to Verdelle Smith had she ever encountered Britain's highways and by-ways.

Unbelievably, this record made it to No22 on the NME Chart in August, when obviously the heat had melted not just the tar but our brains as well, for it contains odd sections of the Highway Code sung delicately and harmoniously in Kings Singers style. So the question remains as to who bought it – and why? While it is a good example of a certain type of singing, one must wonder why anyone thought it was a good idea to try. Yet it sold…

Younger Girl/
All American Girl
THE HONDELLS
MERCURY MF 925

'Younger Girl' was one of the most obviously commercial tracks on the first Lovin' Spoonful album, but was never issued by the New York group as a single because, having such a plethora of great material, they were spoilt for choice.

Others saw the potential. The NY-based Critters took it to No42 on Billboard; this version, from the Gary Usher-produced Hondells, became the West Coast response, though it always trailed slightly, only getting to No52. Usher had used the Hondells' name for a string of motor bike releases, of which 'Little Honda' was the biggest, and this was a change to produce a quieter sound for them, a sound which was to last for several more issues, including a very good cover of Bob Lind's 'Cheryl's Goin' Home'. The flip here, 'All American Girl', is an archetypal piece of Californian cream with the trademark Usher harmonies and chugging guitars.

Just Across The River
THE RAM HOLDER BROTHERS
PARLOPHONE R 5471

Some attention to the Highway Code could well have been in order when Ram John Holder hit on an idea to publicise the release of 'Just Across The River'.

By need of explanation, The Ram Holder Brothers were a duo of Ram John and his brother Jim at the time when they were playing the Witches' Cauldron club in London's Belsize Park, but Jim decided to return to Guyana, leaving Ram John to form a small band (including a 19-year-old Fuzzy Samuels, who later played extensively with Stephen Stills et al) to play local gigs. To gain attention for the record, Ram decided it would be a wonderful idea to push a car over London Bridge… again and again.

The Press were duly invited en masse, but obviously found something better that day, leaving them puffed out after manoeuvring the car several times over the bridge and handing out fliers to bewildered passers-by. The record did actually get plenty of plays on the pirate station Radio London, who saw fit to push it into their top 20.

These days, the R&B/folky/gospel crossover record is collectable, as are Ram John's solo albums such as the fine *Black London Blues*.

The Ram Holder Brothers' gigs were usually around North London, though they did once make it to Stevenage…

Mind Excursion
THE TRADE WINDS **KAMA SUTRA KAS 202**

Writers, singers and producers Pete Anders and Vinnie Poncia had decided to keep The Trade Winds' name alive after the earlier surfy issues, and had started steering the sound towards what is now called Sunshine Pop. They could write great melodies and their voices had just the right plaintive qualities to sit well on this more relaxed form of harmony pop.

The title was deemed suspicious in some quarters, but lyrically it just managed to avoid being seen as too obviously drug-related as the whole thing was light enough in feel to be taken on the daydream level akin to the Lovin' Spoonful hit.

It entered the Billboard Hot 100 twice, eventually making No51. Anders and Poncia had constructed a perfect pop track and vocals, setting the template for later work they did with the Critters – who were just getting their second hit at the time.

Questions And Answers
THE CALIFORNIA IN CROWD
FONTANA TF 779

This was a pure slab of West Coast harmony pop produced by Snuff Garrett in Tokens/ Happenings mode.

It appeared briefly in the US charts, getting to No92, and warranted a follow-up called 'If I Knew A Magic Word'.

There were several groups in the states that used the In Crowd name, and this lot were probably the same ones who had a couple of issues on the Tower label.

The 'California' part of their name was tacked on to the rare British issue to avoid confusion with the Mod group.

Night Time Girl
M.F.Q. RCA 1514

Oh, the joy of taking a chance on a record based on the small print names, and finding that you've come up trumps! The song was written by Al Kooper and Irwin Levine, and arranged and produced by Jack Nitzsche…well that in itself is enough to warrant purchase. Add in the eclectic and talented M.F.Q. and you have to have a winner.

Jack's arrangement must have been done with The Beatles' recently released *Revolver* album in mind, as there is a prominent sitar, tabla and other drones used throughout the well-paced pop song. However, there is no attempt to feature them other than as part of the whole. It only managed to bubble under the US charts, reaching No122, but that was probably several dozens of places better than it reached in the UK.

> "I learned a new tuning on the guitar that was fairly psychedelic and started writing songs in that tuning. 'Night Time Girl' was written for The Byrds, but rejected by them. Aaron Schroeder, my publisher at the time, was a good hustler of material and the song somehow ended up with the MFQ." **AL KOOPER**

Where Did We Go Wrong
THE SANDS OF TIME
PYE 7N 17140

There were always plenty of British groups going for the high harmony approach to songs, some with more success than others.

The Sands Of Time, formed in Ealing in 1962, didn't get their break until they were spotted by Jackie Trent at a club in Manchester. She reported back to her husband Tony Hatch who, having a penchant for harmonies, introduced them to Pye where they had three issues. This slow single, which recalls the Ivy League, was the first.

The group was a foursome comprising Ron Brown (drums), David Booker (guitar), Pete Durham (piano) and Tommy McQuarter (bass). Two of their tracks, including this one, made it onto the first volume of the Ripples series.

My Girl The Month Of May
DION AND THE BELMONTS HMV POP 1565

Did this man ever make a bad record? On occasion, the super-cool Dion re-united with The Belmonts for various reasons, and in this case it was to make two records that emerged on the HMV label: this one and 'Movin' Man' in 1967.

This is quite unlike anything else they cut, and begins with Dion almost scat singing before the verse kicks in. The group provide massed Ba-ba-ba vocals for Dion to soar above and sing against. It's a record that pays heed to the way vocal groups were moving at the time, and yet manages to remain a total one-off.

It later cropped up sung by Richard Thompson on the *Bunch* album in 1972, which was a sort of R&R collaboration between past and present Fairporters, Ex-Eclection members and Linda Peters.

Tell It To The Rain
THE 4 SEASONS
PHILIPS BF 1538

The 4 Seasons, as they were now called, had continued to turn out releases of extraordinary quality and had managed to retain steady sales on both sides of the pond.

This single is slightly different in that it is not written from within the group, and comes from a time when they were looking to widen their influences.

The song, covered well in the UK by The Whales, is as usual full of memorable hooks and a chorus that sticks after one play. Featuring arrangement from Artie Schroeck rather than the tried and tested Charlie Callelo, Bob Crewe's production is as full as ever, with Frankie Valli's three and a half octave voice still at full power at this point.

I Only Came To Dance With You
SCOTT ENGEL & JOHN STEWART CAPITOL CL 15440

As well as being a good record, this is an excellent example of record company opportunism. Scott Engel and John Maus became mega popular with the Walker Brothers, and companies knew that they were active with a number of issues on the West Coast well before the 'Brothers' were formed.

This is one of those earlier projects, originally issued in 1963 as by The Dalton Brothers (years before the Eagles decided to assume the personas of the old outlaw gang) on the small Martay label. Scott had apparently always sought to be in a 'brothers' group since he had heard the Everlys, and this was his first shot at it.

The song, with its big, rolling, almost Spector-like production by his pal Mark Taylor, was written by one Jim Smith, aka James Marcus Smith, aka Jett Powers, aka Orville Woods (especially for black radio stations), aka PJ Proby. Around this time, both Scott and John had been involved with all manner of unsuccessful one-off singles and had been a one-time member of the Routers road band. Tower Records even added the line 'Original Members of The Walker Brothers' to a tie-in album, which includes several lower-grade tracks that may have had no input from the pair at all.

Fragile Child
THE GOLLIWOGS
VOCALION VF 9283

The Golliwogs were soon to become Creedence Clearwater Revival, and this was the second of their singles to get a British release after their version of 'Brown Eyed Girl'.

It is clear that the classic CCR heavy rhythm guitar trademark is already well in place here, which can be found here prominently on both the intro and outro. In other way too, it feels like a CCR record, even through it's not a John Fogerty song. The record doesn't appear to have registered much in the States or here, which goes some way to explaining its ongoing collectability.

Won't Find Better Than Me
THE KIT KATS
LONDON HLW 10075

The Kit Kats were one of Philadelphia's most popular local groups, being able to play long hours in bars and clubs and covering a wider variety of rock, pop and soulish material.

Formed by Kit Stewart and Carl Hausman, this upbeat and bouncy number was one of their mainstays. They first issued it in 1966 as The Kit Kats, and then came back to it in 1970 under the name New Hope, when it sold well enough to make No59 in the States. Both issues came out over here on London Records.

A good recent double CD compilation of theirs on the revived Jamie/Guyden label ended with the real treat of a piece of film showing them performing the song in a club in the Sixties, offering ample proof of their abilities.

Peace Of Mind
THE MAGNIFICENT MEN
CAPITOL CL 15462

'It isn't rhythm & blues…it isn't Rock 'n' Roll…it isn't pop. It's a combination of all these…and yet…' – so wrote Douglas 'Jocko' Henderson (WDAS of Philadelphia), one of the best-known and respected black DJs on the US Sixties radio scene. He was solidly behind the Magnificent Men, who were one of the few white groups to sound convincing on well-chosen material culled from Motown, Stax, Curtis Mayfield and Joe Tex.

The seven-piece played and sung everything themselves, and knew how to present a good show, evidenced by their second 'live' album, which (unlike many from that period) really does sound like the genuine article.

'Peace Of Mind' was a big ballad co-written by lead singer Dave Bupp, who delivers it with a strong and resonant baritone. The studio version was also on their debut album alongside tracks such as Gladys Knight's 'Just Walk In My Shoes', Errol Garner & Johnny Burke's 'Misty', and the classic 'Stormy Weather'. In some ways they were Blood Sweat & Tears before their time, and would have been one of the acts in this book worth seeing live at the time.

"Never seen anything like The Magnificent Men… unbelievable!"
JERRY BLAVAT (WFIL, TV – 'THE GEATER WITH THE HEATER')

It's My Pride
THE GUESS WHO?
KING KG 1044

Canada gets a look in now with The Guess Who? – one of the country's most popular bands in the Sixties.

This is the B side of – and a total contrast to – 'His Girl', which was a faintly soppy song filled with glockenspiel and echoes of McCartney at his most simplistic.

'It's My Pride' is a powerhouse Randy Bachman song that, while borrowing from The Who, was certainly driving towards heavy rock ahead of the pack.

Bachman went on to follow this direction when he formed Bachman Turner Overdrive in 1972, after leaving The Guess Who? in 1970 and cutting his solo album *Axe*. This shows that the roots were firmly in place back in 1966.

Sitting In The Park
GEORGIE FAME
COLUMBIA DB 8096

Georgie Fame helped to stoke much interest in Black American music as on the occasions when he and his band were at the Flamingo Club, for example, they were always willing to chat and hang out with fans who shared the same musical obsessions.

Then, there was the man's voice, with its gorgeous husk that managed to make even his most pop-like offerings attractive.

Then there was his playing. He would sit alone on the stage before a performance, in an empty auditorium, improvising aimlessly on the organ, oblivious to anything around him. To put it simply, the man always loved his music. He didn't just cover this song, but re-worked it into his own interpretation while keeping the languid feel of Billy Stewart's original version.

It's not necessarily better that the original, but it is different, and a genuine appreciation for the song shows through.

John Phillips

As the main writer and acknowledged leader of The Mamas and Papas, John Phillips was responsible for a string of hits that helped to define the middle years of the Sixties. While John was the main writer, each member of the group had a special part to play in the group's success, and for an all-too-brief amount of time they reigned supreme in delivering a light and airy set of sounds that remain timeless.

'California Dreamin'' and 'Monday Monday' set the tone, and from there John led them to re-interpret songs from The Beatles, The Shirelles and even Phil Spector, as well as adding to their own catalogue of songs.

Although schooled in folk groups and folk clubs in New York and elsewhere, their sound was very much a West Coast summery sound as they used the same musicians who made Beach Boys and Spector tracks, with the addition of chaps such as PF Sloan. John also was largely responsible for Scott McKenzie's huge San Francisco 1967 hit, but thereafter ran into personal and drug problems.

He re-emerged in 1970 with his John Phillips – *The Wolf King Of LA* – solo album, which many collectors rate extremely highly.

The sole surviving group member Michelle Phillips remembers him: 'John was a very gifted vocal

arranger, from his days with The Journeymen. He had jazz influences and took from groups like the Hi-Los. He knew who should sing what. He would give out parts to whoever was in the room, convincing people they could do even very complex parts. He expected us to learn them. It could be informal at first, and then he would change parts.

'We wasted quite a bit of studio time because he would change the backgrounds after we had listened to the lead vocals. We were all there for the track recordings, all the way through, up to 17-18 hours at a stretch.

'It was all quite organic, because sometimes we hadn't even finished writing the song!'

Alice Designs
THE SUGARBEATS
POLYDOR 56120

The Sugarbeats, from Hornchurch in Essex, were a breeding ground for future members of Tony Rivers' Castaways and Grapefruit, including as they did Pete and Geoff Swettenham, John Perry and Martin Shaer; the latter later moving to Canada and discovering Bryan Adams. Also included, was Ken Gold who went on to make a successful songwriting career, with hits from The Real Thing among others. At the time of their previous single, 'I Just Stand Here', they were all around 16 years old, still at school, and had to have their parents sign the contracts for them.

Alice Designs was written by Californian scene-maker Tandyn Almer, a man whose work is much revered in some quarters, and the song had a distinct Association feel to it.

"The 2nd (and final) Sugarbeats' record was 'Alice Designs' written by Tandyn Almer. As you are probably aware, 'Along Comes Mary' (his hit with The Association) was wordplay on Marijuana, and 'Alice' was a play on LSD. We had no idea of this as we were six fresh-faced virginal 'surfie' laddies from Essex who had not even taken an aspirin! We thought the lyrics were strange examples of what was coming out of California at that time. We were VERY excited about recording a song written by a hit songwriter, and one from California to boot!"

KEN GOLD

No Fair At All
THE ASSOCIATION
LONDON HLT 10118

The six-piece Association (the classic line-up being Brian Cole, Jim Yester, Russ Giguere, Terry Kirkman, Ted Bluechel and Gary Alexander) had cemented their place with their early hits 'Along Comes Mary' and 'Cherish', which had been produced by cult hero Curt Boettcher.

After the later was dropped by the group, Bones Howe took the board for much of their output, though this song was produced by Jim Yester's brother Jerry from the MFQ (see earlier).

The group specialised in wonderful six-part harmony that interwove vocal lines that were distinctly different from most groups of the day. While they often look as if they had stepped in from behind a bank counter, they were musically quite radical at this stage. 'No Fair At All' builds from a quiet intro that uses Kirkman's flute-playing to the multi-vocal parts that soar above each other.

A 1987 Edsel Records Association compilation delivered a delightful surprise, as its version of this song was quite different from the original issue in that it had extra very effective vocal lines at work, making it an essential gem for fans to find.

Mr Dieingly Sad
THE CRITTERS
LONDON HLR 10071

Bad Misunderstanding
THE CRITTERS
LONDON HLR 10101

Marryin' Kind Of Love
THE CRITTERS
LONDON HLR 10119

These three singles from The Critters are cracking records that fit the criteria for this book perfectly.

The Plainfield, New Jersey, group had first hit with their version of John Sebastian's 'Younger Girl', which they rapidly followed-up with one of their own in the form of 'Mr Dieingly Sad', one of the key tracks that led Sanctuary's John Reed and Kingsley Abbott to the feel and ideas behind the Ripples series of CDs.

Written by Don Ciccone (who was later to join The 4 Seasons), the record reached US No17 and was a perfect sad, summer song with prominent bass and light

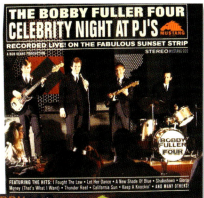

restrained guitars that set the tone for the plaintive feel of many of the group's best recordings.

Other members of the group were drummer Jack Decker and bass Kenny Gorka, while both guitarist Jimmy Ryan and organist Chris Darway also contributed strong material.

While many of their songs came from within the group, the other two singles here came from the Anders & Poncia team.

US No55-hit 'Bad Misunderstanding' can also be found on he *Trade Winds* album where it is easy to hear how close (vocally) Anders and Poncia were to The Critters' voices, and how good they were at producing commercial radio-friendly material. It's a mid-tempo song that builds to a strong and full chorus, that says…gasp… 'The trip was fine, but now we're landing…'

'Marryin' Kind Of Love' is another Anders and Poncia song, this time with input from Doc Pomus, and is a slower love song that again builds to bigger choruses and a hanging high voice and guitar shimmer, using all the commercial production hooks of the last one. Despite this, it only made No111 on Billboard.

The group had five singles and a good album released here without any big sales.

Above: Phil Spector sits in with Bobby Fuller.
Below: A bonus live album in the De-Phi retrospective CD set.

I Fought The Law
THE BOBBY FULLER FOUR
LONDON HL 10030

This is a Sonny Curtis song that first appeared on the *In Style With The Crickets* 1961 album. It is a classic version from Fuller and his gang with heavy rhythm guitar, and really good vocals. It's possibly the best recorded version, despite the popularity of Joe Strummer's one with The Clash. OK, maybe The Clash had the best rock version, and this was the best pop-rock one.

Phil Spector once sat in on piano with The Bobby Fuller Four at La Cave Pigalle in LA, and showed interest in recording Fuller on his Philles label. Maybe this could have happened had it not been for Bobby's mysterious death in July 1966.

Crazy Like A Fox
LINK CROMWELL
LONDON HLB 10040

Although most of us had no idea at the time, Link Cromwell was actually Lenny Kaye, who went on to work as Patti Smith's lead guitarist and to be the compiler of the famous *Nuggets* album of original Sixties punkish material. He worked around the Eastern Seaboard with a group called The Zoo, playing non-prestigious gigs in frat band style, covering songs like 'I'm Crying, She's Not There' and 'Little Latin Lupe Lu'.

'Crazy Like A Fox', a one-off issue, is a bit of an oddity: it is essentially a snarly anti-establishment diatribe in folk rock vein, but it also has the curious injection of the riff from The Drifters' 'I'll Take You Where The Music's Playing' at odd moments. Very New York!

The Misunderstood
I CAN TAKE YOU TO THE SUN
FONTANA TF 777

I Can Take You To The Sun were an American outfit with shifting personnel that John Peel helped bring to England (in fact, this was one of the first groups he helped). Once here, they made this psychy single before their line-up broke up.

The group that cut this track was Tony Hill (keys), Rick Moe (drums), George Phelps (lead guitar), Rick Brown (vocals/harmonica), Steve Whiting (bass) and Glen 'Fernando' Campbell (steel guitar). A previous American member Greg Treadway probably departed just before this single.

Two other strong singles, 'Children Of The Sun' and 'You're Tuff Enough' emerged in 1969.

A steel player in a band in Britain was most unusual at the time, and Glen Campbell's distinctive and attacking style made him popular with several bands. Campbell formed the second version of the band around himself, and the later line-up included assorted future members of The Nice and Van Der Graaf Generator, among others.

This brooding single was way ahead of public taste at the time.

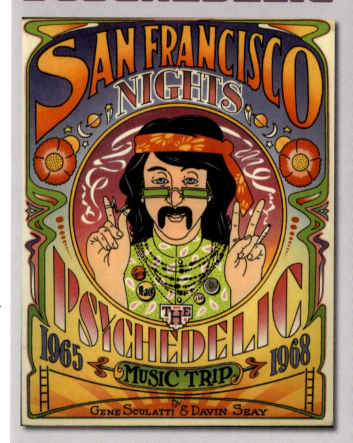

And then Psychedelia came creeping in…slowly at first…but (by the end of 1966) there was an increasing number of strange guitar sounds inspired by the *Revolver* album, vocal distortions, trippy lyrics and other general weirdness.

Album covers went overboard with graphics imported from San Francisco poster art, and light shows and paisley patterns began to invade everything.

The best of early Psych came in rock form, before Los Angeles attempted to subvert it into easily digested pop forms, in the way they had with folk rock. The bands of San Francisco, often rooted in a mix of blues and folk, were far from being pop, but, despite their rootsy and eclectic approaches, were becoming popular far beyond

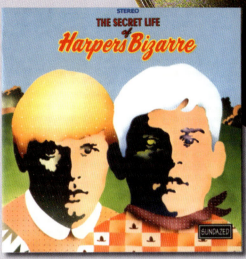

their normal areas. The Charlatans were in the vanguard with their oddball blend of folk, rock and Vaudevillian influences at the Red Dog Saloon. Big Brother and the Holding Company had Janis Joplin to set them apart from a regular blues band, Quicksilver Messenger Service had the folky writing of Dino Valente, and the Grateful Dead were starting out on their own, very particular, road and involving themselves with Ken Kesey's Merry Pranksters, who spread colourful and drug-fuelled aspects of Psych via a series of the famous Acid Tests and other key events.

Promoter Bill Graham opened the Fillmore West as the key venue, followed by the Fillmore East, and the whole scene was soon a cacophony of sound, colour and mixed media events. Jerry Garcia's longtime lady friend Mountain Girl, who was one of the Pranksters, recall's The Fillmore: 'The Fillmore was the best – no contest. It's still the best. It had wooden floors and it was the right shape. No seats so people could move around and dance. Everyone sounded good there.' She describes the Trips Festival: 'It was over three nights and was the first really big collaborative effort in SF. It was in the Longshoremen's Hall, which was the perfect place – an architectural gem – tall, narrow and with mezzanines in various places. There was a mass of different things: film-makers, light shows, and all aspects of the experimental community.'

Something new and radical was happening…

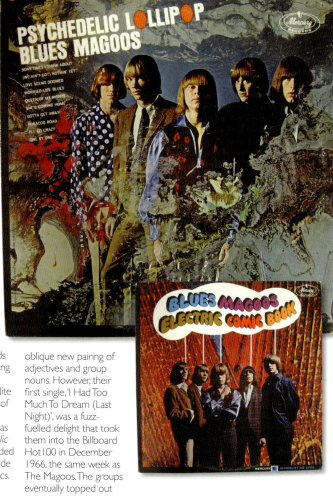

(We Ain't Got) Nothin' Yet
THE BLUES MAGOOS
MERCURY MF 954

I Had Too Much To Dream (Last Night)
THE ELECTRIC PRUNES
REPRISE RS 20532

Before the main effect of the San Francisco bands was felt, some groups were off the mark in seeking to push the boundaries of rock.

The Blues Magoos had begun playing at the Nite Owl Café in Greenwich Village, importing some of the West Coast elements into the similarly arts-based café scene. '(We Ain't Got) Nothin' Yet' was also the first track on their first album, *Psychedelic Lollipop*, on which the key track was their extended version of 'Tobacco Road,' which they turned inside out with all manner of guitar and effects histrionics.

The Electric Prunes could probably have managed to make it on the strength of their name alone, which at the time set the standard for oblique new pairing of adjectives and group nouns. However, their first single, 'I Had Too Much To Dream (Last Night)', was a fuzz-fuelled delight that took them into the Billboard Hot 100 in December 1966, the same week as The Magoos. The groups eventually topped out at No5 for The Magoos and No11 for the Prunes. Britain, by contrast, was not yet ready…

For What It's Worth (Stop, Hey What's That Sound)
THE BUFFALO SPRINGFIELD ATLANTIC 584077

Tudor Records in Muswell Hill was a favourite haunt for many North Londoners. Each week, they always stocked every mainstream single release and duplicated their own lists of them' – which made a very handy reference resource well before publishers realised the usefulness of such things. The line from the song 'There's something happening here, and what it is ain't exactly clear' described it exactly. Although it was lyrically about American events that were not too well publicised at the time in Britain, it ushered in a different style of music.

The Buffalo were one of those rare and wonderful groups whose ranks contained almost too much talent: Steve Stills, Neil Young and Ritchie Furay, along with Dewey Martin and Bruce Palmer, who were to produce some of the most memorable music in the late Sixties before splitting to go separate ways.

The three subsequent Buffalo Springfield albums became almost more important to us than the singles that were taken from them. During the Sixties, album sales began to equal single sales in unit terms, and albums generated more income for the record companies: a change was indeed happening…

CHESS 45 RPM
MADE IN ENGLAND

NORTHERN
SONGS
CRS.8043-A
CRS 8043-A
℗ 1966

DAY TRIPPER
(Lennon, McCartney)
THE VONTASTICS
A St. Lawrence U.S.A., Recording

Stateside 45 R.P.M.
MADE IN GT. BRITAIN

DEMONSTRATION
RECORD—NOT
FOR SALE
Palmina
Music
Shan-Todd
45-KR-4706
(15.7.66)
© 1966
(A 'Swan'
Recording)
S.S 525

HOT SHOT (2.37)
(T. Shannon—C. Cisco—N. Ameno)
THE BUENA VISTAS
Arranged: Mike Terry
A Magi Production
E.M.I. RECORDS LIMITED

The Critters
NEW YORK BOUND

FIVE O'CLOCK WORLD
C&C 1230
The VOGUES
CO & CE

Kama Sutra
45 rpm
KAS 202
℗ 1966
KAS.202-A

MIND EXCURSION
(Andreoli, Poncia Jr.)
THE TRADE WINDS
Produced by Anders-Poncia
ROBERT MELLIN

MCA
EXTENDED PLAY
1-2-3 LIKE A BABY
I STRUCK IT RICH IT'S THAT TIME OF THE YEAR
STEREO
MCEP3
LEN BARRY

THE BATMAN THEME
PLAYED BY THE MARKETTS

Hickory
RECORDS, INC.
NASHVILLE, TENN.
MADE IN ENGLAND
ACUFF-ROSE
45-1387-A
45-1387
℗ 1966

CRYING MY HEART OUT
(Melson, Mathis)
THE NEWBEATS
Produced by Wesley Rose

Mercury
RECORDS

MF 925   45
127248 MCF
MONO
Palace Music   ▽
B
℗ 1966   127248 2F

ALL AMERICAN GIRL
(R. Burns/G. Usher)
THE HONDELLS
with accompaniment directed by
Gary Usher

LONDON
AMERICAN RECORDINGS
45 R.P.M
MADE IN ENGLAND
THE DECCA RECORD CO. LTD
Recorded by
MUSTANG,
HOLLYWOOD
GEMA
BIEM NCB   HL
Acuff-Rose   10030
S

I FOUGHT THE LAW
(Curtis)
BOBBY FULLER FOUR

ember records
45 R.P.M.
EMB S227
ASSIGNING FIRST
PUBLISHED 1966
Sparta/B.I.E.M.

READY, STEADY
(Howard Blaikley, Amurri & H. Tical)
THE CLOCKWORK ORANGES
Produced by Jim Economides
A Vedette Recording

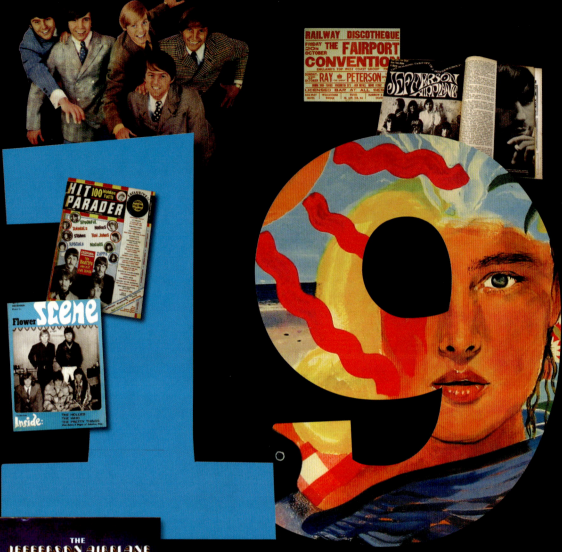

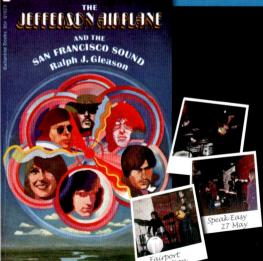

Fairport Convention

Speak Easy
27 May

The Summer Of Love is a conjunction of outlandish fashions, hippie lifestyles, facepaint, San Franciscan influences, aspirations for peace, and psychedelic music experimentations. UK charts, though bookended by hits from the likes of Humperdink, Jones and Frank & Nancy Sinatra, are better remembered for the glorious trio of 'Whiter Shade Of Pale', 'All You Need Is Love' and 'San Francisco (Be Sure To Wear Some Flowers In Your Hair)'.

Media focus on drugs helps police to crack down following some high-profile arrests of three Rolling Stones. The Monterey Pop Festival becomes a real pointer to the future as the audience appreciates Otis Redding, Simon & Garfunkel and Hendrix.

The Beatles release *Sgt. Pepper* to universal acclaim, but Brian Wilson fails to complete his *Smile* masterwork. The Hair musical opens in New York, and the first issue of Rolling Stone magazine emerges with the free gift of a roach clip. Brian Epstein, The Beatles' manager and benign guiding force, dies at the height of their success.

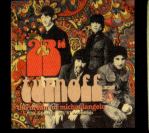

67

Elvis Presley marries , BBC Radio 1 is launched, the Torrey Canyon oil tanker runs aground, Concorde is unveiled and 'In the Heat of the Night' wins best film

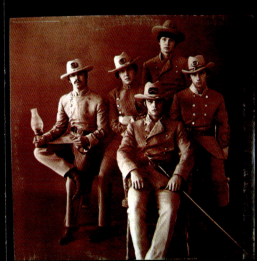

Kind Of A Drag
THE BUCKINGHAMS
STATESIDE SS 588

A fully orchestrated arrangement, built on organ and brass, introduced this US chart topper of February 1967 (despite the UK issue saying 1966 on the label).

The youthful-sounding and attractive lead voice is enhanced by the group's backing vocals, which add immediate warmth to the fast song. The five-piece Chicago outfit comprised Nick Fortune, Dennis Tufano, Carl Giammarese, Jon-Jon Poulos and Marty Grebb and could be described as a poppy version of blue-eyed soul.

They produced a run of good albums in the States including one called *In One Ear And Gone Tomorrow*, moving from a vaguely Beatles look to a double album where they sported both American Civil War Unionist and Confederate uniforms. It's called covering the bases…

Show Me
JOE TEX
ATLANTIC 584102

Joe Tex's career
began in the
mid-Fifties after
he won a talent
contest at the
Apollo Theatre in
Harlem, but despite
several smaller label
issues, it wasn't until
1965 that he found real
success with 'Hold On To
What You've Got'.

That was a slow soulful ballad, whereas
'Show Me' is a fast dancer – which is perhaps
why it wasn't the big hit it should have been,
as the soul hits in the UK at the time tended to
be the mid-tempo numbers from Wilson Pickett
and Eddie Floyd. However, it did reach No35
Stateside.

Tex's voice works well against the bass, chorus
and the rapidly descending brass hook lines, but all
these elements failed to get UK sales.

Ready, Willing And Able
JIMMY HOLIDAY & CLYDIE KING
LIBERTY LIB 12058

'Ready, Willing And Able' is a great duet from
Jimmy Holiday and the experienced session singer
Clydie King, whose voice is mixed high enough on
this song for her to really carry it.

Built on a traditional 1, 1-2 rhythm with bass
heavy, the song's chorus is instantly memorable.
The interplay between King and Holiday, while not
as overt as Otis and Carla, is pitched just right for
the lyrics.

Mississippi-born Holiday had a string of
Bubbling-under US hits, but never quite reached
the same status of his contemporaries, despite
having a voice that could rival any of them.

Clydie King's curriculum vitae covers all manner
of sessions during the Sixties, including the
majestic 'The Thrill Is Gone' on Imperial Records in
1965, which
sadly doesn't
qualify for this
book through
its lack of a
Sixties UK
release.

Everytime
LINDA CARR
STATESIDE SS 2058

Any small-print readers would
immediately pick this as a likely winner
– the writers Oldham/Penn and the
producer Rick Hall being beloved by
rootsy soul fans.

However, what you get here is one of the best
Motown soundalikes of the period, with Miss Carr and
her backing singers recreating the feel of The Supremes at their height,
but without that oh-so-perfect gloss. Their voices have just enough
edgy imperfection to make the record sound like a second-string
Motown group. All the back-up elements are in place, and it's a
strong song.

It was Carr's only UK issue, and it originated from the splendid New
York-based Bell label that was based at 1776 Broadway in the heart of
Sixties music-land.

Linda Carr did pop up briefly in the UK on the Soul Explosion tour
in 1967, very low down on a bill that was led by Sam & Dave, Arthur
Conley and Percy Sledge.

Get On Up
THE ESQUIRES
STATESIDE SS 2048

This slab of early funky soul took the comparatively unknown group up to No11 on Billboard, where this ode to the continued interest in dance crazes – the boogaloo and the shing-a-ling – remained for three weeks in a row.

The song was co-written by Bunky Sheppard, who had led his group The Sheppards on the Chicago scene from about 1959. Mill Edwards of The Sheppards added the distinctive bass voice hook to 'Get on Up' as a foil to the higher floater vocals of The Esquires (who were Bunky's other main group).

It's interesting to muse on EMI's UK marketing at this time, as they had moved from individually coloured label sleeves to ones that pictured albums of their diverse acts. This record came in a sleeve that combined shots of acts as varied as Lee Dorsey, Ray Charles and Stevie Wonder, The Seekers, Nina & Frederik, Herb Alpert and The Singing Postman!

It is reminiscent of the old US inner album sleeve of Capitol's that seemed to refuse to accept that there was any need to differentiate between Fifties style smoochy MOR acts and the new R&R malarkey. Why didn't they ever see the need to have one MOR sleeve design and one aimed solely at the youth markets? What were they thinking of?

With This Ring
THE PLATTERS **STATESIDE SS 2007**

Washed Ashore (On A Lonely Island In The Sun)
THE PLATTERS **STATESIDE SS 2042**

In their Fifties heyday, it would have been difficult to imagine that The Platters could re-invent themselves so effectively. The addition of Sonny Turner's new lead voice took them toward a new Drifters-rooted Sixties commerciality and a run of some fabulous records, of which these are just two.

'With This Ring', produced by New York veteran Luthor Dixon at Mirasound Studios, rushed up to No14 in the States, while 'Washed Ashore' (produced by another vet, Richard 'Popcorn' Wylie) became stuck on the beach at No56 – although it was every bit as good a production.

Trivia buffs please note that 'With This Ring' was recorded at Mirasound on the very day that they had the brand new Ampex G-1000 machine installed. This style of mid-Sixties soul is now referred to as Beach Music in the US, roughly an equivalent to Britain's Northern Soul scene. The common factor is a love of danceable Sixties music.

By the Seventies, there were many Platters offshoot groups on the road made up of members from different eras. There were also others who simply masqueraded under the name. One handbill even proclaimed a 'Drifters' act as Motown legends.

Nobody
KIM WESTON
MGM 1382

Kim Weston was one of the earlier Motown escapees, having moved over to MGM. At Motown, she had produced some of the best-loved collector's records of the era, and had been one of the lesser acts granted a UK fan club charter when the old TMAS club was split up. Yet somehow she was marginalised at the label as the Supremes swept everything before them.

This was the third of her UK MGM releases, which had the commercial Motownesque B side 'You're Just The Kind Of Guy' – which is probably the preferred side for collectors.

'Nobody', by contrast, is a more radical outing with no obvious commercial feel. The song is dominated by an adventurous arrangement with something approaching Indian influences, with clicky percussion and some most interesting string lines. It's as if they had listened closely to *Revolver* and had integrated influences where few had thought to put them.

Rodger Collins
SHE'S LOOKIN GOOD
VOCALION VF 9285

If you're looking for the ultimate dance record, this is undoubtedly one of the best with its bass-led rhythm and Rodger Collins' convincingly macho delivery. Rodger was born in Texas and raised in San Francisco, and this one almost took him into the Billboard Top 100, but it got stuck for two weeks at No101.

Wilson Pickett grabbed the song the next year and took it up to No15, showing that the potential was there all along.

It was Rodger's only UK release, but was a corker of its type and justifiably a popular inclusion on CD compilations.

For Your Precious Love
OSCAR TONEY JNR
STATESIDE SS 2033

Oscar was born in Selma, Alabama in 1939. All of his earlier musical involvement was within the gospel world in various groups, including The Sensational Melodies of Joy. He then moved to a less church-orientated group called The Searchers, and from there into solo work.

'For Your Precious Love' brought him his biggest success, reaching its US peak at No23. Reviving a song normally associated with Jerry Butler and The Impressions, Oscar lets his gospel experience re-surface with the long-spoken section that dominates the first half of the recording, turning it virtually into a sermon. He then sings with a richness and depth that almost seems wrong for a hit record, making it one of the deepest soul records ever to approach the US top 20.

At that stage, few UK buyers would have found it accessible, but over the years its reputation has grown and many more now appreciate its undoubted quality.

We Trust In A Better Way Of Life
THE POOR THINGS **CBS 202431**

She's Dangerous
THE SECRETS **CBS 202585**

Look At Me, Look At Me
THE KOOL **CBS 203003**

Without little accumulated knowledge about these three groups (maybe CBS weren't so hot on biographical publicity sheets in this period), your attention is drawn to them on the worth of their music alone.

The Poor Things, with their sole release, sound like a cross between a 1965-era Animals and Question Mark & The Mysterions with '96 Tears'. They survive a totally naff spoken intro to deliver a Farfisa-filled punkish ode to a better future.

The Secrets were one of Clifford T Ward's early bands, and this represents the musical hot bed of the Kidderminster and Stourport-On-Severn scene.

'She's Dangerous' is the more interesting B side of 'Infatuation', which was a more standard beaty number and their second of three releases. Both were Cliff Ward songs and show just what a good writer he was.

The Kool managed to produce one of the earliest and best UK versions of the Sunshine Music genre. 'Look At Me, Look At Me' can be likened to an update of The Ivy League approach, but a little faster and with added ba-ba–bas counterpointing other group harmonies.

All three of these were solid records that have sadly sunk with very little trace.

What's The Difference Chapters 1, 2 & 3
SCOTT MCKENZIE
CBS 2816, 3309 & 3393 (1968)

While the A side 'San Francisco', issued initially by CBS with a special flower motif in the centre of the label, was heard everywhere to the point of overload, I wonder how many people flipped it to enjoy the B Side 'What's The Difference'. This was a gentle Scott McKenzie song with a lovely melody and restrained singing that always stuck with me.

His follow-up 'Like An Old-Time Movie' almost inevitably didn't repeat the sales of the first one, but tucked away once again on the B side was 'What's The Difference Chapter 2', with 'Chapter 3' following on the flip of the 1968 release 'Holy Man'.

Scott was offering variations on the main theme, and each Chapter added to the whole as well as standing up on its own merits — testament to him being able to work with differing feels.

I Won't Hurt You
NEO MAYA
PYE 7N 17371

This absolutely scrummy one-off is a cover of The West Coast Pop Art Experimental Band's obscure song. It was made as a solo outing by Episode Six member Graham Carter, who used the name Neo Maya to differentiate the work from the group's normal output.

Co-written by the ubiquitous West Coaster Michael Lloyd and a couple from that band, the original was an example of Velvet Underground-styled minimalism with just a heartbeat effect and electric bass for most of the song. Carter, by contrast, uses an acoustic string bass to immediately make the record stand out, and then brings in a huge orchestral blast half way through that further enhances the strange and unusual qualities of the song.

Carter experimented again on the B side with a sound collage called UFO. The man was way ahead of his time.

Summer of Love

Was that summer – the famed Summer of Love – as good as it has been reported? It was a sunny summer, characterised by a burst of genre-defining music that was heard everywhere.

There was a collision of colourful fashion, even more male hair than before, and a genuine feeling of togetherness.

In terms of youth culture, it was the peak of everything the Sixties had been building towards: The Beatles had released *Sgt Pepper* on June 1, and everyone carried copies of it. Many in London had taken to wearing oblique and quaint throwback clothes speedily found in attics or granny's old throw outs, and the talk was of the West Coast 'Love-ins' – which as well as providing a rallying call to oppose the Vietnam War also had interesting sexual connotations that everyone wanted to investigate. And yes, there was a growing supply of drugs around, though perhaps not as many as some suppose.

More importantly, there was openness to the possibilities for the future, where many, possibly naively, believed that we could be at the dawn of a new era of co-operation that would take us further away from the still-recent world conflicts.

Musically, the UK charts were dominated by the middle-of-the-road work of Engelbert Humperdink and Tom Jones, but the actual summer had the trio of year-defining records at the top: 'A Whiter Shade of Pale' (June 17-July 8), 'All You Need Is Love' (July 15-August 5) and 'San Francisco (Be Sure To Wear Some Flowers In Your Hair)' August 12-September 2). Each was the perfect summer hit, and each one wafted around the streets everywhere.

There was an immediate group of hippies visible in London, and in other cities, bells, scarves and flowers were evident, while the smells of pot and patchouli oil mingled in many venues. For a few short weeks it all seemed idyllic.

There were commercial elements determined to cash in on what appeared to be happening, but alongside those there were underground scenes, some dating from late 1965, that were thriving and producing elements of alternative thought, which were well represented in the 2005 Tate Liverpool exhibition representing the year.

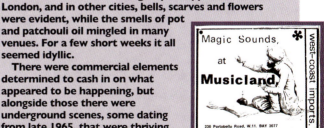

Dathon's Theme
SOUL SURVIVORS
STATESIDE SS 2094

The Soul Survivors were a New York-based amalgamation of The Dedications (Kenneth Jeremiah, Charles and Richard Ingui) and a back-up band of musicians (Ed Leonetti on guitar, Joey Forgiono on drums, and Paul Venturini on the organ) to create a bigger showband type of act.

Under the production of Messrs Gamble and Huff, who were at that point fast-learning their craft, they hit strongly with 'Espressway To Your Heart' (US top 5) and 'Explosion (In Your Soul)'.

This Richard Ingui song on the flip of the latter is a different sound, and revisits the feel of the earlier Righteous Brothers hits. A deep Bill Medley-influenced baritone with a cooing background chorus delivers a 'I can make it – no, really I can' song scenario in classic style.

The group may have been left to their own devices for the production of this side, as it doesn't carry the Gamble & Huff credit of the A side, and, despite some sludgy sounds, it still holds up as a strong number. Imagine if Phil Spector had got his hands on it!

Half Past Midnight
THE STACATTOS   CAPITOL CL 15505

'Half Past Midnight' was a strong commercial record with a big vocal sound. On second thoughts, strike out 'commercial' on the basis that it doesn't appear to have sold anywhere!

There is a possible Canadian link in that the songs are registered there, but otherwise there are no clues.

Using a ticking clock effect to start, the strength of the record is with the song and the layered vocal lines. The lead voice is attractive, and he holds his own within the massed vocals and the big orchestrated backing.

Rosecrans Blvd.
THE 5TH DIMENSION
LIBERTY LIB 12056

Love Years Coming
STRAWBERRY CHILDREN
LIBERTY LBF 15012

Writer Jim Webb was the exciting new kid on the block in 1967, even though he had been learning his craft for some years, including a spell as a staff writer at Motown.

The 5th Dimension had originally formed as The Versatiles and had been brought to producer Johnny Rivers for his newly formed Soul City label. The group consisted of Lamonte McLemore, Billy Davis, Ron Townson, Marilyn McCoo and Florence LaRue, giving the group both a distinctive sound and a spectacular look as the guys were striking and the girls were gorgeous.

Rivers worked them initially in a Mamas And Papas vein but there was more to this group than was immediately apparent and under Webb's writing and direction they moved into increasingly complex fields and arrangements.

'Rosecrans Blvd' was the B side to the poppy 'Another Day Another Heartache', and was really the first track to point to richer possibilities. Webb's song was complex and contained unusual tempo shifts, while the male vocals evoked the heat of the summer city streets of LA.

The Strawberry Children single, a one-off, was Webb's attempt to write with half an eye looking back at the *Pet Sounds* album – it was an exercise in producing the romanticism of some of those vocal layers. It bombed on both sides of the pond, but stands as a delightful summery harmony record.

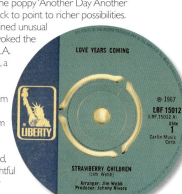

"'Love Years Coming' was my first full release. Strawberry Children was an obnoxious name for a band, but it was the summer of love and the record company saw it as a safe bet that they could sell. It was just me and two chums from college."

JIM WEBB

Let's Live For Today
THE GRASS ROOTS
PYE INTERNATIONAL 7N 25422

This is a good example of how decent vocal group records were attracting a bigger backing sound, ones that often included horns.

The Grass Roots began life as a folk rock alter ego for writer/ producer/singers Phil Sloan and Steve Barri, but had gradually morphed into a real group.

Although still produced by Sloan and Barri at this stage, 'Let's Live For Today' represents their change in style into a mainstream pop rock approach. It steamed up the US charts into the top ten where it peaked at No8, but stubbornly refused to do anything in Britain despite lyrics that were totally in tune with that particular summer.

The revised version of the Grass Roots stayed around a lot longer in The States than many would have anticipated, selling many singles and albums based around the same sound.

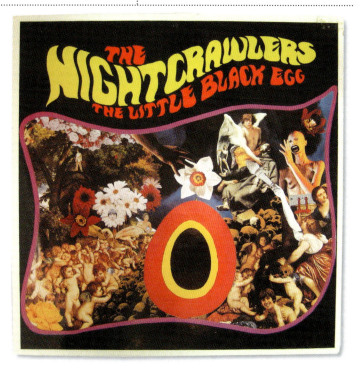

It Could Be We're In Love
THE SHAMES
CBS 2929

The Shames were a six-piece Chicago group who had hit in the US with a decent cover of the Searchers' 'Sugar And Spice', but it was quickly evident that there was ample talent within the band to provide them with strong original material. This is one of the best examples of group member Jim Fairs' work, who wrote the gentler work, and here the group sounds a bit like the Critters' softer songs.

CBS must have believed in them as they issued five of their singles here, but sadly none of their three strong US albums. The final single was called 'Greenburg, Glickstein, Charles, Davis, Smith and Jones', which were not the group-members' surnames but a track from the group's fine third album *Synthesis*, written by group member Isaac Guilory. He later moved on to solo folkier work.

The Little Black Egg
THE NIGHTCRAWLERS
LONDON HLR 10109

The Nightcrawlers were a five-piece group from Florida who really only had this one US hit. They were Charlie Conlon (bass/ vocals), Sylvan Wells (lead), Pete Thomason (rhythm), Rob Rouse (harmonica/ tambourine/vocals) and Tommy Ruger (drums).

'The Little Black Egg' was originally recorded and released in 1965, but it didn't catch on until early 1967 when it finally made No85 on Billboard, enough for it to gain a UK release at that point.

It's basically a good slab of folk rock, but one that is dominated by the striking lead guitar motif that runs throughout. What was it about? Well, that's a harder question…

> "Don't let the lyrics do anything to you because the words are saddening … 'The Little Black Egg' is nothing to do with anything, but part of the reason it caught on was because of the stuff that people read into it."
> **CHARLIE CONLON**

Around And Around (andaroundand aroundandaround)

THE 4 SEASONS
PHILIPS BF1600

The 4 Seasons probably maintained a greater level of consistency than any other act through both the Sixties and the Seventies, when they embraced disco and further developed under the Motown umbrella.

One of their offshoot Sixties ideas was to use Frankie Valli's comic 'Ruby Murray' voice under the name of The Wonder Who?, which brought reasonable hits with 'Don't Think Twice', 'It's Alright' and 'On The Good Ship Lollipop'.

The third track issued under this name was 'Lonesome Road', and it's on this B side that this full-blooded 4 Seasons song appears. It did not appear anywhere else at the time.

'Around and Around...' is another Crewe/Gaudio song with a wonderful chorus. The song is punctuated with big percussive breaks to enhance the power of the vocals.

It's hardly surprising that this is one of the most sought after of The Wonder Who? records.

Lady Friend

THE BYRDS
CBS 2924

At this point, David Crosby was still with The Byrds, and 'Lady Friend' was one of his solo compositions for them.

The full Gary Usher production has McGuinn's highly pitched spacey guitar lines working in parts with trumpets, while the group vocals fill the treble ranges even more than usual.

This is one of the last Crosby-involved songs, as his dissatisfaction with his role in the group was growing stronger. However, it's one that reminds us how important his work was to the group.

Some Other Someday

WEST COAST CONSORTIUM PYE 7N 17352

(The Man From) The Marriage Guidance And Advice Bureau

THE KNACK PICCADILLY 7N 35367

The West Coast Consortium and The Knack show how British harmony groups had really nailed American harmony influences.

The Consortium (as they later became better known) comprised Geoff Simpson (lead/organ), John Podbury (Drums), John Barker (bass), Robbie Fair (lead vocal) and Brian Bronson (rhythm), and this was the first of two singles under this name. As The Consortium they hit with 'All The Love In The World', which made the NME chart at No27 in March 1969.

The Knack were an East London band who started out on Decca with a couple of modish singles, before changing to Piccadilly where, under the watchful eye of John Schroeder, they began producing very good covers from groups such as The Lovin' Spoonful and The Critters.

This piece of British whimsy was the last of their singles, and was sung against a wash of acoustic guitars. The lead voice is supported by high unison backing vocals that give an effect not dissimilar to the one Crosby Stills and Nash were to develop a couple of years later, though with somewhat less reverb!

A version of the group led by Paul Gurvitz (aka Paul Curtis, who would soon form Gun) had previously worked as The Londoners. Two new members, drummer Topper Clay and bassist Gery (aka Gearie) Kenworthy, joined Paul and guitarist Brian Morris when they formed The Knack. Gery has already made an appearance in this book as a member of The Druids.

Echoes

GENE CLARK
CBS 202523

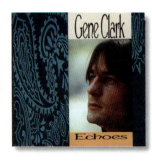

Gene Clark was the first Byrd to jump ship. Those who always considered him to be the best songwriter in the group saw this as a real loss to the band.

Left to his own devices, he was able to develop melancholic folky directions such as this lovely early outing. He also followed a country rock road with a great album that he cut with The Gosdin Brothers.

Clark wanted to move away from pop towards what would later be called a singer/songwriter model. At that stage, this style of intelligent writing was attracting the ear of people such as members of the first Fairport Convention line-up, who became known for their eclectic choices of material to cover. Gene Clark was certainly a favourite of Fairport's Ashley Hutchings, whose early Byrdsian influences came from his songs.

London Underground Clubs

The richness of the London Underground club scene formed the hub of activity in London during the Summer of Love.

The key clubs at first were the already-established UFO in Tottenham Court Road, the new Electric Garden in King Street (in the heart of the-then active fruit and veg Covent Garden market), and Happening 44 in Gerrard Street.

The latter was a strip club by day and some evenings, and converted into a hippie club with light show some nights of the week. It was here that Fairport Convention played their early Soho gigs in June and July, but being a small cellar club, it never quite managed to break free from its seedy feel.

The Electric Garden, renamed Middle Earth by late August after an initial dubious reputation, was a different matter entirely. It was much bigger and had distinct areas within it. Walking in past an office on the left led to the main stage against the right-hand wall, side on to the auditorium. Another smaller stage was in the far right corner in front of the route to the small band back room. Opposite the main stage was a scaffolded lighting gallery where chaps would construct the light shows with the oils, slides, revolves and droppers that gave the club walls quite the best light shows around at the time. There was yet another small performance space near this gantry, which contributed to the club's main nights being able to offer a comparatively seamless transfer between a variety of acts. Sometimes a dry ice machine would add to the ambiance of the club. Depending on the acts, audience numbers varied from two (watching Marc Bolan just before he got Tyrannosaurus Rex going) and the hundreds that turned out for the magnificent stoned gig The Byrds played with Gram Parsons in summer 1968.

Speak Easy

Fairport Convention

UFO was seen as the epicentre, although its big oblong space lacked the atmosphere of Middle Earth. However, it proved fortunate for Fairport because it was during their first appearance there that they met their producer-to-be Joe Boyd.

There were also the 'proper' music clubs like The Speakeasy. They were more like chill out zones for the stars of the day, and were the places where new acts would perform showcase gigs to industry figures. Fairport became regular players here during mid to late 1967, attracting great interest from everyone, including Jimi who would jam with them late at night when all but a couple of dozen people remained in the club.

The Roundhouse at London's Chalk Farm was also rapidly developing as a key venue. At this stage, it was a somewhat tatty and cavernous building quite unlike the feel of the other smaller clubs. Its real heyday came a little after 1967.

The following dozen or so singles are very much what you would have heard in these clubs at the time.

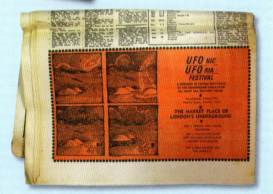

If I Had A Ribbon Bow
FAIRPORT CONVENTION
TRACK 604020

Fairport built their early reputation on a repertoire that took in material from Leonard Cohen, Joni Mitchell, Jim & Jean, Phil Ochs, Donovan, Dylan, Paul Butterfield, Dino Valente, Jefferson Airplane, The Byrds and Jackson C Frank, so when it came to the choice of their first single it was a big surprise that they went for 'Ribbon Bow'.

Ashley Hutchings and singer Judy Dyble took an eager look at Joe Boyd's record collection when they visited his flat in Westbourne Terrace. Joe drew their attention to an LP by Maxine Sullivan containing a 1936 recording of 'If I Had A Ribbon Bow', which they thought was different and off-the-wall.

While not really knowing what would make a good single for the group, the song tickled their collective fancy and it was duly recorded and issued with an accompanying poster campaign. Promo copies were sent out in an envelope with a neat pink ribbon on the top left. The single sunk like the proverbial stone (assuring its ever-increasing value now) as it was quite a long way from what they were performing on stage at the time.

"We were never ones to follow what everyone else was doing I suppose, but 'If I Had A Ribbon Bow' did gather some interest in one unlikely place though. Uncle Frank's Sunday Club in Kidderminster (a dance school during the week) saw fit to organise a Ribbon Bow contest for the local females, which I judged. Real fame that was!"
JUDY DYBLE

Tiny Goddess
NIRVANA
ISLAND WIP 6016

The first Nirvana were marketed as a duo of Alex Spyropoulos (piano/vocals) and Pat Campbell-Lyons (violin/vocals), but, under the overall direction of Island Records' Muff Winwood, they were augmented by Ray Singer (piano/guitar), Sylvia Schuster (cello), Brian Henderson (bass) and others.

'Tiny Goddess' was diametrically opposed to The Soft Machine (see opposite page) in that it was a gentle ballad of descending notes with prominent cello and harpsichord supporting ethereal voices. It was the sonic equivalent to the Elves' kingdom in Lord Of The Rings, when compared with other sounds around then, and yet it fitted perfectly with some elements and feels of The Beatles and Procol Harum.

It was the first of several issues by the strikingly different group, but all stubbornly refused to sell despite the obvious quality and interest.

Defecting Gray
THE PRETTY THINGS
COLUMBIA DB 8300

The Pretty Things, fully committed early on in their career to gutsy R&B, were one of the many bands who took a distinct left turn into psychedelia in 1967. If anyone wants a representative record of what psych sounds like, this is a perfect example.

Starting with vaguely Indian sounding guitars, the lyric tweely speaks of sitting alone on benches before there is a blast of sitar and a further shift into faster sections. Tempo and sound shifts continue with further quiet sections that form an effective counterpoint to the hurly-burly of the other sections.

Throughout their career, The Pretties always followed unexpected directions and their work during the psychedelic era, especially this single, was always exciting.

Say You Don't Mind
DENNY LAINE
DERAM DM 122

Denny Laine's Electric String Band, as it was billed in the clubs, had a very different sound that, without doubt, led directly to Seventies bands like ELO.

Laine left The Moody Blues and set out to combine strings and pop in a unique way. It was a four or five-piece group that played at Middle Earth, with the eccentric and wayward Viv Prince recently of The Pretty Things on drums…so it was obvious that Denny was prepared to live dangerously.

The music, when it came together, was refreshingly brilliant. 'Say You Don't Mind', marvellously produced as it was by Denny Cordell, showed that the magic could be caught on record.

The song has been frequently covered ever since, most notably by Colin Blunstone, but it is this original version that somehow captures the spirit of that summer.

Feelin' Reelin' Squeelin'
THE SOFT MACHINE
POLYDOR 56151

This was one of the first singles that set the Underground tone of the summer. The Soft Machine, then including Robert Wyatt, Kevin Ayres, Daevid Allen and Mike Ratledge, had met maverick producer/hustler Kim Fowley, who produced both sides of what was to become their first single.

The A side, 'Love Makes Sweet Music', was subsequently re-recorded, but 'Feeling Reelin' Squeelin'' on the B side was kept in its original Fowley form.

It is quite unlike anything else before or since, alternating between reasonably straightforward verses and a deep-voiced chorus, backed by single discordant guitar notes before dissolving into a freaky morass before the fade.

Fly Me High
THE MOODY BLUES
DECCA F 12607

Like The Pretties, The Moodies were a group in transition from their first incarnation. Justin Hayward had arrived and this song indicates how he helped the band move towards the approach that led eventually to 'Nights In White Satin'. Not that this is in any way like 'Nights', as it is a happy trippy song that was played a lot in the clubs then. It had the word 'high' in its title so it was immediately accepted!

"Fly Me High was a big underground hit in mid-67 – the title said something to people. I saw the Moodies play this live and their *Days of Future Passed* album in full at the Marquee in Wardour Street about July 1968. In the front row I could see every flick of Justin Hayward's guitar switches, and the Mellotron played to magnificent heights by Mike Pinder – brilliant choral and orchestral effects. Classic gig!"

STUART TALBOT

San Franciscan Nights

ERIC BURDON AND THE ANIMALS

MGM 1359

Another group that went through a conversion was Eric Burden and The Animals, though in his case it was with a different set of Animals.

The R&B-based first set had gone their separate ways: Alan Price had gone solo and Chas Chandler had gone into management, most notably with Hendrix and later Slade. Eric Burdon stuck it out on the road, as he has done ever since, and this single with his new musicians showed how he had been seduced by the West Coast.

Written by the whole band, and arranged by lead guitarist Vic Briggs, it was an appreciative ode to the new Californian lifestyle, and with its relaxed musical approach it fitted right in to that lifestyle. Eric has rarely sounded so laid back…

Granny Takes A Trip

THE PURPLE GANG BIG T BIG 101

This is another of Joe Boyd's musical projects, which pre-date his relationship with Island Records. The Purple Gang have been described as a psychedelic jugband, and they wandered around London dressed in 1920's gear after coming down from Cheshire. They were Peter 'Lucifer' Walker (vocals), DeeJay Robinson (harmonica), Ant Langley (banjo), Geoff Boyer (piano and washboard), Tony Moss (bass) and Christopher Joe Beard (guitar).

Musically speaking, it was probably best described as a whimsical British equivalent of the zanier aspects of The Lovin' Spoonful. The jolly romp on this song was purportedly about an elderly lady going to Hollywood to break into the movies, but the BBC quickly became convinced it was about those nasty drug things, and promptly banned it, scuppering its chances of ever becoming any more than a boppy club fave..

Dantalion's Chariot

THE MADMAN RUNNING THROUGH THE FIELDS

COLUMBIA DB 8260

Zoot Money was always a well respected loony on the scene due to his earlier days with his Big Roll Band (one of the few acts who could rival Georgie Fame at the Flamingo), through to his later time with Eric Burdon, and eventually to his elongated solo spell that continues to this day.

Psychedelia came at a time when the group were ready for a change, like so many of their fellow musicians, and so they dropped the brass section and this one-off single was Zoot's offbeat pitch of his hat into the ring. Along with Andy Somers (guitar) Pat Donaldson (bass) and Colin Allen (drums), Zoot piled everything into the mix. David Wells, the best-known psych expert, called it: "An astonishing, head-swirling slab of kitchen-sink British Psychedelia." But the name and the title was almost too off-the-wall from day one, so EMI didn't support it and no-one bought it, explaining its three-figure appeal now to genre collectors.

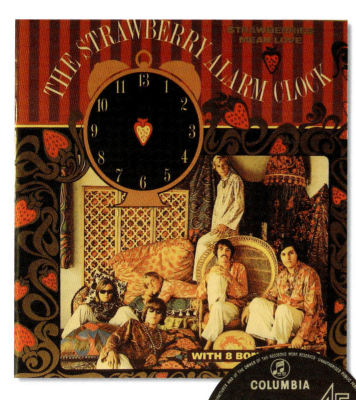

Incense And Peppermints

THE STRAWBERRY ALARM CLOCK

PYE INTERNATIONAL 7N 25436

This one was a US No1 for the Santa Barbara-based group that was previously known as The Sixpence. The song had outside lyrical input from a songwriter called John Carter (not the British one), who ruffled collective feathers by suggesting a different lead voice for the group, who thought it was only going to be a B side.

The song features the same sort of swirly organ that helped the Seeds and The Doors move forward, and the group immediately became seen in the States as one of the groovy new bands on the scene. However, they failed to sustain the success of this one, partly due to frequent personnel changes.

'Incense And Peppermints' remains a classic of its time, though it never attained the same status in Britain as in the States.

Hyacinth Threads

THE ORANGE BICYCLE

COLUMBIA DB 8259

A British equivalent to the Strawberry Alarm Clock in the daft name stakes was The Orange Bicycle.

Unlike many of their contemporaries, The Orange Bicycle managed ten singles, of which this was the first, and one album between 1967 and 1970.

Written by group member Wilson Malone, it was a confident fast-paced debut with high group vocals over a bed of harpsichord and assorted studio trickery.

Members included RJ Scales (vocals), Bernie Lee (guitar), Kevin Curry (drums) and John Bachini (bass).

Despite being largely ignored in Britain, 'Hyacinth Threads' was a huge hit in France, which probably helped EMI to believe they were worth sticking with.

Later, on their album, they covered the Beatles' 'Carry That Weight', The Stones' 'Sing This Song Altogether', four songs by the embryonic Elton John/Bernie Taupin team, and even a version of Denny Laine's 'Say You Don't Mind'.

They were one act that deserved success, but were lost in the crowd.

Sunshine Help Me
SPOOKY TOOTH
ISLAND WIP 6022

Spooky Tooth had just changed their name from Art, under which they had issued a cover of Buffalo Springfield's 'What's That Sound', and 'Sunshine Help Me' was the first of many under the new name. The song was written by new keyboardist Gary Wright who joined pianist Mike Harrison, guitarist Luthor Grosvenor, bass player Greg Ridley and drummer Mike Kellie.

'Sunshine Help Me' was a more rock-oriented sound than many groups were using at the time, and pointed towards a rougher version of Free's later direction. They were prominent on the club scene, but never found the song to capture the public's taste.

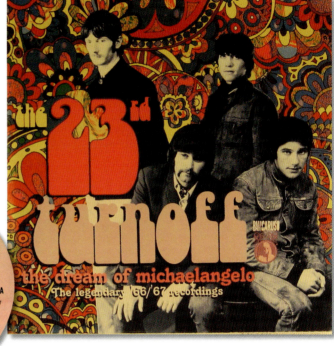

February Sunshine
GIANT SUNFLOWER
CBS 2805

As ever, Los Angeles record producers were quick to apply their gloss to a new genre, and this Lou Adler production is a good example.

It is summery and poppy in a Mamas And Papas vein, with a splendid wash of vocal harmonies all over it. They were, as you probably didn't expect, a bona fide group from Parkersburg, West Virginia, made up of Diana Di Rose on vocals, guitarists James Groshong and John Noreen, William Fleming on piano and bass, and drummer Bruce Boudin.

This one made No106 on Billboard, while their rather strange choice of follow-up, a revival of The Miracles' 'What's So Good About Goodbye', reached ten places lower. They re-emerged soon after as The Rose Garden without any personnel change.

Michael Angelo
THE 23RD TURNOFF
DERAM DM 150

The name 23rd Turnoff had been chosen for a Liverpool band formally known as the Kirkbys. With that moniker, they had been a part of the Cavern-based Mersey scene, but without the success of other local bands.

This was the group's only release under this name, although several other songs were recorded at around the same time. Michael Angelo apparently only features two members of the group, Jimmy Campbell (who wrote both it and the B side) and John JD Lloyd; the other players were hired by Decca for the session. Consequently, famous players like drummer Clem Cattini and guitarist Big Jim Sullivan are among those heard on this highly collectable gem. Its arrangement borrows a little from the Beatles in its use of a trumpet above other instrumentation and, as you may expect, it is a thoroughly professional sound with good vocals from the two group members present.

Next Plane To London
THE ROSE GARDEN
ATLANTIC 584163

After their stint as Giant Sunflower, the newly named The Rose Garden hooked up with experienced producers Charlie Greene and Brian Stone. They took them into Gold Star Studio where they cut an attractive album that re-visited 'February Sunshine' in gentler flute-filled form as well as including a Dylan cover 'She Belongs To Me' and a couple of obscure Gene Clark songs, 'Till Today' and 'Long Time'. However, it was with 'Next Plane To London' that they had their big US hit, with a slow climb to No17.

The song came complete with airport Tannoy voices, and was in part taken as evidence of where the centre of the happening youth world was in 1967 – it was performed in the quieter, almost folky vein that the group had turned to.

The success of the single was probably unexpected because the record company Atco rapidly added stickers to the front of the album cover.

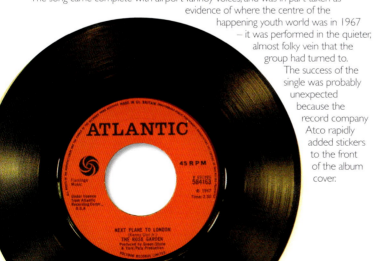

Shake Hands And Walk Away Cryin'
LOU CHRISTIE
CBS 2718

It is impossible to ignore the extended vocal range of Lou Christie, whose tenor to high falsetto graced so many great records through the Sixties, and on such a variety of labels. On this CBS outing, the king of the tortured song story maintains his heartbreak persona on a song that interweaves several song titles from the 1962/63 era – that suggests that it was written a few years ahead of this issue.

The recording, however, uses several later tricks, including a quieter slow section that leads to a full stop, before he powers back in for the final shrieks.

The song was written by Lou with his long-time writing partner Twyla Herbert, who was an attractive and personable older lady.

Robert Plant
OUR SONG
CBS 202656

The remarkable thing about this ultra-rare first Robert Plant single is the vocal range that it displays. Starting out in a low register not a million miles from a cheesy bar singer, the song builds and allows Robert to climb up his range seemingly effortlessly until, by the end, he is singing against soulful brass lines and powering along with some to spare. Although not the most memorable song, it does provide ample evidence of what was to come from the man.

Apples, Peaches, Pumpkin Pie
JAY & THE TECHNIQUES
PHILIPS BF 1597

Producer Jerry Ross really understood how to make soul-tinged pop, and this US No6 hit is a fine example of his talent, though arranger Joe Renzetti must also get credit for the way the vibes are integrated to provide such a danceable undertow to the song.

The group was one of many good multi-membered outfits with a decent lead voice that often graced Ross' records (for example, The Mob or Bill Deal & The Rhondells), and Jay's voice delivers the song with enough lightness to make it the soul equivalent of bubblegum.

The song is built on a memorable re-cycling of the 'Ready Or Not, Here I Come' children's hide and seek call, and it seems odd that no UK act that we know of saw fit to cover it at the time.

The record found favour in soul/dance circles, leading to several other issues or re-issues, and even an album in the UK.

Give And Take
JIMMY CLIFF
ISLAND WIP 6004

Wait A Minute
TIM TAM AND THE TURN-ONS
ISLAND WIP 6007

The re-designed pink Island label quickly became very collectable for fans of danceable pop soul, and these are prime examples why.

Jimmy Cliff had had previous issues in the UK on Blue Beat, Stateside, Fontana and the earlier Island incarnation since 1962, but only really found favour with specialist markets.

The bouncy 'Give And Take', complete with what sounds like a piccolo boosting the repeating riff, had a lot of airplay at the time, and must have sold quite a few copies.

Tim Tam And The Turn-Ons, by contrast, is one of the hardest of the pink Islands to find, as almost certainly no more than a few hundred copies would have been pressed. It was recorded in 1965, and was a throwback to the stompy Four Seasons/late doo-wop sounds. In 1967, it sounded a little dated, but is now sought after for its simple percussive power. It was their only UK issue, although they had other similar-sounding US releases on the Palmer label called 'Cheryl Ann', 'Kimberly' and 'Don't Say Hi', all of which are pretty collectable. Has anyone ever seen a picture of them?

Step Out Of Your Mind
THE AMERICAN BREED
CBS 2972

The title and line 'You gotta get out of your head' were strongly in tune with the accepted druggy lyrics of the year, though strangely this appears to be closer to the idea of 'thinking outside the box' or being prepared to let the inner child out as a way of getting noticed.

This first UK issue for the Chicago-based group came before their better-known 'Bend Me, Shape Me' and 'Green Light' singles. It sets the template for their blend of precision vocals with almost jazz-rock arrangements and trumpets to the fore. They were able to sustain a career for a few years before some later members (keyboardist Kevin Murphy and drummer Andre Fischer) morphed into Rufus in 1973. At this stage they were a four-piece made up of rhythm guitarist Al Ciner, lead guitarist Gary Loizzo, bass Chuck Colburn and drummer/trumpet Lee Grazaino, with all four singing.

When pirates ruled the waves

Without Britain's 1960s radio pirates it is doubtful if the UK music scene would have been able to develop as it did.

Prior to the arrival of the first pirate in the Thames Estuary in Easter 1964 the only place to hear pop music was on the BBC Light Programme's Saturday Club with Brian Matthew or at night on 208 metres medium wave from Luxembourg. A generation had grown up listening under the bedclothes to Radio Luxembourg as the signal distorted with atmospherics and faded in and out. Still, it was the best available. It was the nearest we had in the UK to the big AM stations that inspired the likes of the young Bob Dylan and many other budding stars of the future in remote communities across the US.

Ironically, just before Radio Caroline opened for business a government report had just announced that there was no demand for a 'popular' music station. Within weeks of going on air the station had millions of listeners and a crazy three-year period began which provided a shop window in the UK for performers from both sides of the Atlantic.

Soon Caroline, which mixed white pop with Motown and soul was joined by the American-influenced Radio London. Big L, as it was known, brought a genuine flavour of US-style AM radio. The excitement was infectious and with the pirates as the soundtrack, England swung.

In 1966 a young English DJ joined Radio London after a spell working in the US. After midnight when the advertisers weren't buying airtime and the station wasn't so worried about 'the format' he began playing a strange mix of album tracks from the likes of Tyrannosaurus Rex, Pink Floyd and underground US acts. John Peel's Perfumed Garden influenced a whole generation of rebellious youth and sowed the seeds of his later success on Radio 1.

The pirates were closed down by the government in August 1967. Caroline struggled on for a further six months before being forced off air (though it reappeared four years later). The BBC moved to replace the pirates by renaming the Light Programme Radio 1, but it could never match the anarchic energy of the pirates.

"Instead of Edmundo Ross and his Orchestra playing muzak on Workers Playtime on the BBC Light Programme we had the Beatles, Stones, Byrds and Beach Boys all day long. It was the soundtrack to our lives and we listened wherever we could on portable transistor radios. It was liberation and we drank it in. The pirate stations provided the outlet for all the music coming out of England in the mid-Sixties."

John Peel

Radio Caroline's ship the MV Mi Amigo

Nobody But Me/ Seuno

THE HUMAN BEINZ
CAPITOL CL 15529

Both sides of this US No8 hit are unusual. The obviously commercial topside is a remake of an Isley Brothers number that begins with a No-No-No chant that reminds us of 'Land Of 1000 Dances', before launching into a fratty, bratty version of the 'I'm the best at every dance' macho outlook of the song. It's instantly ear-grabbing, and is enhanced mid-way by a very decent rock guitar break.

The flip side, a total contrast, is more of a gentle soundscape, built around one repeated verse that begins with: 'The breeze, the beach and swaying trees…' The mood piece uses single bass notes, high shimmering guitar lines and an assortment of Brian Wilson-type percussive ideas.

The foursome of Richard Belley (lead), Ting Merkulin (rhythm), Mel Pachuta (bass) and Mike Tatman (drums) were from Youngstown, Ohio. They managed three albums, the last of which, *Evolution*, has found favour with British psych fans through two re-issues on 'See For Miles' (1981) and 'Decal' (1987).

Come And Take A Ride In My Boat

EVERY MOTHERS' CHILD
MGM 1341

Put Your Mind At Ease

EVERY MOTHERS' CHILD
MGM 1350

Oh, if ever there was an all-American group made up of boys-next-door it was Every Mothers' Son – think five Benjamin's from the Graduate and you've got it.

However, they weren't totally manufactured, as three of them, brothers Lary and Dennis Larden and organist Bruce Milner, had worked around the Greenwich Village folk clubs prior to meeting producer Wes Farrell, who pushed them towards MGM.

The trio of folkies added bassist Schuyler Larsen and drummer Christopher Augustine and went electric, and the Farrell co-written 'Come And Take A Ride In My Boat' (titled as 'Come On Down To My Boat' in Billboard, reflecting what they actually sing on the record) floated all the way to US No6 in the summertime. With guitars and organ repeating memorable riffs, and handclaps driving the verses, this is a well-produced bubblegum record ahead of its time.

The follow-up, 'Put Your Mind At Ease', was written by the Larden brothers and is a more adventurous single. Starting with Monkees-sounding guitars and first verse, it switches time and feel for the slower, harmony-filled chorus, but despite the obvious talent it stalled at No46 on Billboard and, after two albums with mostly Larden-penned material, the boys returned to whatever career their college courses had equipped them for.

Please Phil Spector

THE ATTACK **PHILIPS BF 1585**

This one is a real oddity in that it is an American product of the New York music district that does not appear to have been issued in the US at the time. The key characters involved are writer/producer Mike Rashkow (aka Mike Lendell) and Johnny Cymbal (of earlier 'Mr Bass Man' fame). They had produced the A side of this, 'Washington Square', a pleasant bit of NYC pop ode to the key Greenwich Village gathering spot.

Without a B side, this throwaway tongue-in-cheek bit of nonsense designed to catch Spector's attention was decided upon, which the main protagonists then forgot about and moved on to other projects.

For some reason the record emerged in Britain where it probably sold about eight copies, and disappeared until its recent exhumation on Ace Records' 'Phil's Spectre – A Wall Of Soundalikes' various artists compilation.

> **"This was supposed to come out on a label named Attack, which was owned by Jerry Schifrin and Nate McCalla. Jerry, the cousin of Lalo Schifrin, was a nice guy and a good record man, while McCalla was a tough black enforcer of Morris Levy, the owner of Roulette.**
>
> **Attack was an offshoot of McCalla's label Calla, a one-room operation on the second floor of the Roulette building, around the corner from the Brill. On the same floor there was a small demo studio, part-owned by Don Costa and Teddy Randazzo. I worked there.**
>
> **Ellie Greenwich and I were writing and producing together at the time. I wrote 'Please Phil Spector' as a joke in an attempt to get Phil's attention. I did the thing and had her send it to him. He never responded. So we gave the track to Calla to use as the B side to 'Washington Square' because we had nothing else and they didn't care. They bought the master. I never knew the record was ever issued, and I never knew the 'group' was called The Attack."**
> *Mike Rashkow (from the Ace Records' CD notes)*

I Think We're Alone Now

TOMMY JAMES & THE SHONDELLS
MAJOR MINOR D 405

Roulette Records was the US home for this early Tommy James hit. It climbed to No4 on Billboard some six months after the group's first US No1 with 'Hanky Panky'.

Neither song did anything in Britain initially, though a 1988 remake of this one reached the top NME position for Tiffany, and there have been several other covers of the song over the years. Tommy James eventually got his UK biggie with 'Mony Mony', which was also his last Major Minor release.

'I Think We're Alone Now' was the pure pop product of Tommy's work with producer/ songwriters Ritchie Cordell and Bo Gentry at the famed Allegro Studios at 1650 Broadway (aka The Aldon Building, where work had to be arranged around the subway trains rumbling beneath).

James produced many more huge-selling US hits, but never seemed to gain a full foothold over here. Fans of the pure US group style records should also seek out his '(Baby Baby) I Can't Take It No More' and '(I'm) Taken', the latter of which he co-wrote with Pete Anders.

Angel Of the Morning
BILLIE DAVIS DECCA F 12696

Billie Davis, along with Julie Driscoll, was one of the delectable female faces of the Sixties, and both had ample talent to back up their looks.

Billie hadn't had a great time since her hit with 'Tell Him' in 1963, having suffered a bad car crash that removed her from the business for a while, followed by a string of great singles on Columbia and Piccadilly that had not done much for her at the time. This was in spite of a great choice of material that included a fab cover of Gladys Knight's 'Just Walk In My Shoes'.

She moved to Decca in 1967, where this was her second single, and once again shows great taste in material. There are many covers of the Chip Taylor-penned 'Angel Of The Morning', but Billie was one of the first. She delivers it almost in a little girl voice, accompanied by imaginative string lines.

Musical direction was by Mike Vickers from Manfred Mann, and it was engineered by the young Gus Dudgeon. The same team worked on the flip, a most satisfying cover of The Lovin' Spoonful's 'Darling Be Home Soon'.

Western Union
THE FIVE AMERICANS
STATESIDE SS 2012

American writers and producers were past masters at commercial hooks, but none were as pronounced as in this one. It uses telegraphic organ dit-de-dits to introduce the song, which are picked up vocally by the group in the chorus. The song zoomed to No5 on Billboard, but was to be another great pop record that did nothing here, though it did attract a cover from The Searchers, whose good musical understanding of all things American underlines its worth.

"The Chants have been totally overlooked. I would watch them rehearse in a big old house at the bottom of Upper Parliament Street in Liverpool. They would rehearse all day with just a guitarist to get the keys, and they worked so hard on their harmonies. The Beatles backed The Chants at the Cavern – now, that was a memorable gig!"

BILLY KINSLEY OF THE MERSEYBEATS

A Lover's Story
THE CHANTS
DECCA F 12650

The wonderful Chants, who we have already met, were plugging away all through the Sixties, and this sole Decca issue showed that all their previous class was still abundant.

The song is mid-paced, and cleverly uses a variety of book-related terminology to tell the story of a man's feelings for the girl. The background group vocals are sweet behind the fine lead voice, and Ivor Raymonde's arrangement and production swathe it in a more-than-acceptable fashion.

Why oh why did they never get a hit…or at least some reasonable sales?

You're Never Gonna Get My Lovin'

THE ENCHANTED FOREST
STATESIDE SS 2080

This was a studio-based project by Mort Shuman, a while after his peak writing years with Doc Pomus.

It features some adventurous studio work with stops, starts, volume swells and an elongated intro before female vocals take the verses and choruses.

The song owes something to Brian Wilson's 'Good Vibrations' in terms of its feel and multi-sectioning, giving some credence to the 'Variations In Sound' production tag line on the label.

Interestingly it appears to be co-written by Kenny Lynch, which could suggest it was a UK production, but Bell Records and Amy label credits work against this.

Either way, it's a very inventive sound that is effectively a rare example of femme Sunshine Pop. It also benefits from having what must have been one of the earliest covers of Leonard Cohen's 'Suzanne' on its flip.

Guess I'm Dumb

JOHNNY WELLS
PARLOPHONE R 5559

This is another strong cover of 'Guess I'm Dumb', the song that probably takes Brian Wilson closer to Burt Bacharach than anything else. This cover was obviously chosen on the strength of the song rather than any other reason, as there wasn't a US issue then to compete with.

The arrangement is strong and full, and briefly replaces some of the droning sax lines of Glen Campbell's original with a few harmonised vocal lines.

Johnny's lead is strong and assured, and generally fits well on the song. It appears to have been his only Sixties release, partially explaining how little-known it is, even within the Beach Boys' collecting fraternity.

Getting' Hungry

BRIAN WILSON & MIKE LOVE
CAPITOL CL 15513

This one is a Beach Boys oddity that effectively straddles the throwaway 'I'm Bugged At My Old Man' on the *Summer Days (And Summer Nights)* album and of the weirdness of certain *Smile* songs, and what was to come on the *Wild Honey* album. It's the only item from the BB camp to carry the Brian Wilson and Mike Love artist credit on the single, though it is included on the group's *Smiley Smile* album.

It's a stop/start affair that picks up some speed in parts. It contrasts Mike's baritone on the verse with Brian's distinctive higher lines before the chorus that they mostly share. This is set against weird keyboards and plenty of plinky plonky Wilsonian percussive effects, making the whole outing very different to anything else in the group's canon, or anyone else's come to that.

Sunshine pop

The term 'Sunshine Pop' was coined retrospectively in the September 1997 issue of Record Collector by the-then editor Peter Doggett in the light of record collecting activity in the early Nineties that, for a while at least, was led by Japan.

The soft poppy material had its roots in vocal harmony groups such as **The Beach Boys, The Association, The Critters, The Mamas And Papas** and the many US producers who specialised at various stages in such sounds, including **Gary Usher, Curt Boettcher** and **Gary Zekely.**

The popularity in Japan, where US charts were followed more closely that UK ones, is partially explained by the softer vocal feels that sat better on their voices, but it also followed a healthy uptake of all US vocal harmonies since the early Sixties.

By 1967, the genre had become more readily identifiable as it merged into Flower Pop and the lighter examples of psychedelic pop. Lyrical imagery often consisted of flowers, parks, balloons, kites and all things soft and non-threatening, leading to some of it being on the verge of soppy.

However, it was first and foremost in a direct line out of the producer/writer-led pure pop music that was perfected on the West Coast. The records were always well arranged and produced, and always featured good vocals, even if the lyrical content sometimes raised eyebrows.

The advantage of the emerging genre to collectors initially was that few of the records required major investment, though prices have been rising steadily since. Collectors labels have produced good re-release compilations from all parts of the world, including five volumes of *Sunshine Days* from Varese in the US, eight volumes of *Ripples* from Sequel/Sanctuary in Britain, two volumes of *The Melody Goes On* from M&M in Japan, *The Get Easy Sunshine Pop Collection* from Universal/Boutique in Germany and Rhino's recent *Come To The Sunshine* WEA collection.

Many fine examples of the sounds are, as yet, unavailable to the collector. Some examples of the genre follow…

Sunshine Girl
THE PARADE
A&M AMS 701

"Shades of dawn burst into sunshine, I took her hand and ran through the morning." That was the line that ran into the final chorus of 'Sunshine Girl', and somehow this perfectly captures the Sunshine Pop genre in one hit. Produced by one-time Spector apprentice Jerry Riopelle, the song was a most creditable No20 US hit, though the follow-up 'The Radio Song' could only make No127.

The group was basically a trio of Riopelle himself with Murray MacLeod and Smokey Roberds. (MacLeod was also a member of another popular sunshine/soft rock act The Roger Nichols Trio.)

Trivia buffs will also recall that Stuart Margolin was involved with the group, co-writing the B side of 'Sunshine Girl' – he also starred as Jim Rockford's less-than-trustworthy sidekick in the Rockford Files.

Such was the group's popularity in Japan that the only known CD collection of their work was issued there in 1988.

We Can Fly
THE COWSILLS
MGM 1383

The Cowsills had taken their first hit 'The Rain The Park and Other Things' all the way to No2 on Billboard, but were kept off the top spot by The Monkees' own slab of Sunshine Pop 'Daydream Believer'. This one was the ultra-quick follow-up that went up to No21.

The Cowsills were a 'whole family' group, even including their mum and little sis, who were pitched as the ultimately respectable US dream family to the extent that one of the older sons was dropped from the band when their dad found him smoking pot. Their full harmony vocals sat well on the Sunshine Pop sound, and 'We Can Fly' was perhaps a classic example in terms of song, lyrics and overall feel.

The group continued for quite a while, cutting 'meaningful' albums, but it is for their particularly light and breezy material that they are best remembered.

Little Girl Lost And Found
PETER & THE WOLVES **MGM 1352**

Nick Ryan, Jon Richmond, Ken Todd, John Pantry and Garry Nichols had been on the circuit under the name Sounds Around before they ran into independent producer Eddie Tre-Vett who suggested the name change as a possible route to a hit.

The song chosen was an obscure US A&M release by a studio 'group' called The Garden Club, whose 'Little Girl Lost And Found' was an exercise in post-*Pet Sounds* harmony pop. Tre-Vett's production does not attempt to replicate the rounded warmth of the American original, but uses a reedy fairground organ to set up a 'toytown' and essentially British feel to the record. The group do a creditable job with the complicated vocal lines, and the release attracted enough attention at the time from the BBC and Juke Box Jury to warrant them making the name change permanent.

John Pantry continued to be active with studio work and songwriting, and went on to supply the songs and lead and B'vox for the second and very collectable Factory single 'Try A Little Sunshine' in 1968.

MGM 1352

I Could Be So Good To You
DON & THE GOOD TIMES
COLUMBIA DB 8199

Don & The Good Times were major stars in North West America, and had gathered their following with several issues on the Jerden and Dunhill labels.

This one marked their move to Epic Records and a poppier approach through the production involvement of Jack Nitzsche, who co-wrote this great track and poured his magic all over it.

It's a sparkly vocal harmony-filled song with all the ba-ba-bas needed to fill it out. The 1967 version of the group of Don McKinney, Don Gallucci, Ron Overman, Charlie Cox and Bobby Holden dutifully supplied an album that included good re-workings of 'Good Day Sunshine' and 'Gimme Some Lovin''.

The single made it to No56 on Billboard, and despite only being valued at £10, British copies are rare.

California On My Mind
THE EXCELS
ATLANTIC 584133

Both sides of this one-off UK release (the B side was called 'The Arrival Of Mary') are great examples of Sunshine Pop.

There were several 'Excels' working in the States at various time between 1957 and the end of the Sixties. This group were on the US Carla label, where they had at least four issues, the others being 'I Wanna Be Free', 'Gonna Make You Mine Girl', and 'Little Innocent Girl'.

'California On My Mind' revives some of the lyrical themes of the Trade Winds' 'New York A Lonely Town', together with some of the feel of that record.

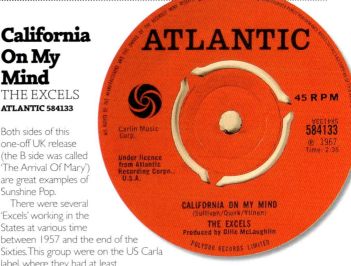

THE YELLOW BALLOON'S

YELLOW BALLOON

JAN & DEAN

YELLOW BALLOON
(Zekley/St. John/Lee)
A Magic Lamp Production

STAINED GLASS WINDOW
(Grady—Zekley)
THE YELLOW BALLOON
Producer Yodar Critch

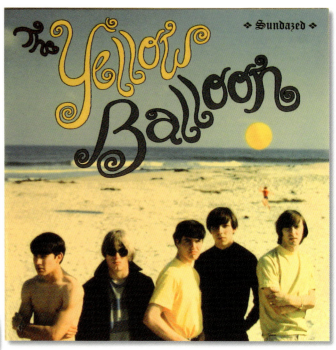

Yellow Balloon JAN & DEAN CBS 202630

Stained Glass Window
THE YELLOW BALLOON **STATESIDE SS 2124**

The link between these two issues is writer/producer Gary Zekely, who was working in Los Angeles, with more than half an eye on anything Brian Wilson was doing. He had co-written the song 'Yellow Balloon', which had reached the ears of Dean Torrence. Dean was, at that time, in the process of cutting *Save For A Rainy Day* to try to keep the Jan & Dean name alive while Jan Berry was still recovering from his accident and subsequent coma.

Dean quickly saw the song's potential and recorded a version. When Zekely heard it, it didn't tally with his production conception for it because it reflected the plainer, almost stripped-down approach that Dean was using for the album, while emphasising the ba-ba-bas in the song that recalled the duo's earliest hits.

Zekely rapidly realised he needed to record his own version the way he wanted, so his studio musician version (under the name of The Yellow Balloon) arrived in time to get a Billboard ad right next to an ad for the Jan & Dean version. Zekely's version won the chart battle hands down, making No25 while Dean's Balloon got stuck in the trees at No111.

Swiftly, Zekely said "Uh Oh…hit record…no group…" and assembled a real Yellow Balloon for promotion and to front the inevitable follow-up album. This group included one Don Grady in disguise. Grady was known to all Americans as one of Fred McMurray's sons in the hit TV show, My Three Sons. He wanted to make it as a bone-fide musician without relying on his name, but inevitably the secret soon came out.

Grady also wrote with Zekely, and 'Stained Glass Window' was one of theirs. It was the last of the group's three singles, and failed to chart anywhere, though it did become a particular favourite years later with the Paisley Underground LA subset in the mid-Eighties. It alternates Left Banke-style baroque feels with the more usual full-blooded Sunshine harmonies. The Yellow Balloon album was consistently tasty, with fine production by Zekely on a set of strong pop songs.

"'Stained Glass Window' was easy to write. It was like one of those jolts of lightning – it was 'Ooh! What is that?' I think it was a bit ahead of its time, and it had that string quartet stuff happening. It just laid out real nice."

DON GRADY

Back On The Streets Again
SUNSHINE COMPANY

LIBERTY LBF 15034

The Sunshine Company were another LA act that almost certainly encountered The Yellow Balloon. The group had sold well with their version of 'Happy' (competing with another version by The Blades Of Grass) and had almost issued a version of 'Up Up And Away' before they realised they were up against the 5th Dimension and the radio-friendly Johnny Mann Singers.

'Back On The Streets Again' was their second single and their biggest US hit, reaching No36, some 14 places higher than their 'Happy' release. It was enough for the five-piece group of Merel Bregante, Doug Mark, Mary Nance, Maury Manseau and Larry Sims to keep going and release three strong albums and to appear alongside all the biggest West Coast acts of the day at all the key venues. Their albums were splendidly crafted affairs that showed great taste in outside writers, and a real respect for well-arranged songs.

My World Fell Down
SAGITTARIUS **CBS 2867**

Covering an Ivy League song written by the talented Brits John Carter and Geoff Stephens was an unusual move for a hotshot West Coast producer, but that's exactly what Gary Usher did with this single from his Sagittarius project.

Another one with an eye on his old mate and songwriting partner Brian Wilson, Usher was eager to push the boundaries with this one on Columbia's still quite new eight-track machine, turning it into a sound collage in parts, as opposed to the straightforward Ivy League incarnation.

Glen Campbell takes the lead voice and Beach Boy Bruce Johnston is also in there fattening out the background vocals. Usher serves it up in different sections, each with its own distinct ambiance and feel, varying from full-on pop and quiet sections, to a bewildering array of noises-off that included (as listed on the Columbia Recording Studio sheet): tractor, baby cries, horse race, alarm clock, teletypes, gun battle, symphony orchestra tuning and a pile driver! All the way through, though, the accent

was on the vocals, making it one of the most memorable of the period.

Possibly too radical for major sales, it did manage to get to US No70, and its collectability in Britain suggests that it sold diddly-squat here.

My Friend Jones
RAM JOHN HOLDER
COLUMBIA DB 8262

By now, Ram John Holder was firmly following a solo path with the re-location of his brother Jim to Guyana, and he was moving towards his best musical period of his London Blues work.

This was a good step along the way, with help from Paul Jones (his friend in the title) and some Manfred Mann members. Everyone involved lived quite close together around the Finchley Road/Swiss Cottage area of North London, which is how Paul and Ram first linked up.

This difficult-to-characterise record was never going to be a hit, but it sounds as soulful and as earthy today as it did then.

Extra Terrestrial Vistiations
ART NOUVEAUX
FONTANA TF 843

This is another of those real oddities that emerged on the Fontana label that no-one seems to know about.

The producer credit of Steve Douglas suggests a Los Angeles product as it is the same Douglas sax player who was a famed member of Spector's Wrecking Crew.

It's a gentle ode to UFOs and visitors from outer space, which had long been a fascination of Americans. It sounds a little like something Simon and Garfunkel might have cooked up while fooling around, but with electronic werps and whibbles strategically placed to provide interest.

Presumably a one-off studio idea, it doesn't appear to have sold in the States, and, for some oblique reason, had a UK release that is now rated at over £20 in the Record Collector Price Guide.

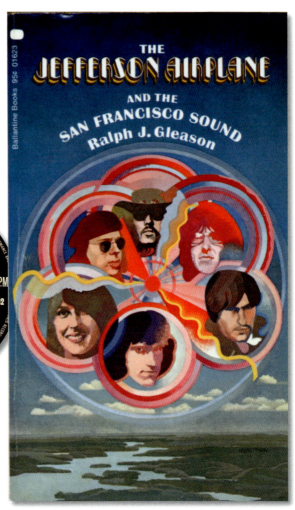

Ballad Of You & Me & Pooneil
JEFFERSON AIRPLANE RCA 1647

As if to confirm that 1967 was taking music into very different directions, this one from the Airplane eschewed the intensity and commerciality of 'White Rabbit' and 'Somebody To Love' and let the Paul Kantner song explore much more of what the band were like on stage.

Rather than being a Grace Slick-led item, Marty Balin takes most of the frontline vocal chores with Grace swooping erratically in the background and joining him in an approximation of unison in certain sections.

Although similar to 'Somebody To Love' in tempo and feel, it is more freeform and, for the times, avant garde. Despite that, it rose to No42 in America at a time when the charts were still reflecting commerciality, but it made enough of a showing to become one of the records that really began to lift rock music into a separate place from pop.

The Airplane quickly became darlings of the teen mag scene.

PLEASE tell me something about the Electric Prunes, who I believe are coming here soon. — Anne Raymond, 75 London Road, Bath.
● Quite correct, Anne. The Prunes are already here, and will be in Bath on December 4. Group is based in sunny Los Angeles on the American West Coast and comprises: James Lowe (22)—lead singer and harmonica; Michael Gannon (20)—rhythm guitar and harmony vocalist; Michael Weakly (21)—drums; Ken Williams (19)—lead guitar; and Mark Tulin (19)—bass guitar. And when you hear them stand by for blasting—they use eight separate amplifiers, which is pretty powerful stuff!

Get Me To The World On Time
THE ELECTRIC PRUNES
REPRISE RS 20564

Producer Dave Hassinger guided the group to another powerhouse performance on this US No25 hit, which is as equally collectable in the UK as their preceding 'I Had Too Much To Dream Last Night'.

This is dominated by an oscillating and shuddering guitar effect that is mixed even higher than the snotty vocals, leaving us in no doubt that, coupled with Hendrix's arrival and the stirring of embryonic heavy rock that was emerging from blues bands, the future of the guitar on record had changed beyond all recognition. This one made No42 in Britain, bettering its predecessor's No49 showing. The group was originally from Seattle, and built a cult following with the fuzz effects, acid guitar and echo-laden drum sounds that they evolved over a series of albums cut in LA.

Baby Your Phrasing Is Bad
CALEB
PHILIPS BF 1588

The young Caleb Quaye was embracing phasing on this ultra-rare first release, of which reputedly only around 300 were pressed – and many of them were given away to friends.

Although around 19, Caleb was already involved with session work, and was well-known on the London R&B/rock scene through work with Long John Baldry and Bluesology. The latter's involvement suggests to some that Elton John was on this track, although there is no immediate aural evidence of a piano. Instead, there is total phasing overkill with Lennon-inspired 'Tomorrow Never Knows' vocal effects.

It is certainly one of the most collectable British records of the era, and one that distinctly evokes the experimentation of 1967.

Caleb also worked with Cochise, Hookfoot and Elton, when the latter's solo career had properly taken off.

Reflections Of Charles Brown
RUPERT'S PEOPLE
COLUMBIA DB 8226

Another disc that perfectly evokes the summer of '67 is this one from Rupert's People, which was so obviously modelled on 'A Whiter Shade Of Pale' in feel and melody.

No matter, it is a well formed recording with a tasteful guitar looping in and out of the arrangement.

It was supposedly recorded by Les Fleur De Lys (and there were at least two sets of them); a Rupert's People 'group' was assembled, but they apparently fell out with manager Howard Conder and were replaced by another group who had previously worked as Sweet Feeling. Included in these comings and goings at various stages were Paul and Adrian Gurvitz (see also The Knack and Gun) and ex-Merseybeat John Banks, while at one point the 1967 personnel were listed as Rod Lynton (guitar/vocal, who also wrote the song), Ray Beverly (bass), Dai Jenkins (rhythm), John Tout (organ) and Steve Bendell (drums).

Life's too short to spend time agonising over names, just go back and listen to a splendid record that was very indicative of the times.

Summertime Blues
BLUE CHEER
PHILIPS BF 1646

Blue Cheer, from San Francisco, were part of the expansion of that local scene. They were the first act to play the newly opened Denver Dog when promoter Chet Helms was convinced to extend his West Coast operations into that city.

Cheer were quite possibly the first act to warrant the description of Power Trio, which this first UK issue of theirs testifies in bucketloads.

Taking the basic structure of the old Eddie Cochran hit, they ripped it apart to reform it as something that could lay claim to being the first slab of heavy metal.

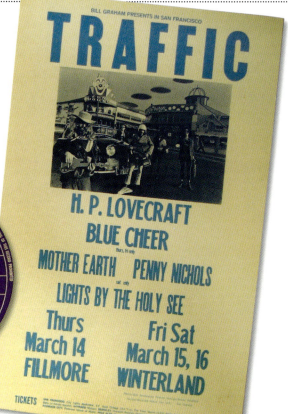

TeenSeT

LOVE YEARS COMING

STRAWBERRY CHILDREN
(Jim Webb)
Arranger: Jim Webb
Producer: Johnny Rivers

LIBERTY

℗ 1967
LBF 15012
(LBF.15012 A)
Side 1
Carlin Music Corp.

Capitol
A CAPITOL RECORDS, INC. U.S.A. Recording
DEMONSTRATION
RECORD
NOT FOR
SALE

BMI CANADA
LTD.
(9.6.67)
HALF PAST MIDNIGHT (2.06)
(Emmerson)
THE STACCATOS
A Dasanda Production

CL 15005
CC 1-72453 45
℗ 1967

MAJOR MINOR

MAJOR MINOR RECORDS LTD 45

e Knack
Time Time Ti
plete UK singles (and more) 1965-1967
The pre-Gun recordings of Paul Gu

island

WIP-6016-A
℗ 1967
Time: 5:58
4:10
Copyright Control

TINY GODDESS
(G. Spyropoulos—R. Singer—P. Campbell-Lyons)
NIRVANA
Produced by: Muff Winwood and
Jimmy Miller

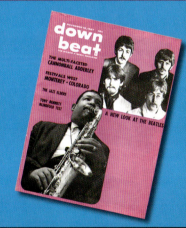

down
beat

THE MULTI-FACETED
CANNONBALL ADDERLEY

FESTIVALS WEST
MONTEREY · COLORADO

THE JAZZ ELDERS
TONY BENNETT
BLINDFOLD TEST

A NEW LOOK AT THE BEATLES

© Transatlantic
Records Ltd. 1967
Produced by
Joe Boyd

45 r.p.m.
BIG 101

Side One   GRANNY TAKES A TRIP
(Bowyer, Beard)
THE PURPLE GANG
Essex/Heathside Music
MCPS

SUNSHINE GIRL
(Riopelle, Roberds, MacLeod)

45 R.P.M.
Made in England

A&M
RECORDS

AMS.701
℗ 1967
AMS 701-A

THE PARADE
Produced by Jerry Riopelle
COPYRIGHT CONTROL

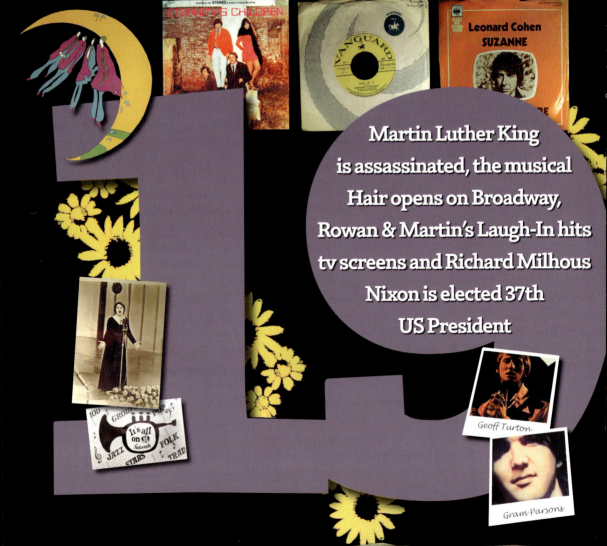

1968

Martin Luther King is assassinated, the musical Hair opens on Broadway, Rowan & Martin's Laugh-In hits tv screens and Richard Milhous Nixon is elected 37th US President

Geoff Turton

Gram Parsons

This was a year known for its student sit-ins and street protests, with the French Government almost toppled as workers join the students.

Anti-Vietnam War feelings intensify, both Martin Luther King and Bobby Kennedy are assassinated, and Soviet tanks roll into Prague, giving the year a very different feel.

Country Rock emerges with The Band's first album and Gram Parsons' work with The Byrds, Cream falter and break up, but rock music finds new strength and power as album-based bands begin to take centre stage.

Groups seek more grandiose projects like The Who's *Tommy* and The Stones' *Rock 'n' Roll Circus*, and Graham Nash leaves the Hollies to co-form Crosby, Stills and Nash.

The music business is changing and artists are starting to seek creative control as evidenced by the Beatles setting up Apple Corp and releasing the White Album.

Eli's Comin'
LAURA NYRO CBS 3604

Bronx-born Laura Nyro was strikingly different from
the word go, which explains why so many diverse artists
quickly sought to cover material from her first album,
on Verve, *More Than A New Discovery*. The album's
'Wedding Bell Blues' and 'Stoney End' were covered by
The 5th Dimension and Barbra Streisland respectively.
Laura moved to CBS with the marvellous Eli and the
Thirteenth Confession album, from which 'Eli's Comin'
was taken.

From the first moment of a hanging keyboard and
vocal note, this track is different. It surges forward with a
passionate urgency – Laura drawing on her love of R&B
and gospel works – and she soars and sweeps around the
main melody before returning to a bold hanging section
that takes us to the fade. The strong flip 'Sweet Blindness'
was characterised by subtle time shifts.

She went on to cut the *New York Tendaberry* album in
1969, and the *Gonna Take A Miracle* album in 1971, when
she was joined by Labelle in an affectionate re-visiting of
the R&B girl group material of her youth.

Magic Garden

THE 5TH DIMENSION

LIBERTY LBF 15052

The 5th Dimension had begun on Johnny Rivers' Soul City label as a soul version of The Mamas and Papas, and progressed musically through their covers of Laura Nyro's material, including Stoned Soul Picnic. However, their best-known hits came from the pen of Jimmy Webb.

Webb quickly realised that the vocal talents and diversity of the group allowed him to further develop the sectionalised aspects of his songwriting. Marilyn McCoo, Florence LaRue, Billy Davis Jnr, Lamont McLemore and Ron Townsend had taken Webb's 'Up Up And Away' high up the US charts, and went on to issue two albums of virtually entirely Webb songs.

Experienced producer Bones Howe, who had worked alongside so many West Coast artists, knew just how to bring out a mix of commerciality and adventurism in the records.

'Magic Garden' was the flip side of the upbeat and oft-covered 'Carpet Man', and the keystone track of the album of the same name. Its combination of bouncy uplifting verses that lead towards a quieter, ethereal section near the end make it the closest anyone has come to capturing the feel and warmth of a hot summer's day. The whole thing becomes quite magical, either as a single song, or as a descriptor to an album that many people see as one of the best of the Sixties.

The 5th Dimension with Bones Howe and Jimmy Webb during the 'Magic Garden' sessions in Hollywood.'

Piece Of My Heart

BIG BROTHER & THE HOLDING COMPANY

CBS 3683

If the breathy and seductive females in the 5th Dimension were at one end of the spectrum, then Janis Joplin's vocal on 'Piece Of My Heart' is surely at the other. Big Brother And The Holding Company (was there ever a more restricting group name?) were one of the mainstays on the San Francisco scene of The Fillmore and Winterland but, despite their signing to Columbia, they never managed to become the major act that the company envisaged. Janis Joplin was another matter entirely, as her gut-wrenching cover of Erma Franklin's original song shows.

Akkord record
player 1968 (below)
and Dallas record
player in 1962
(right)

Fender adverts in 1968(left)
and 1962 (right)

Lah-Di-Dah
JAKE THACKRAY
COLUMBIA DB 8364

Everyday People
SLY & THE FAMILY STONE
DIRECTION 58-3938

Sly & The
Family Stone

Jake Thackray

It may seem particularly odd to group these two together; but they are both records that leave you smiling. Jake Thackray had the most mournful face, which made him a popular choice for several TV shows at the time.

He was a wry observer of human foibles, and 'Lah-Di-Dah' which examines the difficulties of a young man's integration into his beloved's family was probably his most-played song on radio or TV. It contains probably the only rhyming of 'acquiesce' and 'caress' in a song, and is certainly the only mention of a rupture in this book!

Looking at any picture of Sly & The Family Stone would raise an inevitable smile, as they were certainly a wacky mixed bunch.

Built around the writing and production talents of Sly Stewart, the group had burst onto the scene with the still influential 'Dance To The Music'. 'Everyday People' was a huge US No1 hit, staying at the top for a month after a 12-week gradual climb. Built on a steady drum and cowbell groove, interspersed with brief fuzz guitar notes, the song is a plea for tolerance – different strokes for different folks. The whole thing is so laden with vocal and instrumental hooks at every turn that it's hard to understand why it could only struggle up to No36 in Britain in early 1969.

Mrs Bluebird
ETERNITY'S CHILDREN
CAPITOL CL 15558

Co-produced by Curt Boettcher with his look-alike sidekick Keith Olsen, this is one of the most perfect of the many Sunshine Pop records. It only managed to get to No69 in the States where it stayed resolutely for three weeks before dropping back down. Because of the way the American charts worked, for the record to even get that high it had to have been in the top ten in some markets.

It seems that in this case, the company did not follow through with the necessary promotional pushes on radio and in wider markets to push it higher, which explains why many US hits reached a certain level and then seemed to disappear.

The group came from Biloxi, Mississippi, and consisted at this stage of Linda Lawley, Mike 'Kid' McClain, Charles Ross and Roy Whittaker. They cut two albums for Capitol's offshoot Tower label, the second being produced by Gary Paxton rather than Curt ' n' Keith.

'Mrs Bluebird' has all the Association-styled harmonies you could ever want, and was enhanced by a strong guitar solo. The song was apparently sparked from the 'Mr Bluebird on my shoulder…' line from Disney's 'Zip-A-Dee-Do-Dah'.

Silly Grin
THE FAMILY DOGG
FONTANA TF 921

The Family Dogg (not to be confused with the West Coast hippie organisation) were a London studio-based outfit with a lot of diverse talents.

The key man was producer Steve Rowland, but alongside him were writers Mike Hazelwood and Albert Hammond, blonde singer Christine (Crackerjack!) Holmes and brunette Zooey (aka Pamela).

This was their second single, and was a more heavily orchestrated Spector-influenced re-make of a track from the first Critters' album written by that group's Jimmy Ryan. It made full use of all the group's voices on the choruses, while their subsequent album, *A Way Of Life*, gave all the group, except Christine, the chance to be lead vocal. This Bell Records' album, on which 'Silly Grin' features, is pretty collectable, partly for the interest in the group and their eclectic choices of material (which included Jimmy Webb, Paul Simon and Dylan alongside their own works), but also for the small print, which reveals credits for John

Paul Jones (bass), John Bonham (drums) and Jimmy Page (guitar) among others. Also pictured on the album were the group's technical advisors Panda and Tanya Doggage, two Tibetan terriers whose stated ambition was to kill The Singing Postman.

The lovely Zooey could also be found working in the Speakeasy's restaurant most evenings.

Montage (from the film 'How Sweet It Is')
JEFFERSON
PYE 7N 17634

When Geoff Turton left the Rockin' Berries, he took on the solo persona of Jefferson, and started to work with producer John Schroeder.

According to John: "Geoff had a good middle-of-the-road pop-type voice, like the 4 Seasons or the Tokens. Back then, the single was the be-all-and-end-all – you needed a hit…"

Their first choice for Jefferson was a cover of a song that had led off the third album of The Love Generation in the States, a flowery, harmony-lite band who had scored a couple of hits.

'Montage' was another Jimmy Webb song from a film, and Geoff's version captured all the magic and feel of soft sunshiny music with his version, but had spectacularly little sales success. This came for him with a British hit 'The Colour Of My Love', and a surprise American one with 'Baby Take Me In Your Arms', though he wasn't able to sustain success for long in either markets, and eventually returned to touring Berries line-ups.

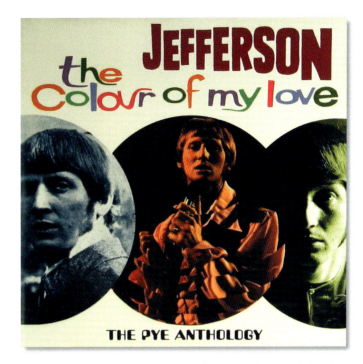

"With the Berries, it was all blokes together and I had been a bit of a stooge for the comedy, which was okay, I suppose. When I made the break, I thought I wanted to be another Andy Williams, but John insisted we went for songs that would make a real impact to overcome the image I had as a bit of a 'hairy fairy'. 'Montage' was one of those – an intelligent song." **GEOFF TURTON**

Mythological Sunday
FRIENDS **DERAM DM 198**

John Carter is one of the best-known unknowns in the business. He was known as a member of Carter-Lewis and The Ivy League, but gradually worked his way into being a behind-the-scenes musician, recording many of his own or friends' projects. He was, to give two examples, responsible for The Flowerpot Men's 'Let's Go To San Francisco' and was the lead voice on The New Vaudeville Band's 'Winchester Cathedral'.

'Friends' is one of many studio names he concocted for release, and the song has subsequently popped up in re-mixed form on various Flowerpot Men CDs. It is a fine example of John's modus operandi, in that he always gives good value with lengthy sectionalised tracks – and when anyone re-releases his material, he will often go back and tweak tracks to offer new sections or mixes for collectors.

This was originally the B side of the release, 'Piccolo Man' being the more commercial top side, but it has been one for John to re-visit on more than one occasion.

" It's a favourite track of mine – another mini-epic with diminished chords. I like the mix with me singing, but this one has Tony Burrows on lead. I think it is one of the most psychedelic ones, with strange lyrics, a floaty sound and soldiers marching – a sort of flowery/psychedelic movement."
JOHN CARTER

Suzanne
LEONARD COHEN
CBS 3337

With the emergence of certain key 'student bed-sit' albums, in 1968 this song, from *Songs Of Leonard Cohen,* became a part of many people's lives.

Wikipedia describes the song as 'beginning and ending as an ode to a half-crazy woman capable of personal connection, containing an unconventional discussion of Jesus in the second verse which has been removed in at least one cover of the song,'

Suzanne was the subject of disagreement between Cohen and producer John Simon who wanted to add piano and possibly drums. Speaking some years later Cohen was clear that there was no way he was having drums or piano on the record.

Someday Girl
THE MOON LIBERTY LBF 15076

The Moon included Matthew Moore, who wrote this song, and one-time Beach Boy David Marks, who still remembers the Moon period with fondness.

This was the first single of two and has a wonderful haunting quality about it, enhanced by sweeping strings that help build the crescendos. It's the sort of song that if it were to be written by someone like Coldplay today it would be hailed as a classic, but then, very few heard it, and even fewer bought it.

A UK album was also issued, called *Without Earth.*

"We worked so very hard on The Moon; we practically lived in the studio. We listened to The Beatles' *White Album* a lot during that time."
DAVID MARKS

She's A Lady
JOHN SEBASTIAN
KAMA SUTRA 618026

John Sebastian had left the Lovin' Spoonful at a time when the personal relationships within the band had been soured by drug-related problems.

His solo career looked promising – everyone had looked to him as the driving writing force in the group, and this first single seemed to fulfil all that was expected: gentle instrumentation wraps around his warm and pleasing voice on a song that struck the right note from the start.

His career however got bogged down and despite some solo success Sebastian never kicked his Spoonful roots or delivered the promise which many had predicted.

Path Through The Forest
THE FACTORY MGM 1444

This highly collectable rarity was produced by Eddie Tre-Vett. The Factory were akin to a Psychy power trio, and this blend of feedback, freaky guitar and insistent rhythm was pressed in small enough quantities for some to believe that the demos are more common than stock copies.

The group comprised three teenagers: guitarist Ian Oates, bassist Jack Brand and drummer Bill MacLeod, and the song appears to have been written by Clifford T Ward under the pseudonym of his wife's maiden name.

An NME review in October 1968 referred to 'plenty of excitement' on the record, certainly alluding to the mass of effects, electronic and otherwise, that pervade it.

The group managed one more single, 'Try A Little Sunshine', on CBS, which is also mega-rare and sought after, commanding prices approaching four figures. That one was written by John Pantry and co-produced by their manager Brian Carroll, who recalled both records in Record Collector's August 1996 issue: "We wanted to add effects [to 'Path Through The Forest'], but someone from the record company straightened their tie and said no. So the single was re-mixed to get rid of some of the weirder psychedelic sounds… It's good that The Factory have finally got the recognition they were denied all those years ago. Their two singles were classics. There's no doubt about it."

Give A Damn
SPANKY & OUR GANG
MERCURY MF 1052

And She's Mine
SPANKY & OUR GANG
MERCURY MF 1123

The eclectic Spanky & Our Gang were a harmony group unlike any other, always prepared to take on the unusual in terms of both material and arrangements.

The various original members assembled more by chance than design, though some shared a folk background. They were picked up by Chicago's Mercury Records, who appeared content for them to work in a happy, light, poppy vein, as evidenced by their first big hit 'Sunday Will Never Be The Same' and its follow-up 'Making Every Minute Count'.

The initial foursome became a sextet of Elaine 'Spanky' McFarlane, Nigel Pickering (rhythm), Malcolm Hale (lead), John Seiter (drums), Kenny Hodges (bass) and Lefty Baker (another lead guitar). They developed a 20s/30s period look that affected their musical choices and visual appeal, but tragedy struck when Malcolm Hale died in 1968.

Their albums had always been varied affairs (Suzanne to Stardust on the second), often including spoken sections between tracks, and by the time of their third album *Without Rhyme Or Reason*, from which these two singles are taken, they were looking for even more variety.

'And She's Mine' is a simple love song with a gorgeous melody, unusual group vocals and a bridge that strongly harks back to early Beatles.

'Give A Damn', by contrast, is a late Sixties protest song that calls for everyone to open their eyes to the social ills around them. It was strong enough to be banned on several US radio stations, which stopped it getting higher than No43 there. Otherwise, the song, written by their producers Stu Scharf and Bob Dorough, certainly would have gone higher as it had a particularly strong melody, production and group performance.

Sha La La La Lee
SYMON & PI
PARLOPHONE R 5662

The record credit reads: 'Arranged & Produced Mark P Wirtz as a tribute to Phil Spector', which straightaway tells you that this is a soundalike record. Since 1963, producers in both the US and the UK had attempted to replicate the 'Wall Of Sound' with variable results. Even leaving aside the make-up of the sound – Spector's unique instrumental combinations – each studio room has its own special sound and ambiance, so they could never quite catch the feel of Hollywood's Gold Star or New York's Mirasound (Spector's most used studios). For anyone to come close was quite an achievement.

Mark Wirtz was able to do it better than most, and this track shows how close he could get. He recorded the track first, before trying a variety of voices as leads over it. The line up of session players and singers was as rich as London could provide at the time. The resulting record, a full-blooded remake of The Small Faces' 1966 hit, has since become one of the real hidden treasures of the end of the Sixties.

Simon and Pi were Robert Simons and Linda Day, who used to sing with an Irish showband.

Symon and Pi—Robert Simons and Linda Day—used to sing with an Irish showband and they make their disc debut with Sha La La La Lee (Parlophone). The song was originally a Small Faces hit and, if you think the disc sounds like a Phil Spector production, it is intentional. Producer Mark Wirtz is an admirer of Spector and the arrangement by these two 20-year-old Londoners is intended as a tribute.

> "Much to my embarrassment, there isn't much to say about the Symon and Pi recordings (four sides in total, the 'Sha-la-la...' and 'Love Is Happening To Me' A-sides and the 'I-don't-remember-what-they-were' B-sides).
>
> I recorded in Motown-style back then, namely cutting tracks randomly and whimsically, then trying different artists on them. Symon and Pi (I don't remember their real names) happened to fit the part, so I recorded them.
>
> My regular studio band back then was Clem Cattini and Rex Bennett (drums), Russ Stableford (bass), Nicky Hopkins (piano), Ray Cooper and Denis Lopez (percussion – lots of it), Big Jim Sullivan and John McLaughlin (guitars), and a combined background vocal ensemble made up of John Carter, Ken Lewis, Chas Mills, the Ladybirds and the Breakaways..."
> *Mark Wirtz*

John Carter (Ivy League, Flowerpot Men etc) who added backing vocals adds: "I guess this was just another session...get to the studio...ooh and ah a bit, and then..over to the pub. It's a hard life!"

Witchi Tai To
EVERYTHING IS EVERYTHING
VANGUARD VA 1

Throughout the Sixties, there were always records that were totally unlike anything else around and this is a case in point. Witchi Tai To starts with a gentle organ not dissimilar to Procol Harum, from which comes a repeated chant that may or may not be of native North American origination.

Gradually, more instrumentation is added, tambourine, guitars and a cool-sounding tenor sax, which take the chant loping on to the fade. It's all pleasantly hypnotic.

The group was an aggregation of New York jazz/rock musicians built around Chris Hills and Chico Waters, who also had out an eponymous album in 1969 and another interesting one in 1971 called *Comin' Outta The Ghetto*.

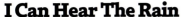

I Can Hear The Rain
REPARATA AND THE DELRONS
RCA 1691

Weather Forecast
REPARATA AND THE DELRONS
BELL BLL 1021

Two splendid records from Reparata and her gals with producers Bill and Steve Jerome, prove yet again what a great outfit they were. Using inclement weather as a motif for sadness is a well-trodden musical path, but it is played to its kitsch hilt with these two.

'I Can Hear The Rain' is a big girlie sob. The group uses the traditional girl group harmonies and feel, and builds to big choruses and crescendos. 'Weather Forecast' warns of rain too, but against a perkier, more upbeat background, that was more akin to the group's Captain Of My Ship sound.

A sombre female radio voice warns of clouds and rain, while Reparata agrees that all the sunshine has gone from her life.

There had been several personnel changes in the group by this time, members joining and leaving with confusing rapidity. However, Mary Aiese' strong lead is still evident on the RCA disc, which reportedly had back-ups from the-then unknown Melba Moore.

Mary 'Reparata' Aiese signs up.

Your Mind And We Belong Together
LOVE **ELEKTRA EKSN 45038**

The *Forever Changes* album had yet to really settle into the collective consciousness when this one-off oddment single came out.

At four minutes 22 seconds long, 'Your Mind And We Belong Together' allowed the group to almost present a sampler of the *Forever Changes* styles, though this certainly would not have been the intention as these two sides were the last recordings by that line-up of Love, cut at Sunset Sound on January 30, 1968.

The song's first section is most reminiscent of the album with its oblique Arthur Lee lyrics and feel, and several different, quieter sections follow this, until the last third is taken up by a searing guitar solo. The A side took 44 takes, as the band discussed as they went along how to stitch it all together.

The other side, 'Laughing Stock', was cut the same day with ten takes in two distinct sections – acoustic and electric. It begins in the gentler Bryan MacLean-influenced acoustic style, but then burst into a faster electric group thrash in the style of the Da Capo album's wilder moments. Clearly a studio try-out of ideas, the song then withers on the vine as everything simply teeters to a gradual stop. At that point, these Arthur Lee-produced cuts were both non-album sides, making the single now quite collectable.

Gentle On My Mind
GLEN CAMPBELL
EMBER EMB S249

Love him or hate him for his later descent into all-too-easy-listening recordings, Glen Campbell was a classy guitar player and singer who appeared on many West Coast hits as a session player.

By now, he was beginning his solo career with the A side of this one, Jimmy Webb's 'By The Time I Get To Phoenix'. It was issued in the UK as a bit of an oddity: a three-track single, you could find his version of John Hartford's great mid-tempo song 'Gentle On My Mind' as one of the flip choices. Without doubt, it was a potential A side in its own right, and Glen sings it as if it was all his own.

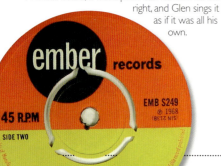

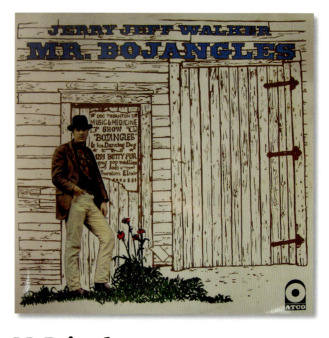

Mr Bojangles JERRY JEFF WALKER
ATLANTIC 584200

The superb Austrian guitarist Thomas Leeb recently played this one as a part of his set, yet he was unaware of Jerry Jeff Walker, only knowing the song from the Nitty Gritty Dirt Band version, with whom he had worked briefly in the States.

Jerry Jeff is a happy-go-lucky Texan singer, who has made a series of heart-warming albums since 1968, most of which can be recommended to anyone who likes laid-back country with a rock twist, sung in a dark brown relaxed drawl. Jerry Jeff's song about the famous black dancer is one of his best known, and brought him a No77 US hit, held back by sales being split with a rival cover version from Bobby Cole. Jerry Jeff had previously been part of a group called Circus Maximus on Vanguard Records.

On the Mr Bojangles follow-up album, he was produced and engineered by the famed Tom Dowd, who was also credited as 'Patron Saint', 'Voice of Reason' and 'Vestige Of Sanity'.

Volume 1 of the Ripples CD series

Bitter Thoughts Of Little Jane
TIMON
PYE 7N 17451

Timon was a young lad from Liverpool, who emerged to cut this oddity on Pye. It is very obviously Beatles-influenced, but has a charm all of its own.

It benefits greatly from an attractive arrangement that features good bass and guitar lines, flute and varied string sections, making it a well-formed and executed record that really justifies its three-figure collector price. He put out one further single in 1970 on the Threshold label as Tymon Dogg, before re-appearing under the new name on later Clash recordings. You can find it on *Ripples Volume One*.

Mendocino
SIR DOUGLAS QUINTET
MERCURY MF 1079

Doug Sahm was another laid-back Texan character, who found his sound early on. He stuck with it through any number of back-up players, though they almost always included his organ-playing sidekick Augie Meyer.

As The Sir Douglas Quintet, they enjoyed their 'She's About A Mover' hit both in the US and, albeit smaller, in the UK, and had issued a string of similar-sounding songs. The Mover turned up in remade form on the *Mendicino* album, showing how much the groove meant to Sahm and his usual cohorts.

Alongside Sahm and Meyer on this one were John Perez, Harvey Regan and Frank Morin, and together they made a lovely lazy sound that made listeners think they had just turned up at the studio, got their groove going and almost made it up as they went along.

The song itself is a bit of nonsense about how he wants his new young lady to stay with him in his lovehouse in Mendicino, and was typical of the songs that Sahm wrote. The album is full of great bluesy/rock/pop crossover tunes in a similar groove.

Gram Parsons

The place was the Middle Earth club in London's Covent Garden in summer 1968, the occasion was a gig by The Byrds and it was packed out. Round the back, the Byrds roadie Jim Seiter was looking anxious because he was having to borrow a PA system – what he had was inoperable.

It turned out to be a great gig. The Byrds, made up that night of Roger McGuinn, Chris Hillman, Kevin Kelly (drums), Doug Dillard (electric banjo) and Gram Parsons, were absolutely magnificent. Responding to the nature of the club (ie they were all stoned), they played for about an hour delivering all the expected Byrds hit material and key album tracks.

At one point Gram Parsons, resplendent in an all-white Nudie suit, stepped forward and took over leading the band through material from their new *Sweetheart Of the Rodeo* album on which he had been a major guiding force.

The sound changed from loud rock/pop to old-style laid-back country, which at that point was pretty new to a London audience. Despite that, it was very well received. The band ended up playing a two-and-a-half-hour set with more crowd-pleasing Byrdsongs.

Gram Parsons made more of an impression that night than almost anyone else. He sounded great, he looked great, and it was obvious that he was a major talent, emphasised later by his solo albums on Reprise. Like other southern boys who blazed a trail in country rock he immersed himself in the rock and roll lifestyle and ened as one of its most famous victim. Certainly more famous in death than during his short life.

It's All Over Now
THE VALENTINOS
SOUL CITY SC106

This is the original version of the song that had previously been a hit for The Rolling Stones. At that time, this version had not emerged in the UK, but, in 1968, the influential Dave Godin arranged a release on his Soul City independent label.

The Valentinos were in fact The Womack brothers who had begun as a gospel group, influenced by The Soul Stirrers and the Five Blind Boys of Alabama. They signed to Sam Cooke's SAR label in 1961, and this was their fourth single. With the lead voice from Bobby Womack, it scraped into the Billboard Hot 100, reaching No94 in July 1964.

Of course, The Stones' version did a bit better…

Eleanor Rigby
RAY CHARLES **STATESIDE SS 2120**

Ray Charles' output throughout the Sixties, in such a wide variety of styles and with such consistent quality, has to be admired. His version of 'Eleanor Rigby' changes the feel and tempo of it, the principle difference to be found in the string arrangement. In place of George Martin's string quartet triumph on the Beatles' original, there is an uncredited arrangement that sweeps around the main melody rather than being in opposition to it.

Ray gives the song a new sadness and melancholy as sings with deep feeling for the characters within the lyrics.

Timi Yuro
IT'LL NEVER BE OVER FOR ME
LIBERTY LIB 15182

Timi Yuro had been around all through the Sixties, but never attained the star status she so richly deserved.

This very rare UK single, enhanced by a striking and strident string arrangement, finds her in commanding form on the mid-tempo song of heartbreak and parting.

The wonderfully soulful performance was popular with the Northern Soul crowd, who could easily identify with the title as a rallying call. It's one that crops up reasonably regularly on decent soul compilations from the EMI group.

Let's Copp A Groove
BOBBY WELLS
BEACON 3-102

Shake Your Mini
SHOW STOPPERS **BEACON 3-106**

Beacon Records was a small London-based independent label, who, unsurprisingly, used a flame logo. Their flame burned briefly, giving them a few hits, the biggest being the Show Stoppers' 'Ain't Nothin' But A Houseparty' that reached the UK Top Ten in April 1968.

'Shake Your Mini' was the more collectable follow-up to Houseparty, but disappeared without trace at the time.

Bobby Wells' record is also pretty collectable, especially in the yellow label format, and both records were licensed in from US labels – The Showstoppers from Showtime, and Wells from Romur.

Both dance-based songs share the same bass-led urgency, explaining the collectability, and the status of Beacon as a label to look out for. The label itself may have had people involved who were suspected of using it as a front for other less acceptable activities, but do record collectors care about such things?

Big Bird
EDDIE FLOYD **STAX 601035**

When he cut 'Big Bird', Eddie Floyd was at an in-between stage of his career. He had had an initial major phase of providing a thousand groups with material to cover with 'Knock On Wood' and 'Raise Your Hand', but was still awaiting his early Seventies heyday with great songs like 'I'll Never Find A Girl'. He reputedly started to write this one at Heathrow while waiting for a flight to the States, Otis Redding's still-recent death in his mind.

It's a mighty powerful piece, driven in this instance by his voice, the guitars and drums. The brass boosts the sound, but does not take the normal specific Stax lines.

Floyd repeatedly calls in the chorus for the plane to 'Get on up Big Bird, to my baby's love', imbuing the whole thing with an urgency and emotionality that was different to the label's and the artist's normal output.

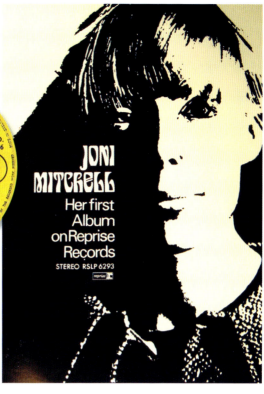

Night In The City
JONI MITCHELL
REPRISE RS 20694

Joni's original version of this song is light and bright, with David Crosby's production really letting all the chorus hooks from her voice come through strongly. The single is taken from Joni's first solo album *Songs to a Seagull* which was originally released without a title due to a record company mix-up.

Touring the songs from this album allowed Mitchell to spread her wings and her second album *Clouds* contained her versions of two song she had written that were being performed by other artists: 'Chelsea Morning' and 'Both Sides Now'.

Although Mitchell was to have success herself with 'Big Yellow Taxi' later on, 'Night in the City' failed to chart.

She was part of the West Coast-based singer-songwriter movement like fellow Canadian Neil Young.

Please (Mk. II)
ECLECTION
ELEKTRA EKSN 45046

Eclection was a London group who followed a not-dissimilar path to Fairport in their early days – the two groups were appealing to basically the same audiences and often played the same venues, such as The Country Club in London's Belsize Park.

Both groups had a female singer up front, who changed as they progressed: Fairport began with Judy Dyble and then worked with Sandy Denny, while Eclection changed from Australian Kerrilee Male to folk singer Dorris Henderson.

Dorris fronts this strong folk rock song, which was Eclection's third Electra single after 'Nevertheless' and 'Another Time Another Place'. The Mk.II in the title refers to the fact that 'Please' had first been issued a month earlier with a different B side.

The various members of Eclection came from different parts of the world: Kerrilee and guitarist Trevor Lucas were from Australia, guitarist/trumpeter Mike Rosen was an American,

bass George Hultgren was European and drummer Gerry Conway was British, living near London's Finchley Road.

The close ties with Fairport continued. Trevor Lucas later worked in both Fotheringay and Fairport and married Sandy Denny., and Gerry Conway is the current Fairport drummer. George Hultgren re-appeared as George Kajanus and had several big hits with Sailor.

Eclection with Dorris Henderson. This postcard was inserted into promo copies of the record

"It was no surprise to me, even on first hearing, that 'Meet On The Ledge' would become an enduring anthem. After all the many years, to me it still sounds fresh and relevant."
ASHLEY HUTCHINGS

"It is more Fairport's song than my own, I suppose, but it has every right to be there and I am still very proud of having written it."
RICHARD THOMPSON

Meet On The Ledge
FAIRPORT CONVENTION
ISLAND WIP-6047

After the oblique first issue of 'If I Had A Ribbon Bow', Fairport's manager Joe Boyd guided them to the emerging writing talent of Richard Thompson, the man who Joe saw as Fairport's biggest asset.

On this original version of the song (it is one Fairport recorded on a number of occasions), the verses are taken by Ian Matthews and Sandy Denny in turn, with everyone and their dog joining in on the choruses.

'Meet On The Ledge' has received many explanations as to its original meaning, including reference to a particular tree climb that Richard used to do with teenage chums.

There have been many other suggestions as to the meaning, ever including explanations bordering on the metaphysical, and over the years Richard himself has remained uncommitted as to his original thoughts.

However, it is what the song has become, rather than how it began, that is the key element to every Fairport fan around the world as it holds a unique place in the repetoire as a rallying anthem at the end of every Fairport concert.

It was also the track chosen to represent Fairport on the famous Island Records sampler *You Can All Join In* which was present in almost album collection of the period. It is credited with speeding the careers of the bands featured including Free, Jethro Tull and Traffic.

MAGIC GARDEN
(Jim Webb)

℗ 1968
LBF 15052
(LBF.15052 B)
Side 2
Carlin Music

5th DIMENSION
Produced by Bones Howe
LIBERTY

fontana
TF 921
267 827 TF
45
MONO
A
Kama Sutra
Music Ltd.
℗ 1968
267 827 1F

SILLY GRIN
(Ryan)
THE FAMILY DOGG
Accompaniment directed by Reg Tilsley
A Double-R Production by Steve Rowland & Dave Dee

MGM
DEMO RECORD
NOT FOR SALE
EDDIE TRE-
VETT MUSIC
LTD.
7XSM 1587 45
℗ 1968
MGM 1444
(18.10.68)

PATH THROUGH THE FOREST
(Rollings)
THE FACTORY
An Eddie Tre-Vett Production
Produced by D. Lyon-Shaw and
B. Carroll

LOOK at the Sunshine

CAPITOL

BELL
RECORDS
TRADE MARK OF BELL RECORDS INC.
MADE IN GT BRITAIN
THE GRAMOPHONE CO LTD.
United Artists
Music Ltd.
BLL 1021A 45
℗ 1968
19.7.68
BLL 1021
(A Mala Recording)

WEATHER FORECAST
(T. Michaels—V. Gormann)
REPARATA and The Delrons
Arranged John Abbott
Producers Steve & Bill Jerome
for Real Good Prods.

VANGUARD
VA 1
45
Lovetruth Music,
USA
VA1 1F
Apostolic
SIDE A
℗ 1968

WITCHI TAI TO
(Pepper)
EVERYTHING IS EVERYTHING
Produced by Danny Weiss
for 10th Street Productions

DIRECTION
DIRECTION
THE FAMILY STONE
EVERYDAY PEOPLE

mercury
MF 1123
127 466 MCF
45
MONO
A
Spanky &
Our Gang
Music (USA)
℗ 1968
127 466 1F

AND SHE'S MINE (2.34)
(Hodges)
SPANKY & OUR GANG
Produced by Scharf & Derough
Sound by Joe Sidore

Kama Sutra
℗ 1968
MADE IN
ENGLAND
Robbins
Music
618026A
618026
Produced by
Paul
Rotherchild
Arr. & Cond.
by Paul Harris

SHE'S A LADY (1.45)
(Sebastian)
JOHN SEBASTIAN
A Product of Koppelman-Rubbin
Assoc., Inc.

Apollo 11 takes men to the first lunar landing, Sharon Tate murdered by Charles Manson gang and The Woodstock festival is held in upstate New York

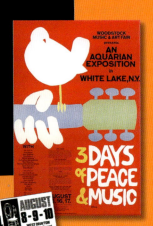

Rock Music comes of age in 1969 as better equipment allows outdoor festivals, and concerts attract huge numbers. Woodstock is wet but full of stars, Dylan plays the Isle of Wight, The Stones leave the Altamont festival with a bitter taste after the Hells Angels murder of an audience member, and the Toronto R&R Revival concert shows there is still life in the Fifties rockers. Cutting edge music has shifted to album formats, with the charts full of a wide variety of styles; Bowie and Elton John get going with 'Space Oddity' and 'Your Song' respectively, and the Jackson Five arrives. The Beatles play their last gig on Apple's roof and release their last studio album, while hundreds queue for the round-the-clock showings of Easy Rider at the Classic Cinema at Piccadilly Circus. The Archies' 'Sugar Sugar' shows that pop isn't dead, though all around progressive rock is getting louder and more grandiose.

Black Pearl
SONNY CHARLES & THE
CHECKMATES LTD. **A&M AMS 752**

Proud Mary
THE CHECKMATES LTD.   **A&M AMS 769**

Through controversial work with the Beatles and a supposed rescue bid on their various projects, producer Phil Spector refused to end the Sixties with a whimper. In 1969, he made a deal with A&M

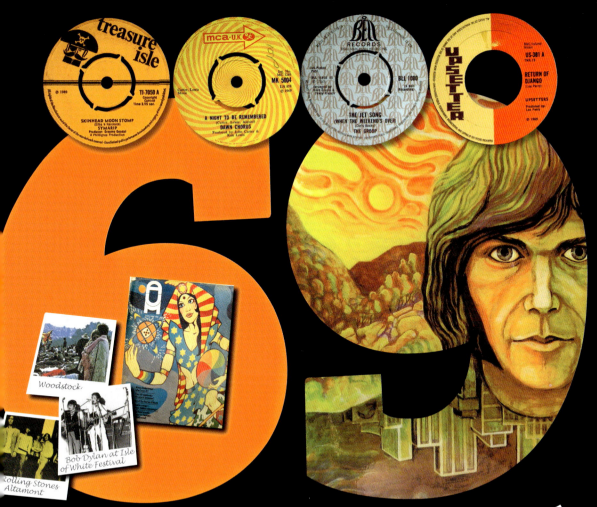

Woodstock

Bob Dylan at Isle of White Festival

Rolling Stones Altamont

Records for some issues under a Phil Spector Productions logo for newly produced material. Unfortunately, it produced little of note: there was the new Ronettes' record 'You Came You Saw You Conquered', but while welcomed by fans this bore little of the magic of the past.

The only jewel in the crown, and a partial one at that, was Spector's work with what appeared to be an oddball supper club group called The Checkmates Ltd. They included two frontline singers – Sonny Charles and Bobby Stevens. In the case of the former, Spector heard a very special voice that could ride atop of all the backing tracks he could amass. The group also included lead guitarist Harvey Trees, bassist Bill Van Buskirk and drummer Sweet Louie. One single, 'Love Is All I Have To Give', featured Stevens' anguished lead, but the other two, 'Black Pearl' and 'Proud Mary', gave full rein to Sonny Charles' soaring tenor. His voice had the sweetness and clarity of Sam Cooke, but the power to project and rise to the falsetto range.

'Black Pearl' was an immediate classic with a Spector/Toni Wine/Irwin Levine writing credit, into which Spector poured all his earlier instrumental elements. In its way, the record

is every bit as good as 'Lovin' Feelin' or 'Be My Baby' or any of the other classic hits but, because it was seen as Spector being a one-trick pony, it was broadly ignored by many in the industry.

However, it did make it to US No13, although there were only really two or three above it that deserved the higher rating…

The version of 'Proud Mary', a recent hit for Solomon Burke and Creedence, was an absolute stormer, but could get no higher than No69.

On this version, Spector provided a massive churning backdrop for Sonny Charles to let rip on, leading to a quite breath-taking record.

There was one album that had all the singles, including a fully Spectorised version of his own Spanish Harlem, and somewhat of an anti-climatical B side that had a Hair suite; topical but music that bore little relationship to the main thrust of the work. File under wasted opportunity.

Jackson 5

'An absolutely definite number one smash' - Penny Valentine Disc & Music Echo 1st November 1969 on Proud Mary

'UPSETTERS play peg leg style on 'Return of Django' - a hop, hup, lurch blue-beat record.' Penny Valentine Disc & Music Echo 20th September 1969

BELL RECORDS

Return Of Django
UPSETTERS
UPSETTER US 301

Liquidator
HARRY J ALL STARS
HARRY TR 675

Skinhead Moon Stomp
SYMARIP
TREASURE ISLE TI 7050

One reason for great records like 'Black Pearl' not finding favour was because the peak of pure pop power had passed, and in its place was a desire from record buyers to investigate other forms of music: rock, folk and reggae. West Indian-originated recordings had been popular with cult audiences and in specific markets since the start of the decade, but by 1969 their sounds were all around, especially since Desmond Decker's huge 'Israelites' hit made UK No1 in April.

This trio proves how infectiously good and dancable the releases were. We break the non-big-hit rule of the book as The Upsetters got to No4, and Harry J bounced around the lower reaches of the Top 20.

The first two were instrumentals. 'Return Of Django' featured a nicely loose sax break, while 'Liquidator' was dominated by a simple organ melody. 'Skinhead Moon Stomp', with its semi-spoken, semi-chanted lyrics, was more than a nod to one of the music's key British audiences, exalting them to get up on the floor and have a good time.

There had always been specialist small labels for the reggae scene, but in 1969 it was a time for real expansion.

The Jet Song (When The Weekend's Over)
THE GROOP
BELL BLL 1080

Will You Be Staying After Sunday
THE PEPPERMINT RAINBOW
MCA MU 1076

Grazing In The Grass
THE FRIENDS OF DISTINCTION
RCA 1838

While other musical genres were rapidly taking shape, pure pop remained as a force in the singles market. Ever since The Mamas And Papas and the 5th Dimension, full-blooded mixed vocal-led records, that were radio-friendly and hook-laden, had been released.

Partly Australian The Groop made No112

The Cooks Of Cake And Kindness

THE CALIFORNIANS

FONTANA TF 991

This is a very collectable release on Fontana, a label that features heavily in this book.

This was the B side to the more immediately commercial Happenings-styled vocal harmony item 'Mandy', but has since become the more sought-after track.

It was written by John Carter and Russ Alquist, and features a blistering and trippy high guitar line behind the more traditional song structure.

The group was from the Birmingham/Wolverhampton area, and, as their name suggests, they were fans of West Coast harmony pop – they had covered songs from The Beach-Nuts and Spanky & Our Gang among others on previous Decca releases. Personnel is thought to have included Mike Brooks, Robert Trewis, John O'Hara and PJ Habberley.

CHART BOUND

Friends of Distinction
"Grazing In The Grass"
c/w "I Really Hope You Do"
RCA 1838

> **"I wrote this with Russ Alquist and this was one of his typical hippy lyrics. It didn't have to mean very much as long as it was weird!**
> **This was around the same time as we wrote the Laughing Man. I think the little banned substances really worked for Russ! We recorded this for the Flowerpots *Peace* album, but when I shelved that we told Southern Music to go after a cover. Hence The Californians record.**
> **I didn't know they had done it and I was in Trident studios cutting something else when I heard this record coming from another room and thought, hang on, I wrote that.**
> **I was actually delighted with their version. It was better than ours and should have been a hit. Oh, and no, I wasn't on the record."**
> *John Carter*

on Billboard with 'Jet Song', while Peppermint Rainbow topped out at No32; but The Friends Of Distinction went all the way to US No3. Between them, they probably only sold a couple of hundred copies in the UK.

The Peppermint Rainbow, from the evidence on the back cover of their album (above), were ill-advised satorially as well as in terms of their name, although the production and arrangement guidance from Paul Leka ensured the album was substantially better than you'd expect from the cover!

The Friends Of Distinction (Charlene Gibson, Barbara Love, Harry Elston and Floyd Butler) were produced and arranged by Roy Cork Jnr. who swathed 'Grazing In The Grass' in a trumpet and woodwind-led orchestration that supported the fine and exuberant group interchange vocals. The record cleverly uses the full panorama of instrumental sounds, including percussive breaks, as a backdrop to the group's 'Shigga-a-digga' vocal hook.

Chelsea Morning
JONI MITCHELL
REPRISE RS 23402

It says something about a singer/songwriter's talent when a song such as 'Both Sides Now' can be issued as a B side, as was the case with this Joni Mitchell release.

'Chelsea Morning' had cropped up as a cover on the first Fairport Convention album, along with 'I Don't Know Where I Stand', but now the lady herself was starting to make waves.

While some writers mature into their best work, Joni Mitchell (along with Laura Nyro) came up with her best right from the start – though some may disagree and point to her *Blue* album.

But to be able to release 'Chelsea Morning' with 'Both Sides Now' on the flip shows an unrivalled quality at the outset of her career.

> 'JONI MITCHELL gives 'Chelsea Morning' her usual perfect treatment with that lovely catch tripping up her voice'.
> - **Penny Valentine Disc & Music Echo 2nd August 1969**

Morning Way
TRADER HORNE
PYE 7N 17846

The female lead voice on both of the Joni Mitchell covers on the first Fairport album was Judy Dyble, but it was not long before the group, under Joe Boyd's eye, replaced her with Sandy Denny.

Sandy was a wonderful singer and a great writer, and brought much to the group, but Judy's subsequent career is not without note. After briefly working with Giles, Giles and Fripp at the dawn of the formation of King Crimson, Judy formed Trader Horne as a duo with Jackie McAuley, late of Them and the Belfast Gypsies. The unlikely pairing worked well, producing this, another single and one album, interest in which has remained high over the years.

Love (Can Make You Happy)
MERCY **WARNER BROS. WB 7291**

This went all the way to the No2 spot on Billboard, kept off the top only by The Beatles' 'Get Back'.

It's a deceptively simple piece – its gossamer acoustics and little plinks are, at times, reminiscent of a slowed-down 'Groovin'', with tambourine and relaxed vocals.

It's an unashamedly middle-of-the-road record, but one that somehow still appeals across the board.

A Night To Remember
DAWN CHORUS **MCA-UK MK 5004**

This is a product of John Carter, his mate Ken Lewis and, once again, Russ Alquist. It is nothing short of a complete tour-de-force, and is the link between Carter's better-known work with the Ivy League and the Seventies First Class records. It has class in all areas: a great song with a memorable chorus, imaginative arrangement, huge vocal harmonies and it is long enough (a Carter trademark) for all the ideas to develop fully.

There are obvious Brain Wilson influences in terms of structure and instrumentation choices, including theremin-type sounds, but here they produce something new, rather than slavishly copying, as so many others were doing.

Different tempo passages, quiet and loud sections, and the vocal power all combine to produce something much better.

> "'A Night To Be' was one of my favourites of our one offs. There were Pet Sounds influences but I think it had a really nice atmosphere. I had the chance on this to use a couple of instruments I'd been messing around with, the autoharp and the ukulele, which made it a little different. It could have been a Flowerpot record and by the way it's being used on the RPM comp of Flowerpot Men and associated tracks 1966-1968--- available soon at your favourite record store." **JOHN CARTER**

Sugar Mountain
NEIL YOUNG
Reprise RS 20861

Another writer to produce good work early in his career was Neil Young. His songs with Buffalo Springfield and his first couple of solo albums for Reprise have unique qualities to them.

Around the same time, he put out a cover of Hank Williams' 'Oh Lonesome Me' and 'Sugar Mountain' was the non-album song on its B side.

It's a gentle acoustic song about idyllic and utopian existence. It runs for 5.36 minutes, and it is not until the very end that it becomes evident that it is, in fact, a live recording.

Get Together
THE YOUNGBLOODS RCA 1877

Chet Powers (aka Dino Valente) wrote this song and it was already established as a hippie anthem through many cover versions by bands on both sides of the Atlantic when it had its second coming in the US charts in 1969. It was a surprise to everyone as it had been around for a while that the Youngbloods' version was such a big US hit in 1969.

It had previously reached No62 on Billboard in October 1967, but a re-release saw it make No5 in September 1969, the strongest placing of the many versions of the song.

The quirky Youngbloods were reminiscent of The Lovin' Spoonful in terms of their eclecticism, specifically on good-time knockabout tracks like 'Grizzely Bear.'

The Youngbloods foursome came out of similar NY folk settings to the Spoonful: Jesse Colin Young, who had been following a solo path, was joined by Jerry Corbitt, Joe Bauer and Lowell Levinger (aka Banana).

As well as this delightful hit, their early albums were both varied and interesting, *Elephant Mountain* being a particular mellow favourite of many.

Neil Young

Between April 11 1966 and May 5 1968, Neil Young played as a working band member with Buffalo Springfield, providing what many see as their finest moments: 'Nowadays Clancy Can't Even Sing', 'Do I Have To Come Right Out And Say It', 'Mr Soul', 'Broken Arrow', 'On The Way Home', and their tour-de-force 'Expecting To Fly'.

When the group broke up (which was almost inevitable, given its contrasting talents), Young emerged almost straight away with two magnificent solo albums on Reprise: *Neil Young* and *Everybody Knows This Is Nowhere*, both of which are gradually being re-discovered after decades of attention on the later Harvest era.

Young's mercurial talents were most obvious in his writing, but his singing and guitar playing should not be overlooked. When he was eventually drawn back into Stephen Stills' orbit with Crosby, Stills, Nash and Young, it even seemed that his talent dwarfed the other three. The inter-group musicianship was probably at its height when the foursome played a memorable concert at the Royal Albert Hall, which, except for an accapella encore, they finished with an extended version of 'Down By The River' from Neil's second album. Young was in the driving seat, coaxing the others to ever-greater heights, who responded and in turn drove him on. At the triumphant end they rushed together for a massive group hug.

Years later, when they reconvened to make *American Dream*, Young's songs once again carried the work.

His career has taken him through a wide variety of albums, some of which pale by comparison with others, but the work with Buffalo Springfield and immediately afterwards in the final years of the Sixties is still one of the musical high points of the whole decade.

It should also be noted that Neil Young was one of the first, and definitely the most stylish, wearer of suede fringe jackets!

To B Without A Hitch
BRIDGET ST JOHN
DANDELION K 4404

Bridget St John, a lovely female singer on the scene at the end of the Sixties, was one of the favoured acts signed by John Peel and Clive Selwood for their newly formed Dandelion label.

Bridget's slightly husky voice has an intimacy and warmth missing from artists today, and all of her early albums, especially the Seventies' *Jumblequeen*, make wonderful listening.

'To B Without A Hitch' was her first single, and Dandelion's second, and was inspired by a hitch-hiking holiday with a friend to Italy in summer 1966. The song's format reflects the difference between the rush and urgency of travel, and the quieter and more reflective moments in between, when one is more involved with eating buttercup sandwiches.

Everybody's Talkin'
FRED NEIL
CAPITOL CL 15616

This song, in its Harry Nilsson cover version format, is forever associated with the thought-provoking Midnight Cowboy film that introduced Jon Voight to our screens and showed Dustin Hoffman's fine acting talent. The producers of Midnight Cowboy had wanted to use Neil's version of his own song, but had requested that it be re-recorded somewhat faster to fit the escapist mood of the film. Neil didn't want to comply, so it fell to Nilsson to score the worldwide hit, though Fred would have collected royalties to spend later on his beloved dolphins, which have taken up much of his later life.

Fred Neil had been around the New York folk scene since the early Sixties Bitter End club days,. 'Everybody's Talkin'' was another of his lyrically elusive works, and was partly the result of the way producer Nik Venet was working with Neil at the time: setting him up with sympathetic musicians and keeping the tape running. Before this song, he was best-known for his haunting song 'The Dolphins'.

Bluegreens On The Wing
WILLIAM TRUCKAWAY WITH LILLIAN, NETTA AND JO
REPRISE RS 20842

This final track from William Truckaway sums up what this book is all about: introducing odd records to people who may not have been aware of them. Even with the lyric sheet, many are still no nearer to knowing what it's all about – other than it being a delightful bit of nonsense with its AA Milne-inspired references to Piglet and Heffalump.

It was produced by William with the better-known Erik Jacobsen at Wally Heider's studio in San Francisco, and the associated album included session talent from steel guitarist Buddy, violinist Richard Green and flautist Charles Lloyd. It doesn't appear to have sold anywhere.

'Bluegreens' features William playing Moog amid this cheerful and gentle acoustic track, with some handclaps and very attractive harmonies from his girls.

The album reveals him to be an affable-looking denim-clad hairy-hippie type, whose music is as laid back as he looks on the cover, slumped on the wicker chair.

Mr Truckaway's real name was William Sievers, under which name he had been a member of Sopwith Camel of 'Hello Hello' fame. This partially explains his easy-going, Lovin' Spoonful-style approach and lyrics that invite you to sing along, because "the ever-there hefflebear couldn't be wrong". I think we should all settle for that...

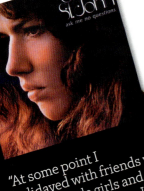

"At some point I holidayed with friends who had two little girls and, as far as I remember, I read them Beatrix Potter stories. One of them was The Tale Of Jeremy Fisher, which is where the buttercup sandwich allusion comes from. The B is for Beatrix or Bridget, whichever, but it's also for 'be'!"

BRIDGET ST JOHN RECALLS THE HOLIDAY WITH HER FRIEND

RETURN OF DJANGO
(Lee Perry)
UPSETTERS
Produced by: Lee Perry
US-301 A
TMX.73
B&C/Island Music

reprise
WILLIAM TRUCKAWAY
with Lillian, Netta and Jo
BLUEGREENS ON THE WING
(William Truckaway)
Produced by William Truckaway
for Sweet Reliable Productions
GREAT HONESTY MUSIC
45 RPM
RS.20842
RS.20842-A

WARNER BROS.
LOVE (CAN MAKE YOU HAPPY)
(Jack Sigler Jr.)
MERCY
45 RPM
WB 7291
WB-7291-A

BELL RECORDS
THE JET SONG
(WHEN THE WEEKEND'S OVER)
(Chris Ducey)
THE GROOP
BLL 1080
Arranged by Dave Grusin & Torrey French

HARRY
LIQUIDATOR
(H. Johnson)
HARRY J. ALL STARS
Produced by Harry J.
TR 675
TMX.314
B&C Music

reprise
NEIL YOUNG
SUGAR MOUNTAIN (5.36)
Produced by Neil Young
45 RPM
RS.20842

NEIL YOUNG
with CRAZY HORSE
EVERYBODY KNOWS
THIS IS NOWHERE

PROUD MARY
(J. Fogerty)
(From The A & M Album AMLS 943)
A&M RECORDS
Phil Spector PRODUCTIONS
THE CHECKMATES LTD.,
featuring SONNY CHARLES
Producer Phil Spector
Engineer Larry Levine
BURLINGTON
AMS 769
AMS 769-A

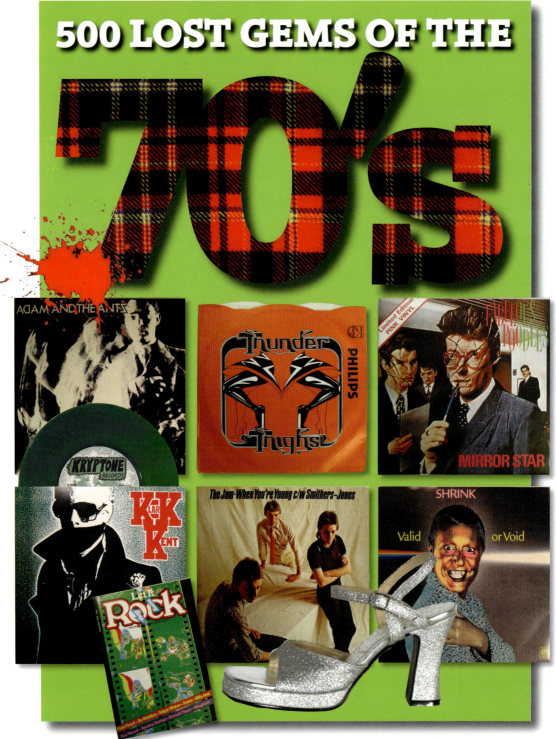

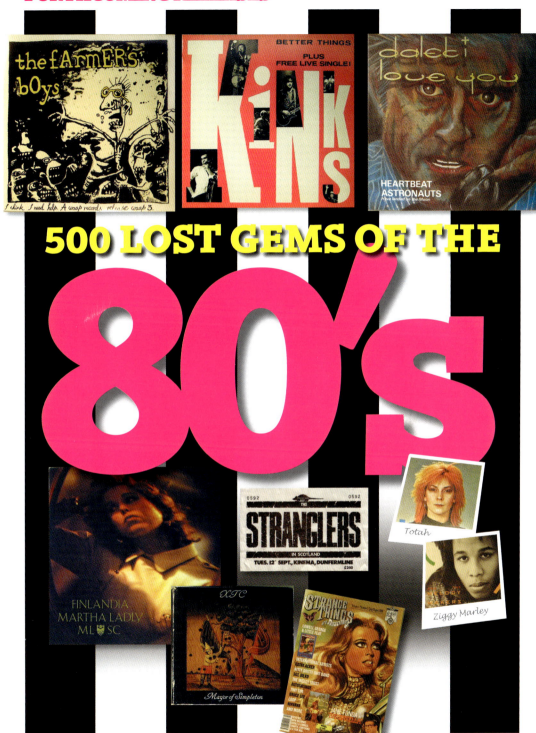

500 LOST GEMS OF THE
80's

Yet more stunning singles from the lost archives of oblivion! from post punk through new romantics to the indie scene. Visit www.lostgems.co.uk for more info

SIXTIES LOST albums

With two pages
to each album
discover the story
of some of the
decades great
'lost' classics.
Visit www.
lostgems.co.uk
for more
info

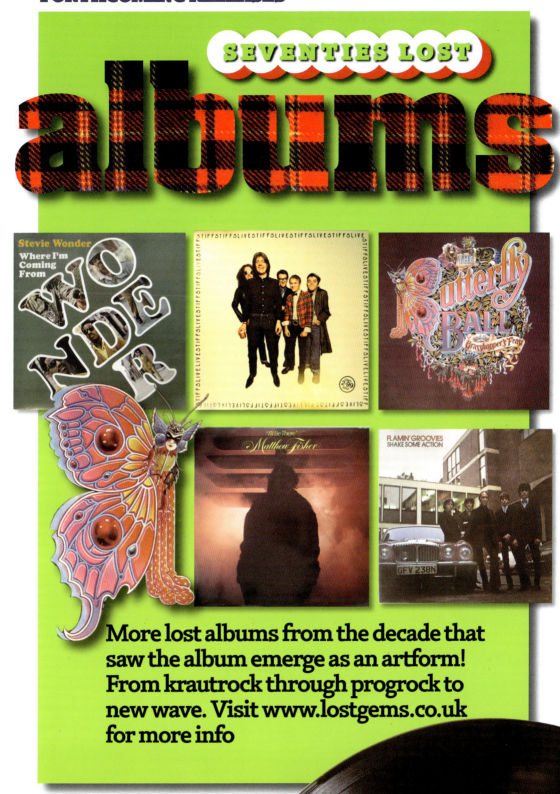